THREE BITS OF
Fry & Laurie

Stephen Fry and Hugh Laurie started writing and performing together in 1981 while at university. They have since appeared together on *Alfresco*, *Saturday Live*, *Blackadder*, *Jeeves and Wooster* and a BBC series entitled *A Bit Of Fry & Laurie* (also available in book form), while doing a variety of other writing and performing separately. They are currently eating, sleeping and spending a more or less average amount of time in the lavatory while working on a new series of *A Bit Of Fry & Laurie*. Stephen is the taller of the two, while Hugh isn't. Stephen hates the word 'while' while Hugh also hates it, while Stephen hates it a tiny bit more, while Hugh is inclined to think enough is enough, one doesn't want to get things out of proportion. They both live in While in Devon. Stephen is thinking of moving.

STEPHEN FRY and HUGH LAURIE

Three Bits of
Fry & Laurie

HEINEMANN : LONDON

First published in Great Britain 1992
by William Heinemann Ltd
an imprint of Reed Consumer Books Ltd
Michelin House, 81 Fulham Road, London SW3 6RB
and Auckland, Melbourne, Singapore and Toronto

A CIP catalogue record for this title
is available from the British Library
ISBN 0 434 27193 4

Printed and bound in Great Britain
by Clays Ltd, St Ives plc

Caution
All rights whatsoever in these sketches are
strictly reserved and applications for permission
to perform them in whole or in part must be made
in advance, before rehearsals begin, to
David Higham Associates Ltd,
5-8 Lower John Street,
Golden Square, London WIR 4HA

This book is dedicated to the memory of Margaret Thatcher, which would appear to be rather faulty.

Acknowledgements

The BBC series *A Bit Of Fry & Laurie* would in theory not have been possible without the producing-directing, producing and script-editing services of Kevin 'His Grace' Bishop, Nick 'Mind Out' Symons, or Jon 'I'm Sure I Had It On When I Arrived' Canter. It was also theoretically impossible without Johnny Morris and A.S. Byatt, but in the event a certain amount of Dunkirk spirit prevailed and we struggled along happily enough without them, only losing a cuff-link just before the recording of the last episode. Which goes to show that a lot of these so-called indispensable people are just so much hype and the sooner the Olympic Committee comes to realise it the better for all of us.

A Fryetty-Laurietty Cheque Book And Penis also heading towards Mr James Moir, Head of Light Entertainment at BBC TV, who is very good at his job and very nice with it. And very with it. And nice.

Contents

A BIT OF FRY & LAURIE

Introduction

Stephen   Well, Hugh?

Hugh   Fine thanks.

Stephen   Exactly. Now that, I believe, is an example of the kind of 'joke' the ladies and gentlemen are entitled not to expect over the coming . . . oh, how long d'you reckon?

Hugh   I think the average person could get through this book, cover to cover, reading every single word, in something under three months. Give or take. I mean don't rush it. Don't forego quality weekend time with your spouse or partner just to make that deadline. It's simply a rule of thumb.

Stephen   Mm. You're not a fast reader, are you Hugh?

Hugh   What I like to say is, I may not be fast, but I'm gentle.

Stephen   All right, that's enough soft-soap and fragrance-free conditioner. What about the hard facts and odour-rich detail? Will this book mean an increase in personal taxation?

Hugh   Certainly our hope at the moment is that the book will be financed largely by the tooth fairy.

Stephen   Hmm.

Hugh   Stephen?

Stephen   Yes, my old pen-caddie?

Hugh   I noticed that when you made that 'hmm' noise, your eyes flicked towards the telephone, as if to say I wonder what my chances are of calling for help before I am horribly butchered in another one of those cases one seems to read about almost every day now?

Stephen   Hmm.

Hugh	There you go again.
Stephen	Right.
Hugh	Now I can't help but observe that you're moving sideways towards the door, while keeping what seems to be a relaxed and cheerful expression on your face.

There follows an incredibly long pause which, thanks to the miracle of modern book technology, you can experience in a fraction of the time – leaving you free to get on with the things that really matter. Your garden, for instance – or perhaps you're a bit of a DIY addict? Or maybe it's just a question of loafing round the house in a comfortable pair of hats.

Stephen	OK. Time to get serious.
Hugh	Crikey.
Stephen	The more observant among you will have noticed that this collection of scripts from *A Bit Of Fry & Laurie* is a 'tad' fatter than in days gone by.
Hugh	Fatter?
Stephen	Plumper. Wider. Broader in the beam. Differently-girthed. Widthly-challenged.
Hugh	Fatter.
Stephen	Precisely. Now there's a reason for this. And that is that this great lardy zeppelin of a blubber-book contains not one, not two, not four, not five, but six, yes, that's right, *three* whole editions between the covers.
Hugh	Stephen, have they gone mad, the publishers and retailers of this book? Do they not realise that this in itself represents quite extraordinary value for money?
Stephen	I don't know, Hugh. I really don't. You try to reason with people, to steer them in the right direction, but sometimes you may just as well wear a calf-length purple kaftan and have done with it.

Hugh   You're trying that course of action now, I see.

Stephen   I had to, Hugh. It may be futile, but I had to try it. If I ever thought there was a chance of saving this once-mighty publishing empire from financial ruin, and that I hadn't taken that chance, I just wouldn't be able to sleep with myself. I'm a giver, you see.

Hugh   Stephen, sometimes I quite admire you.

Stephen   Oh stop that. It's fool's talk, and we haven't much time.

Hugh   Ten-four.

Stephen   The threeness-in-oneness of this book is being talked about in pubs and clubs up and down the room we're now in. Not since the Ford Motor Company published the Workshop Manuals of the Cortina Marks 1, 2 and 3, in the same handy stowaway folder, has such a publishing phenomenon occurred. History may look upon it as a grandiose folly. Or it may say, hell, they took a chance, they rode the tiger, they caught some stardust, who are we to say they were wrong? We can't predict. We simply do not know whether *A Bit Of Fry & Laurie* will even be on the History syllabus in fifty years' time.

Hugh   Stephen, the picture you're painting is a horrifying one.

Stephen   I know. But it helps me to concentrate. Just lift your chin a little. There, that's perfect.

Hugh   Well I suppose it falls to me to restate the dull, dry legal warnings. To the effect that you may not perform any of the material contained herewithin to a fee-paying audience without the prior written consent of the authors. And that your home is at risk if you do not keep up repayments on any loan or mortgage secured against it. And that the manufacturers accept no responsibility for you driving into a motorway bridge at eighty miles an hour on your way back from a Cluedo party. And that in the event of you ever wanting to make a claim against this policy, we moved, we never heard of you, whistle for it suckers. And so on and so forth.

Stephen   But hey, in the words of the song, it's not all doom and gloom.

Hugh   No, of course not. Lots to be cheerful about.

Stephen   Tons. Sally Gunnell got that gold medal in the 400 metres hurdles.

Hugh   Well there you are. The Hexham bypass has been shelved until at least 1996 . . .

Stephen   *Bob's Full House* has moved to the earlier time of 7.15 . . .

Hugh   In fact a whole raft of feel-good factors seem to be at work, making Britain a happier place to live.

Stephen   And if we've done our part . . .

Hugh   Thrown our twopen'orth in . . .

Stephen   . . . then . . .

Hugh   . . . then . . .

Stephen   . . . maybe . . .

Hugh   . . . just maybe . . .

Stephen   . . . it's all been . . .

Hugh   . . . a massive error.

Stephen   Unforgiveable.

Hugh   We're very sorry.

Stephen   Very sorry indeed.

Fry & Laurie
... THE THIRD BIT

To Sir Garfield Lineker

A Word, Timothy

*Stephen is in his study at home. There is a knock
at the door.*

Stephen   Come in.

Hugh enters.

Hugh   Hello, father. Mother said you wanted to see
me.

Stephen   Yes, Timothy. A word. I want to . . . *(He is
trying to open a drawer in his desk)* Damn this
drawer, I just cannot open it, would you mind, I
wonder Timothy?

Hugh goes round and easily opens the drawer.

(Eyes rolling to heaven) Yes, yes. I knew it. I tried to
go on fighting it, but I could not. It is true. Every
word is true.

Hugh   *(Puzzled)* Father?

Stephen   Timothy, it is time you knew who you were.

Hugh   But I know who I am, father.

Stephen   No, child, you do not.

Hugh   I am Timothy Forrest.

Stephen   No. I wish it were true, but no. Sit. Twenty-four
years ago a doctor told your mother and me that it
was impossible that we could ever have children.

Hugh   Oh. Why not?

Stephen   I can't remember the precise reason. It was

5

something to do with penises I think. We decided to adopt a child.

Hugh   I see. And you chose me.

Stephen   After a great deal of shopping around, yes. From a new edge-of-town orphanage that had just opened in Royston.

Hugh   Did they tell you who my real parents were?

Stephen   They told us that you were an orphan, that your real parents had died in a walking accident shortly after your birth. But that was a lie as we subsequently had cause to understand.

Hugh   They're still alive?

Stephen   Let me tell this in my own time, in my own way, in my own clothes, Timothy.

Hugh   I'm sorry, father.

Stephen   On your seventh birthday a man called round to this house. His name was Furlo Roth. He took out a silver multi-bladed knife and placed it in this drawer, the one you have just opened. *(Stephen takes out the knife)* He closed the drawer and said that only the Chosen One could open it. You, Timothy . . . you are the Chosen One.

Hugh   I am?

Stephen   And this *(indicating knife)* is Berwhale. The avenger. The weapon of the Chosen One. Tomorrow is your twenty-fifth birthday and you must leave us to go in search of Pewnack, the Destroyer, the Dark One, the Beast.

Hugh   Golly.

Stephen   When the fourth moon of Trollack rises above the Cylinder of Eyelass then Pewnack will strike. His kingdom shall be numberless and darkness will blight the land, all men shall be slaves and the time

6

of weeping will begin. So it is written in the runes of Ollerman-Goth, so it must be. Only the Chosen One can stop him, and only Berwhale, the avenger, can pierce the armour of the beast.

Hugh   I knew it! It sounds funny, father, but in my heart I *knew* there was something. I realise now that I have been waiting for this moment all my life.

Stephen Yes! Yes, it must be so.

Hugh   Where do I find this beast, this Pewnack the destroyer?

Stephen He lives in Saffron Walden.

Hugh   Saffron Walden, right.

Stephen You must go there. Surprise is the key. If he knew you were after him he would set the minions of Threek on you. Become a part of the community. Get a job in a canning factory. Bide your time.

Hugh   Yes. How will I know this Beast?

Stephen Only Teece, the Wise One, can tell you.

Hugh   Teece.

Stephen Teece. In six months, when you have been accepted by the Saffron Walden community Furlo Roth will come to you and tell you how you might find Teece and begin the battle to free us of Pewnack.

Hugh   Yes! Yes! It shall be done.

Stephen Now take Berwhale, the avenger and go upstairs and wash your hands for lunch.

Hugh   Right.

Exit Hugh.

Stephen looks sorrowfully after him.

Enter woman.

Woman   Well?

Stephen   I think he swallowed it.

Woman   Thank God.

Stephen   We'll get that lazy sod out of the house and earning his living.

VOX
POP

Stephen   Only one decent brothel left in this part of town now. I remember when it was built. I fainted halfway through the topping-out ceremony as a matter of fact.

Love Me Tender

Stephen addresses the audience.

Stephen   I wonder if you can remember what you were doing at half past three on the sixteenth of August, 1977. I remember exactly. I was revising for my insect-killing exams. In those days you could never call yourself educated unless you knew how to kill wasps. Anyway, as I say, I was swatting away for these exams, when I felt a sudden rush in my soul, a sense of something incredibly beautiful and mysterious passing into me. An extraordinary feeling, not unlike an evening with Cliff Michelmore, but somehow more peaceful. What could this feeling portend? Two hours later I discovered its meaning exactly. For it was precisely at that time that Elvis Aaron Presley died. I knew then that the soul of Elvis had passed into me. And since that day I have, more or less, been Elvis. I have spent nearly all my time eating ice cream and Big Macs and popping Percodan and Quaalude pills. Eerie isn't it? But I am, of course, not the only person into whom Elvis, with his customary generosity, breathed his soul. My colleague and bitter, sworn friend Hugh Laurie had a similar experience and here he is to tell you about it in the only way he knows.

Hugh sitting on a stool singing 'Love Me Tender'. Shot develops to reveal that he is singing it to Nicholas Parsons, who is sitting on a stool next to him.

Hugh   Love me tender, love me sweet
Never let me go
You've made my life so complete
And I love you so

9

Love me tender, love me true
All my dreams fulfil
For my darling I love you
And I always will.

VOX
POP

Stephen I have to read when I'm on the
throne. Have to read. Harpic
bottle, tube of toothpaste, doesn't
matter what it is. Even a book
sometimes.

Milk Pot

Stephen and Hugh enter as medieval clerics. A pot of UHT milk is on the table between them. They play the whole thing to camera as if the camera is a judge.

Stephen Behold. The Court under the eye of God finds itself convened this day of our Lord, Tuesday which is called Tuesday.

Hugh So be it. Be it so. And not otherwise.

Stephen Nay.

Hugh Moo.

Stephen As witness my hand hereunto bearing the great seal of Rotherham.

Hugh Miaow.

Stephen All who do have righteous business before these presents make sign or else say this court nay.

Hugh Or moo.

Stephen Or, possibly, moo.

Hugh The charge. Make known the charge.

Stephen Fourteen guineas per calendar hour.

Hugh Cheap.

Stephen Woof.

Hugh Be it appended and known in these our records that this chalice of Ultra Heat Treated milk being appointed in the wisdom of our Lord God to accompany the coffee of the most reverend and holy Bishop of Uffington did fail to yield up its juices therefore most basely causing that holy and right goodly man

11

to snag his fingernail against the tab the which is provided for the opening. Of. Thereunto.

Stephen   Of it.

Hugh   Slightly.

Stephen   This snagging the devil having achieved, for it must rightwise be known that the devil hath possessed this chalice . . .

Hugh   Or pot.

Stephen   Hath possessed this chalice or pot . . . the lid did then open in an irritating little 'V' shape and most lewdly disgorge its opal fluids upon the chaste and seemly waistcoat of our most Godly bishop.

Hugh   Thereat proving that the pot is a most wicked pot . . .

Stephen   Or chalice.

Hugh   A most wicked and contumely pot or chalice wherein Satan doth play Jackalawkins.

Stephen   This being said . . .

Hugh   And neighed.

Stephen   This being said and neighed unto the articles where of it is written that it should be said or neighed we do make most erotic demand that this pot or chalice be cast out, excommunicated, denied the blessing and eucharist of our Saviour and be tossed unshriven, unhouseled, interdict to the condign flames whence it most surely rose. Prepare the chasting dish. Prepare the chasting dish.

Hugh   It is prepared.

Stephen   The chasting dish is prepared and now the pouring.

Opens milk and spills it.

Bugger.

The Department

*Hugh is returning to his flat with some shopping.
Echoing stairwells etc. Stops outside door and reaches for
key, but something is wrong. Ears pricked. He carefully
puts down shopping and removes an automatic from his
belt. He works the slide to load the chamber, the way one
has seen countless times, but instead it comes away in his
hand.*

Hugh   (*Mutters*) Shit.

*Hugh puts the gun down and gently nudges the door
open with his foot. Nothing. He moves stealthily through
the flat. Nothing. A lavatory flushes. Hugh whirls round
in a martial-looking crouch. Stephen emerges from the
bathroom, drying his hands.*

Stephen   Alan, my boy. Good to see you. I hope you
don't mind, but I was . . .

Hugh   What the hell are you doing here? How did you get in?

Stephen   Your landlady. Charming woman. It turns out that
she and I are great fans of Johnny Mathis.

Hugh   So what the hell do you want?

Stephen crosses to a fish tank in the middle of the room.

Stephen   Mmm. I'd forgotten your obsession with Japanese
fighting fish. You're quite an expert aren't you?

Hugh   Never mind that. Just say your piece and get
the hell out of here.

Stephen   Never could really see it myself. What is it about
them that interests you?

Hugh   Japanese fighting fish? They're loyal. Honest. They

13

don't send you to Aylesbury on half-arsed operations
and then sell you down the river.

Stephen Now that's hardly fair, Alan. The Department . . .

Hugh The hell with the Department. That's finished,
over. Finished with. Over. Finished and done with.
It's over. Completely finished.

Stephen You're right, Alan. I shouldn't have come. You have
your own life now, I can see that. Your flat. Your fish.
And there's a girl now, I gather. Deborah, is it?

*At the mention of 'Deborah' Hugh snatches up a banana
from the fruit bowl and holds it under Stephen's throat.*

Hugh You want to know something, read the file. Sir.

Stephen Of course, Alan. Of course. I'll leave you now.
Thanks for the use of the lavatory. Oh by the way . . .

Hugh What now?

Stephen We're reopening the Steinbeck case. I thought you
might like to know . . .

Hugh Steinbeck? What the hell . . . ?

Stephen You and Steinbeck were pretty close, weren't you?
Both orphaned at an early age. Both took excellent
degrees at the Sorbonne. Both had trials for West
Bromwich Albion. You at inside right, Steinbeck in
goal, if I remember rightly. Both have an account
with John Lewis at Brent Cross.

Hugh Is that a crime?

Stephen Of course not, dear boy. I'm just pointing out the
similarities, that's all. And then of course, you both
adore fish. Really quite remarkable.

Hugh You bastard.

Stephen He trusts you Alan. You're the only one who
can get him back for us.

14

Hugh   It's your damned porridge, use your own damned spoon.

Stephen   Please Alan, don't throw porridge in my face. That's completely over. Finished. Done with. Over and finished. Done over and finished with. Over. You understand? Finished over with. Done.

Hugh   Hello! I seem to have touched a nerve.

Stephen   All right Alan, blast you. Fifteen all. We need you and you need us.

Hugh   I need nothing and nobody.

Stephen   You need an import licence for those oh so pretty Japanese fighting fish of yours.

Hugh   You bastard.

Stephen   *(Throwing documents on to the table)* First class flight to Chichester. Table for two in the sleeper from Chichester to Stroud. *(Puts down a gun and some bullets)* Hair-trigger, fur-barrel and soft-eared bullets. Just as you like them.

Hugh   You certainly came prepared didn't you?

Stephen   I prefer to put it this way. I certainly came prepared. *(More documents)* Welsh passport, hotel reservation at the Welcome Break, Low Wycombe, all in the name of one Lewis Potter.

Hugh   And the real Lewis Potter?

Stephen   A chartered prostitute from Hereford. Killed two years ago in a smiling accident. Will you do it, Alan?

Hugh   You said table for two . . . ?

Stephen   Of course, Alan. Allow me to introduce your wife.

A woman emerges from the bathroom.

Hugh   What the hell . . . ?

Woman	You need a new ballcock.
Hugh	I beg your pardon?
Woman	On your cistern. I've fixed it for now, but it needs replacing.
Stephen	I know you've always worked alone, Alan, but under the circumstances the Department felt . . .
Hugh	The Department can go to hell. I'm finished, done away with, at last, period, no more, full stop, the end, full period. You can shove the Department up your arse.
Stephen	Well of course I can't do that, as you well know Alan. The Department is a huge building housing hundreds of people – not the sort of thing you can shove up your arse without a great deal of . . .
Woman	Excuse me, Admiral.
Stephen	What is it, my dear?
Woman	Major Tarrant seems to doubt my abilities.
Hugh	You're damn right.
Woman	Would it make any difference if I said that I was the case officer on Operation Richard Whitely?
Stephen	Since your time Alan. Ugly business. Russians tried to flood Europe with counterfeit Richard Whitelys. The Department was on a Code 1 for three months.
Hugh	All I'm saying is, I don't carry passengers.
Woman	Neither do I, Major.
Stephen	Ho ho ho. Looks like you've met your match at last, Alan. Now, I'll leave you two to get acquainted, while I have another go on that excellent lavatory of yours. *(Sotto voce to the woman as he passes)* Don't worry. His bark's worse than his bite.

16

Exit Stephen.

Hugh   Did he tell you what happened to my last partner?

Woman   Shot dead on the steps of the Prague Embassy. I've read the file.

Hugh   Yeah? Well files ain't a lot of use when you're staring down the barrel of a knife.

Woman   I'll try and remember that, Major.

Hugh   Yeah, you do that.

Woman   Nice flat.

Hugh   *(Refusing to be charming)* It gets me from A to B.

Woman   Quite a collection of Japanese fighting fish. Are they good?

Hugh   At fighting?

Woman   At being Japanese.

Hugh   *(Grudgingly)* The one on the left has a black belt fourth dan, the one on the right has retired.

Woman   Look, if we're going to be working together we might as well be friends.

Hugh   I work faster alone.

Woman   Perhaps it would be a good idea if we went to bed together.

Hugh   Like I just said, I work faster alone.

Woman   Me too. Have you got two bedrooms?

Hugh   Sure.

Woman   I'll take that one. You take the other.

They both disappear into separate bedrooms. Almost a split second later they re-emerge, both smoking cigarettes.

Woman	Better?
Hugh	Much. Dammit, I don't even know your name.
Woman	Does it matter?
Hugh	I guess not. Well if you want to be useful, you could start by fixing us both a drink. You'll find some whisky . . .
Woman	Above the sink, I know. I've read the file, remember?
Hugh	Huh. You minx.

Stephen emerges from the lavatory.

Stephen	Hmm. That really was most enjoyable. Would anyone else like a go?

There is no response.

No? Well in that case, I think *I* might have another turn. Really most excellent.

Stephen bumbles off again.

Woman	What does he *do* in there?
Hugh	I've really no idea.

Cut to Stephen's song.

> VOX
> POP
>
> **Hugh**   I can't stop now, my wife is being
> towed away.

Stephen's Song

*This is a spoken song, done against a backing of
high strings. Not unlike Eamonn Andrews's unforgettably
majestic 'The Shifting, Whispering Sands'. It is a kind
of spoken 'Windmills of your Mind'.*

*Stephen is dressed in a very new-agey sort of way.
Possibly a caftan, possibly not. His hair is silky. The
microphone is long and is held between his slim, sensitive
palms.*

Stephen   The world is ever sliding
Ever gliding, ever turning;
Ever yearning and colliding.
The stairs begin to creak
You turn but cannot speak
When the bubble starts to squeak
And you find the truth you seek

Chorus:
You, yes, you, you, you
It's you I'm speaking to.
You . . . the starling of my night
The goddess of what seems
You . . . the sparkle of my fright
The parcel of my dreams
(Slowly) Just . . . the . . . parcel . . .
Of my . . . dreams. *(Whispered)* Yes

The you, why, you, you, you
The you who do what none can do
The you that haunts my ears
On the shortlist of wasted rains
The avenue of chandeliers

19

That shames my frozen veins
(Slowly) That . . . shames . . . my . . .
Frozen . . . veins. *(Whispered)* Not yet

The world is ever hiding
Ever riding, ever burning;
Ever churning and dividing.
For the horse bestrides the cart
And the temple rent apart
Thou wilt be what thou art
As your hand becomes your heart

You, yes, you, you, you
You who knows what once I knew
The you that spits my blood
And stares at both my clouds
You wear a sleeve of mud
Your cuffs become my shrouds
(Slowly) Your . . . cuffs . . . become . . .
My shrouds. *(Whispered)* Oh why?

You, yes, you, you, you
Which you the what how who
You crumple the skirts of need
In the belly of desire
Where my freshly planted seed
Can spin its tangled wire
(Slowly) Can . . . spin . . . its . . .
Tangled . . . wire. *(Whispered)* Oh
Certainly

Thank you.

Psychiatrists

Doctor's surgery cum office. Hugh and Stephen are on chairs. Each has a notebook on their lap.

Stephen   I think it might be helpful to start off with your telling me something about your state of mind at the moment. Would you say you were generally happy, depressed, confident, unsure . . . what word comes into your mind, would you say? Take your time.

Hugh stares at Stephen for a moment, deeply interested.

Hugh   This is fascinating. Quite fascinating. Your problem seems to centre around the delusion that you are a psychiatrist and that everyone you speak to is some kind of patient of yours. This is a rare, but not unheard of syndrome.

Stephen   Mm-hm. Perhaps it would help if we talked a little about your mother at this point.

Hugh   Extraordinary. Very interesting. Why 'Mother'? Was your mother affectionate when you were small?

Stephen   Affection! Affection. Now perhaps we're getting somewhere. You felt a lack of affection. I wonder if you happen to know whether you were breast-fed or not?

Hugh   Ah! Ah-ha! Breasts. Already we've focussed in on breasts. What are your feelings about breasts, I wonder? Do they frighten you? This is not uncommon.

Stephen   *(Writing)* 'Breasts and fear' . . . intriguing. And where do you think your father fits into all this?

Hugh   Father . . . father. Mm. So let's imagine a line, shall we, with fear at one end and breasts at the

21

	other. I want you to tell me where you think your father fits on this line.
Stephen	Lines, interesting, lines. Why 'lines' I wonder? Lines are very male, aren't they? Very forceful. They thrust, they penetrate, don't they? They urge onwards.
Hugh	At last the layers are beginning to unpeel. Urging, penetrating, maleness, breasts. How often would you say you masturbated?
	Pause.
Stephen	Yes. I really do think if you don't mind we had better get back to me asking the questions. I think it is important, if you're to be helped, to remember who is the doctor here and who the patient. I will ask the questions.
Hugh	And I'll pretend to be the patient, all right. That way I can tell from the questions you ask me, what it is that is truly disturbing you. All right. Good.
Stephen	Now, come on I'm going to be quite firm. You are the patient.
Hugh	*(Humouringly)* Yes . . . that's right.
Stephen	I want to hear you say 'I am the patient.'
Hugh	What was that?
Stephen	'I am the patient.'
Hugh	*(Writing this down)* Good! That's a breakthrough. Now that you know that, let's proceed.
Stephen	*(Exasperated) You* are the patient!
Hugh	*(Shrugging)* I am, you are – perhaps we're all patients.
Stephen	*(Really quite angry)* I am not a patient!
Hugh	Please remain calm, Mr Windrush.
Stephen	*Doctor* Windrush.

Hugh	(*Lifting telephone*) Yes. You know. I only have to lift a telephone and you will be restrained.
Telephone V/O	Yes, hello.
Stephen & Hugh	It's all right Rebecca, I'm in a session.
Stephen	Look, I'm sorry, I really cannot help you unless you stop playing this ridiculous game.
Hugh	Extraordinary. I really don't think I have ever detected a more deeply embedded illusion.
Stephen	It's not an illusion!!
Hugh	I'm trying to be as understanding as I can, Mr Windrush.
Stephen	You came asking for help. I am prepared to offer that help, but really Mr Johanssen . . .
Hugh	Tony. I've told you, call me Tony.
Stephen	Really Mr Johanssen, that help can only be forthcoming if you are honest . . . not only with me, but with yourself. Now please . . . no more tricks, no more games. I am a very busy man. I have another patient coming in any minute now. So let's be reasonable. Hey? What do you say?
Hugh	Your last doctor tried a course of lentizol, I believe? Did you find that helped at all?
Stephen	All right. Let's begin very simply, shall we? If you are, as you say, a doctor . . .

A sort of egg-timer type device goes off on the desk, it rings.

Hugh	I'm sorry, Mr Windrush. That's the full hour. Shall we say, same time next week?
Stephen	Yes, I think I can fit you in then. This time bring

some photographs of your parents, if you have any. I think that might be useful.

Hugh   I might try a little hypnosis I think.

Stephen   Perhaps you would be kind enough to confirm that appointment with Rebecca on your way out.

They both stay where they are.

Hugh   Mm.

Stephen   Mm.

The door opens. In comes Kay.

Kay   Oh, you're both here. I think I'm seeing you first, Mr Windrush. Would you mind waiting outside Mr Johanssen, you're a little early. Rebecca – two cups of tea please.

Hugh   Extraordinary.

Stephen   So deep-seated.

Hugh   Simply fascinating.

Stephen   Do sit, Mrs Medlicott. Make yourself as comfortable as you can.

VOX
POP

Stephen   You see what worries me about education is this. Where are the future Ned Sherrins? Mm? Who are the young Sherrins of tomorrow? Are they being trained up? No. I shudder for the sake of our children.

Condom Quickie

A chemist's counter: Hugh strides up to confront the shop assistant.

Assistant Can I help you?

Hugh Yes please. I'd like eight packets of condoms, please.

Assistant Eight?

Hugh Eight. Four of them Fetherlite, three of them ribbed, *(half sotto voce)* the new single by Jason Donovan, *(loud again)* and one multi-coloured pack of Fiestas.

Assistant Jason Donovan?

Hugh That's right. Can you make sure they're all sensitol lubricated?

VOX
POP

Stephen Hoo, that's a tricky one. Er, dinner with Melvyn Bragg, cooked by Keith Floyd, followed by sex with Madonna, and then breakfast in bed, served by Chris Patten in a yellow jumpsuit.

Embassy

Stephen   (*Singing*) But in spite of all temptations
To belong to other nations
He remains an Englishman
He remains an Englishman
For in spite of all temptations
To belong to other nations
He remains an Englishman
He remains an Englishman

Hugh enters bearing a piece of paper.

Hugh   Ambassador.

Stephen   Ah, Witty, isn't it?

Hugh   That's right, sir. A message just came through for you from the Vice-Consul in Al Rahad. Marked most urgent.

Stephen   A message. Then read it dear boy. Our esteemed Vice-Consul is not the sort of man to bandy the words 'most' and 'urgent' without that he has cause.

Hugh   Right, sir. 'Twelve armoured divisions heading south. Infantry build-up along border continues. Every indication, repeat every indication that invasion is imminent repeat imminent.'

Stephen   Hmm.

Hugh   What should we do, sir?

Stephen   Good question, Witty. Very good question. My feeling is that we should do *The Mikado*.

Hugh   I'm sorry, sir?

Stephen   I know that some of the younger fellows in

26

the chancellery feel that it's time for a *Pirates of Penzance*, but there isn't a part for me in it, you see.

Hugh   I'm sorry sir, but I don't quite . . .

Stephen I don't want to seem like a spoilsport, but I do feel that there must be a part for me in it, and *The Mikado* seems to be the most appropriate.

Hugh   Surely sir, there are more pressing calls upon our time.

Stephen The gymkhana? Oh I think we can let our wives sort that one out. I've agreed to pin the winning rosette, Julia is going to have to be satisfied with that.

Hugh   The invasion, sir. Unless he is stopped now there'll be the most appalling catastrophe. Surely we must at least issue an ultimatum.

Stephen All right, Witty, all right. Despatch this. 'Unless you withdraw soonest your ticket allocation for our next Gilbert and Sullivan production will be severely reduced.'

Hugh   Ambassador. For heaven's sake.

Stephen Too strong, you think? Perhaps you're right. 'Unless you withdraw soonest Derek Nimmo's touring production of *Separate Tables* will not be cancelled.'

Hugh   Ambassador, he's about to invade! Within a matter of hours we could be on the brink of a world war.

Stephen You've not been long in the Foreign Office have you, Witty?

Hugh   Three years, sir.

Stephen Ah. Really? So you missed our last production of *Pirates*?

27

Hugh	I'm afraid so, sir.
Stephen	Hm. Pity, pity. I wore one of Julia's dresses.
Hugh	I'd heard that, sir.
Stephen	Little tight under the arms, but otherwise surprisingly comfortable.
Hugh	Really, sir? But shouldn't we be . . .
Stephen	There was the most wonderful moment in the second act when I was supposed to go to the front of the stage and kiss the wife of the second secretary. Well, I tripped on one of the steps going down . . .
Hugh	Sir. I'm sorry to interrupt you, but we are facing an extremely dangerous situation and it is our duty to inform London that invasion is imminent and request instructions.
Stephen	I'll be honest with you, Witty.
Hugh	Sir?
Stephen	I don't like you.
Hugh	Why not, sir?
Stephen	Because you're a troublemaker, Witty, that's why. Because you think you know it all.
Hugh	No I don't sir. But with respect we are paid an astonishing amount of money, given servants, wine cellars, automatic knighthoods and fantastic privileges just so that when moments like this arise we will be able to avert war. That is our one function, sir and we owe it to the peoples of the world to start earning our money and actually do something.
Stephen	A pretty speech, Witty.
Hugh	Thank you sir.
Stephen	Pretty and convincing.
Hugh	Thank you very much sir.

28

Stephen   The Victoria Club in Daar al Rashchid holds a public speaking competition every April, first prize is only a silver cup, but this Embassy hasn't won it for over a hundred years. Think I might enter you.

Hugh   But sir, in twenty four hours, there isn't going to be a Victoria Club.

Stephen   What are you talking about?

Hugh   It's slap bang next to the Sheik's Palace. So if there's a war, sir, it'll be the first target. Bound to be the first target.

Stephen   Hell's bells. We must do something. Get me the Foreign Secretary, who's the Foreign Secretary? And how do we get hold of him?

Hugh   We signal from the cypher room.

Stephen   Cypher room. Where's that?

Hugh   It's where we rehearsed *The Gondoliers*.

Stephen   Oh yes, a very attractive room.

VOX
POP

Hugh   We had our first child on the NHS, and had to wait nine months. Can you believe it?

Duel

*Hugh and Stephen in period dress on a misty heath,
about to duel. There is a referee, and possibly some seconds.*

Referee   Gentlemen, I believe you both know the purpose
of this meeting.

Stephen   Thank you Mr Tollerby, but we have no need of
explanation. The circumstances are well known to us.

Hugh   Quite right. Let us be about the business.

Referee   Very well, gentlemen. Sir David, I understand
the choice is yours – sword or pistol?

Hugh   Sword.

Referee   As you wish.

Hugh takes the sword and swishes it expertly.

Hugh   Ha. The only weapon for a gentleman.

Referee   Quite so. That means, Mr Van Hoyle, that you
have the pistol.

Stephen   Thank you, Tollerby.

Referee   When I give the command, I shall expect . . .

Hugh   Wait a minute.

Referee   Is there something wrong, Sir David?

Hugh   Well . . .

Stephen   Quick man, the hour grows late . . .

Hugh   Well it's just that when you said sword or pistol, I
sort of assumed that we would both have the same
one, if you know what I mean . . .

Referee	Ah.
Stephen	I'm not with you.
Hugh	Well I said sword, assuming that meant we would both have a sword . . .
Stephen	Oh I see.
Referee	Mmm. Thing is, I've only brought one of each, unfortunately.
Stephen	Oh damn and blast.
Hugh	Sorry to make a fuss, but it seems a bit unfair otherwise.
Referee	No, I take your point, Sir David.
Stephen	Well is there somewhere we could get a sword?
Hugh	I doubt there'd be anywhere open at this time . . . Excuse me!

Hugh dashes off and stops a pair of joggers in dayglo strip.

	You wouldn't happen to have a sword on you, would you?
Jogger	*(Not stopping)* Twenty past seven.
Hugh	Damn.
Stephen	Well . . . we're a bit stuck, really, aren't we?
Referee	Gentlemen, I realise that this is a bit of an improvisation, but needs must when the devil . . .
Stephen	Get on with it.
Referee	Right, how would it be if Mr Van Hoyle were to take the pistol but promise not to fire it?
Hugh	You mean, use the pistol as if it were a sword?
Referee	Exactly.
Hugh	Well, suits me.

31

Stephen   Wait a minute, wait a minute. That's hopeless. Wouldn't cut anything, look.

Stephen prods Referee with the pistol.

See?

Hugh   Perhaps you're right.

Referee   Well it was just an idea.

Stephen   You could try shooting with your . . . no, that won't work. Forget I spoke.

Hugh   Mm. How about fists?

Referee   You mean boxing?

Stephen   Oh Lord no. I'm no good at that at all. It hurts your knuckles.

Hugh   Well, I can't think of anything else . . . hang on I've got some matches here I think.

Stephen   What, you mean set fire to each other?

Hugh   Better than nothing. Oh no, actually look, there's only one match left in fact.

Stephen   We could nip across to that café and see if they have any forks . . .

Referee   Gentlemen, if you'll bear with me – I have one last idea up my sleeve.

Stephen   Well?

Referee reaches up his sleeve and pulls out a handkerchief.

Hugh   A handkerchief?

Referee   No, Sir David. *Two* handkerchiefs.

Stephen   You're suggesting that we duel to the death with a pair of handkerchiefs?

32

Referee   I realise it's not ideal, Mr Van Hoyle, but it would at least be fair . . .

Stephen   It would take for ever. I've got to be in town by eight.

Hugh   Well we haven't got anything else.

Stephen sighs.

Stephen   Oh all right then. Better be clean, that's all.

Referee   Perfectly clean, I assure you.

They each take a handkerchief.

Gentlemen, I believe you both know the purpose of this meeting?

Stephen and Hugh start hitting each other with handkerchiefs.

> VOX
> POP
>
> **Stephen**   You see it's a slippery slope. It starts by reading the *Daily Mail*. Within a few weeks that's it. You're a witless, heartless lump of shit.

Ass-Kickers Song

Hugh and Stephen are a pair of country boys: Hugh has a guitar and Stephen has a very creepy look.

Hugh   My brother Oren and I would like to sing for you now, but we can't. At least my brother Oren can't, bein' as how he suffered a strange musical accident when he was young, that caused lasting and considerable damage. So if it's all the same to you, my brother Oren will just sit here and tap along to the strange rhythms in his head. This song is called 'There Ain't But One Way'. *(Starts to play)*

(Sings)
The world is facin' problems,
Gettin' bigger every day,
We got a greenhouse over Texas,
And recession's on the way,
There's hunger in the third world,
There's anger in the first,
Half the world is floodin',
And the other's dyin' of thirst,
But tho' people they may tell you,
That this planet's dyin' fast,
I ain't seen a problem yet,
Can't be solved by kickin' ass,
Kickin' ass!

Stephen   Kickin' ass!

Hugh   Kickin' ass is what we do,
Kickin' ass,

Stephen   Kickin' ass!

Hugh   Iron foot in the velvet shoe,
We don't care whose ass we kick,

34

If we're ever all alone,
We just stand in front of the mirror,
And try to kick our own,
We kicked ass in Grenada
We kicked ass in Iraq
We've kicked the ass out of the ozone layer
Now they say we gotta kick it back,
We'll kick the ass of cancer
We'll kick the ass of AIDS
And as for global warming
We'll just kick ass wearing shades.

Stephen   Kickin' ass!

Hugh   Kickin' ass is what we do
Kickin' ass

Stephen   Kickin' ass!

Hugh   Iron foot in the velvet shoe
We don't care whose ass we kick
If we're ever all alone
We just stand in front of the mirror
And try to kick our own
Yes you can move your ass
Haul your ass
And bustin' ass is fine
And there ain't a better place to put your ass
Than on the line
But if you're like us
And you won't take second best
You'll put your kickin' boots on
And kick like all the rest.

Petrol Attendants

Stephen and Hugh are dressed as estate agents, but are working behind the counter of a petrol station.

Hugh   . . . pity you couldn't make it down to that club the other night.

Stephen   Down to Shaggers?

Hugh   Yeah. Cracking club, that. The crumpet there is first rate. I mean really excellent. Absolutely excellent.

Stephen   I heard that. I had heard that the crumpet was top drawer stuff.

Hugh   Oh it's excellent. Excellent.

Stephen   You're a what, gold member there?

Hugh   At Shaggers? Platinum member.

Stephen   Right, 'cos I just got given membership at Screwers.

Hugh   Really? Platinum?

Stephen   Diamond, with strontium edging.

Hugh   Oh that's excellent.

Rebecca enters.

Rebecca   Excuse me, I'm trying to get some petrol out of pump number four.

Hugh   Yup?

Rebecca   Well it doesn't seem to work, can you . . . wait a minute. Don't I know you two from somewhere?

Hugh	Don't believe I've had the pleasure, no. Have you had the pleasure, Simon?
Stephen	Don't believe I have had the pleasure of having the pleasure, Nick, no.
Rebecca	Didn't you used to be estate agents?
Hugh	Er . . .
Rebecca	You did! You were estate agents at . . . where was it? Wilson and Routledge.
Hugh	Er, we did at one point dabble in the property game, yeah.
Stephen	And it is a game, isn't it?
Hugh	Oh hell yes, it's just a game. Stakes are high of course, not everyone can take it, but it's a game nonetheless.
Rebecca	And now you're running a petrol station?
Stephen	Now we're in the petrol game, yeah.
Hugh	And it is a game.
Stephen	Oh yeah.
Rebecca	Well do you mind moving into the switching on pump number four game, because I'm in a bit of a hurry.
Hugh	Yes, can I ask first of all how much you were thinking of spending?
Rebecca	I beg your pardon?
Stephen	M'colleague is trying to get an idea of your price bracket.
Rebecca	Look, I just want some petrol out of pump number four.
Hugh	That would be the Super Plus?
Rebecca	Yes.

Hugh	Simon?
Stephen	Nick?
Hugh	Details on the Super Plus? Lady's in a bit of a hurry. *(To Rebecca)* M'colleague won't keep you a moment.
Rebecca	Details . . . ?
Stephen	*(Reaching into a filing cabinet)* Super Plus, Super Plus. There we go. 'A fine, well-produced petrol in an increasingly sought after octane range, ideal for the professional person.'
Rebecca	Yes, yes, can I have some please?
Hugh	Simon, do we have the keys to pump number four?
Stephen	*(Looking at a board behind the counter)* I believe they're out at the moment, Nick. There's been quite a lot of interest in the Super Plus, as it happens.
Hugh	Oh a great deal of interest. We've had several motorists in here this afternoon, offering cash deals.
Rebecca	Well look, I'm offering a cash deal. I want ten pounds worth of petrol.

She puts a tenner on the counter.

Hugh	Yowzer. Looks like the lady means business.
Stephen	Surely does and then some.
Hugh	So ten pounds of Super Plus would be what, Simon . . . ?
Stephen	I'm on the case. *(Taps away at the till)* That would buy you . . . about two pints.
Rebecca	Two pints?
Hugh	Forty pounds a gallon, Simon, am I right?

Stephen	Right as ever you be, Nick.
Rebecca	Forty pounds for a gallon of petrol?
Hugh	For a gallon of Super Plus.
Stephen	It's a top drawer petrol, that, no question.
Hugh	Oh it's excellent. Absolutely excellent.
Rebecca	But . . .
Stephen	Tell you what. D'you mind, Nick?
Hugh	Carry on ahead.
Stephen	Lady's obviously keen . . .
Hugh	I read the lady as keen myself, Simon.
Stephen	What we might be able to do is ring Mobil and ask whether they'd take an offer.
Rebecca	What are you talking about?
Hugh	Tscch. Very unlikely, Simon.
Stephen	I'm not saying it'll work, Nick, I'm saying give it a try.
Hugh	K.

Stephen dials a number.

	So, what does yourself do in the evenings, I'm wondering?
Stephen	Good question there from m'colleague. Does yourself ever get down to Shaggers in the Kings Parade?
Hugh	Or Screwers in Horley Street?
Rebecca	I'm afraid not.
Hugh	That's a shame. Excellent clubs. Absolutely excellent.
Stephen	*(Into phone)* Hi, Mrs Mobil? Simon Pointless here.

39

About that Super Plus . . . yeah, well I have a
lady here who says she's interested, but wondered
whether you'd be at all flexible on price? Sure I'll
hold. She's gone to check with Mr Mobil.

Hugh   Presumably you're hoping for a more attractive price?

Stephen   Well I'm going to try for a sensible price.

Hugh   Good move. Try for a sensible price first, then
an attractive price later.

Rebecca   I wouldn't mind if it was cheaper.

Hugh   Cheaper. Long time since I've heard that one.
What's 'cheaper' in new money?

Stephen   Beautifully priced.

Hugh   That's it. Let's see what old Simon can do.

Stephen   *(Into phone)* Still here, Mrs Mobil. Lady's looking
for a beautifully priced package. Can do. *(To Rebecca)*
Mrs Mobil is anxious to dispose of the property and
feels she can let it go for 195 a gallon, immediate
sale.

Rebecca   Fine.

Stephen   That's fine Mrs Mobil, we'll get back to you.

Rebecca   Can we get on with it?

Stephen   We're expecting the keys back in a couple of days,
so how about we fix up an appointment towards the
end of the week?

Hugh   Friday at 11?

Stephen   Ah, I'm showing some first-time drivers round
pump number four at eleven on Friday . . .

Hugh   Some time early next week then?

Rebecca   Twenty five thousand estate agents who were safely
confined in offices only a year ago have been forced
by the property slump out into the community. It's

40

a dreadful situation. But you can do something to help. Five pounds will help towards an assault rifle or handgun. Even 50p will buy enough ammunition to deal with a team like Nick and Simon. Please. Give generously. In the meantime, I'm going to have to decide which of these two to shoot first. Goodbye.

Points gun at Hugh & Stephen.

Hugh   Bye.

Stephen   Bye.

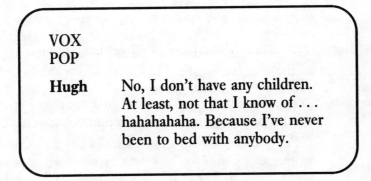

VOX
POP

Hugh   No, I don't have any children.
             At least, not that I know of . . .
             hahahahaha. Because I've never
             been to bed with anybody.

Jobs

Hugh addresses the camera:

Hugh   Hm. Yes. Jobs. I've had a variety of jobs since
I moved to London. I started off, let me see,
running a mobile twenty-four hour discothèque
for the St John's Ambulance Brigade, for when
they had those big functions, and they needed a
discothèque standing by, just in case. And then after
that I set up as a freelance nudist, doing odds and
ends, weddings, supermarket openings, that sort of
thing. A lot of work for Securicor, funnily enough.
But then there was the great nudism crash of '87
and I got in with a removals firm in Notting Hill,
doing a job for an Iraqi diplomat called Nigel Havers.
You can imagine the stick he used to get, having the
same name as Nigel Havers. But he was a nice chap,
and we moved house for him. He wanted his house
moved to the end of the street, because he said it
was easier to park there. Funny thing was that by
the time we'd finished, and put the last slate back
on the roof, an Austin 1100 went and parked in the
space in front of the house, so we had to move it
all back again. Happy days, though. And then, let's
see, I had a couple of months in the white slave
trade – on the selling side, I should point out. Just
on the telephone, really, it was mostly mail order
work, pretty dull, but it did get me into my next
job which was director of pharmaceutical research
at ICI. God knows how I got it, because I don't
know the first thing about drugs, although I was
pretty good in the interview. But they rumbled me
eventually. All I could think of to say was that the
pills ought to be oblong instead of round, and after

a couple of years of that they threw me out. Then I thought I needed a break so I joined a group of travelling loss adjusters. They used to tour round the seaside resorts every summer putting on loss adjusting shows for children. That was very good fun, although I used to drink far too much. God those loss adjusters can stick it away. Unbelievable. Then I was Princess Anne's assistant for a while, but I chucked that in because it was obvious they were never going to make me Princess Anne, no matter how well I did the job. It was a question of who you were, rather than how well you did, you know, and I hate that. After that, let me see . . . etc

VOX
POP

Stephen So I said 'Why don't you shove it where the sun don't shine' and so he did. He put it in the cupboard under the stairs and it hasn't been mentioned since.

European Deal

Hugh   First may I say what an honour this is for my company. I hope this will be the start of a long and fruitful business relationship. Now shall we begin? First of all, Mrs Carry Bannerchief.

Stephen   Tistrada mempot cloonystart, wekwester memenchyfud, lililili hi mau Carrybannerchief . . .

Hugh   My company . . .

Stephen   Hip lokerbelly wimey wimey bobular custole fiper . . .

Hugh   Would . . .

Stephen   Ststerharbulan cotrotty bububub whesker . . .

Hugh   . . . like . . .

Stephen   Marpy fanholer crikerbomb yelymasterman incy gobtratter . . .

Hugh   . . . to tie up a European deal with your company.

Stephen   Ti.

Hugh   But I hope you'll agree . . .

Stephen   Wop bum bum bum bum bum bum bum bum bum . . .

Hugh   That the price must be fair to both parties.

Stephen   Linhakky tutular . . . er . . .

Hugh   Problem?

Stephen   I'm afraid there's no such word as price in Strom.

Hugh   Oh. Er . . . cost?

Stephen   Not really.

Woman   *(Worried)* Hinty p-pepular?

Stephen	*(Reassuring her)* Streen hathock.
Hugh	You must have a word for the amount that is to be paid for something.
Stephen	Not really. There's 'hifty bewn-hate'.
Hugh	What does that mean?
Stephen	It means price in the sense of 'exploding vest'.
Hugh	There's no sense in which price means exploding vest.
Stephen	It's the closest we get.
Hugh	All right – the exploding vest must be fair to both parties.
Stephen	Hifty bewn-hate. Happy hip-wipe.
Woman	Niling clover bolips weethle-fwisk prenty arse.
Stephen	That's perfectly sofa factory.
Hugh	Now – any long-term contracts?

Stephen & woman laugh.

Stephen	Long-term contracts – ha ha ha.
Hugh	Wha . . .
Stephen	You see 'long-term contracts' in Strom means 'wee-wee'.
Hugh	Really?
Stephen	Yes . . . ha ha ha.
Hugh	Yes, well, the only thing left is the outstanding 'long-term contracts', ha ha, for after sales service.
Stephen	What?
Hugh	After sales service.

Woman stands up looking furious.

Woman	Fudd nob.

She smacks Hugh hard in the face and stalks out of the room.

Hugh	What !!!???
Stephen	I do apologise.
Hugh	What on earth did she do that for?
Stephen	Well I think she is not so happy that you would be insulting her.
Hugh	All I said was 'after sales service'.

Stephen slaps Hugh.

Stephen	So you do speak Strom after all.
Hugh	No. What does it mean?
Stephen	What?
Hugh	After sales service.
Stephen	Ah well. I could show you, but I'd have to have a goat and four pairs of Marigold washing-up gloves.
Hugh	Oh dear.
Stephen	Oh you really are cruising for a bruising.
Hugh	Now what? What does 'dear' mean?
Stephen	In Strom, dear means a large animal with wet noses, the soft brown eyes, and the antlings. I suggest you speak with your principals, and I will go and try and placate Mrs Carrybannerchief.

The set is empty. There is a long-ish pause.

Caption
'I expect they'll be back in a minute'

46

Pause.

Caption
'Oh dear'

Pause.

Caption
'In a way, it's surprising that this doesn't happen more often.'

Pause.

Caption
'After all, rooms spend a lot of their time being empty, don't they?'

Pause.

Caption
'Not that this is a real room, of course.'

Pause.

Caption
'I mean, since there's nothing else going on you might as well take a peek round the sides.'

The camera slowly pans off the set and shows a bit of wall. It returns to the centre and looks off the other side. We catch a glimpse of the rear of a naked man just slipping behind a flat. Camera returns to the centre again.

Caption
'There's an audience as well'

The camera goes all the way round and looks at the audience. Returns to the room.

47

We hear Hugh and Stephen re-entering the set.

Hugh   *(Off camera)* Ah. Any luck with Mrs Vetsach?

Stephen *(Off camera)* I'm afraid she's inconsolable.

Caption
'Hello. Sounds like they're off again.'

The camera pans round to the set again: Hugh and Stephen are back.

Hugh   Well this is more than a little embarrassing. I'd certainly hoped to have this entire deal wrapped up by the end of today.

Stephen You don't know where to stop.

Caption
'There's quite a good film on the other side, if you're interested.'

Pause.

Caption
'I think it's got Rod Steiger in it.'

Pause.

Caption
'And I believe there's a thriller on Channel Four.'

Cocktail Ending 1

Hugh and Stephen address the camera at the end of the show: they are in black tie and Hugh is sitting at the piano.

Stephen   Well that's just about it for this week.

Hugh   That's right. Time the old enemy . . .

Stephen   Oh shut up. So it's good night from me . . .

Hugh   And it's good night from me.

Stephen   We're going to leave you with tonight's cocktail recipe. This one's called 'A Slow Snog With A Distant Relative'. For this you'll need two measures of brandy, three of rum. One measure pink gin, one white. A dash of lemonade, a sprint of orange juice, a spoonful of crushed Sugar Puffs, two hard-boiled eggs and an open-toed sandal, size nine if you can get it. Hit it Mr Laurie, if you'd be so very kind.

Hugh strikes up a jazzy sort of riff while Stephen mixes a 'Slow Snog With A Distant Relative', spilling drinks everywhere.

VOX
POP

Stephen   My only criticism of David Icke is that he doesn't go far enough.

49

We Haven't Met

A drinks party. Hugh approaches Stephen.

Hugh   Hello. We haven't met, Terry Swale. My wife tells me that you're new to Yorkshire.

Stephen   Yes, I'm a bit of a southerner, I'm afraid.

Hugh   Whoops! Can't have that. *(Laughs)*

Stephen   No! *(Laughs)* My mother's family came from Sheriff Hutton, though.

Hugh   Ah, well perhaps there's some hope for you! *(Laughs a great deal)*

Stephen   *(Also laughing a great deal)* Yes!

Hugh   So.

Stephen   Ng.

Pause.

(At length) I must say everyone seems very friendly.

Hugh   Well it's not all whippets and cloth-caps, you know. *(Laughs)*

Stephen   No. No. *(Laughs)*

Hugh   We have heard of avocados and hot and cold running water. *(Shrieks with laughter)*

Stephen   *(Also laughing)* Hot and cold running water! Avocados! That's lovely. So, you live . . . ?

Hugh   Boroughbridge way.

Stephen   Ah, lovely.

Hugh   Well, you know. We've got the Moors handy and the

50

	Dales. Ten minutes and you can be in York, Ripon or Harrogate. We like it.
Stephen	Right. Lots of good air and lovely walks, I should imagine.
Hugh	Ye-e-s. But we have all got cars, you know.
Stephen	Well, naturally.
Hugh	I mean it's not all fell-walking and climbing boots.
Stephen	No. Right.
Hugh	You should see some of the traffic we get in Thirsk and Harrogate.
Stephen	Oh.
Hugh	And the pollution in Leeds can rival anything you've got down south, we like to think.
Stephen	Mm.
Hugh	Oh yes. Sometimes takes me two hours to get to work there are so many cars.
Stephen	Well, right. It can be terrible, can't it? I always used to go to work by bicycle when I was living in London.
Hugh	You can't move in Ripon for bicycles. Worst bicycle jams in Britain.
Stephen	Right. Still, it's a much better place to bring up the kids. I mean, quality of life and everything. Less of the seamier side of life to . . .
Hugh	We have heard of sex and violence up here, you know.
Stephen	Well, obviously.
Hugh	We like to think that there are more drug-related muggings, rapings and beatings in the Vale of York than anywhere outside America. See that woman over there? Sally Oldcastle. She runs the biggest

crack ring in Europe. And what's more she's not stuck-up.

Stephen Good Lord. So there's not much that's different from London, really.

Hugh You said it, mate. Whatever they've got down south, there's more of up here and it's cheaper and more expensive and you can't park.

Stephen Right, right. Well it's getting late, I think I'll just translocate myself home now.

Hugh Beg pardon?

Stephen I must translocate myself home with my personal translocation podule.

Hugh What the hell's that?

Stephen Well it's basically just the same as a domestic translocation podule, but you wear it on your wrist, that's all.

Hugh Yeah, what does it do?

Stephen I punch in the grid coordinates of where I am now, then the coordinates of wherever it is I want to go, press the button on the side and hey presto.

Hugh Hey presto?

Stephen My molecular structure disintegrates and reassembles within a matter of seconds at my chosen destination.

Hugh Hang on, hang on . . .

Stephen What?

Hugh You mean like *Star Trek*?

Stephen I'm sorry?

Hugh You mean you go all wobbly and then disappear?

Stephen My God.

Hugh	What?
Stephen	You mean you've never seen one of these before?
Hugh	Er . . .
Stephen	They're all the rage down South. My daughter bought me this at a petrol station. It's the Sinclair version, but some of the Japanese ones are really fabulous.
Hugh	Wait a minute.
Stephen	What?
Hugh	If you've all got these things . . .
Stephen	Yes?
Hugh	What do you need petrol stations for?
Stephen	For everlasting life.
Hugh	I'm sorry?
Stephen	Everlasting life. They discovered it a couple of years ago in Southampton. If you drink a gallon of petrol every day, you'll live for ever. You must have heard that?
Hugh	That? Oh yeah. We drink petrol up here, all right. Yeah. Live for ever, we do, sometimes longer.
Stephen	Well I should hope so. I'm just amazed you don't have personal translocation podules.
Hugh	Who said we don't have them?
Stephen	Well I just thought . . .
Hugh	Bloody designed and built up here, those things. We've had 'em for years. In fact, they've come and gone.
Stephen	Have they?
Hugh	Oh yeah. They were a sort of craze for a while, but nowadays . . . no, I was just surprised to see

53

people still using them after all this time. It's been years since I've seen one of them things.

Stephen   Oh, well would you like to have a go on mine? For old time's sake.

Hugh   No thanks.

Stephen   Sure?

Hugh   I've had a couple of drinks. Don't want to get pulled by the law when my molecules are all over the place.

Stephen   Fair enough. Well, I'll be on my way.

Stephen grabs a cloth-cap and puts it on his head. He collects a leash on the end of which there is a whippet.

Hugh   What are those?

Stephen   Cloth-cap and whippets. All the rage down south. Bye.

He presses a button on his watch and disappears.

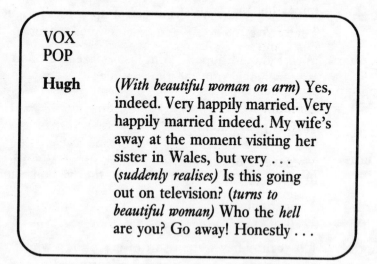

VOX
POP

Hugh   (*With beautiful woman on arm*) Yes, indeed. Very happily married. Very happily married indeed. My wife's away at the moment visiting her sister in Wales, but very . . . (*suddenly realises*) Is this going out on television? (*turns to beautiful woman*) Who the *hell* are you? Go away! Honestly . . .

54

Names

Stephen and Hugh are going through letters.

Hugh   Hello.

Stephen   Certainly. You know, we've had, as you can see
from these post bags, the most marvellous response
to our Name Quest.

Hugh   That's right. We know that a lot of you out there
have known or met people who have amusing and
unusual names.

Stephen   So we asked you to write in and tell us about them.

Hugh   And what crackers you've told us about!

Stephen   *(Reading)* 'There is a man who comes to wash
my windows once a month whose name is Jervillian
Swike. It always makes me laugh a great deal.' That
was sent in from a Mr Suckmaster Burstingfoam of
Ipswich.

Hugh   I'm rather fond of this one: 'Dear *A Bit Of Fry
and Laurie*, I was at school with a boy called Donald
Duck and later went out with a woman named Soilia
Piffin. Yours etc. Peter Cummin-Myear.'

Stephen   Five pounds on its way to you for that one Mr
Cummin-Myear. Or how about this one 'Dear *A
Bit Of Fry and Laurie*, My wife's first husband
was called Simon Coggie. I still split my sides
whenever I hear that name. Yours faithfully Frigmy
Popplehate-Fresharse.'

Hugh   Tremendous response all around. Many thanks
to all of you who wrote in. Meanwhile . . .

The Other Department

On Film: Hugh is loitering on a street corner, looking hard. He looks around him, and then enters one of those Pay-Az-U-Krapp public lavatories: cut inside to the interior of a dingy office, which, in a tardis sort of fashion, is larger than it ought to be. Hugh looks round him and then approaches a desk, behind which Stephen is being measured up by a tailor.

Stephen Alan, dear boy, glad you could make it. Shan't keep you a moment.

Hugh No problem.

Tailor Three or four buttons on the cuff, sir?

Stephen Oh, I'm not sure. What do you think, Alan?

Hugh *(Shrugs)* Three's plenty.

Stephen You think?

Hugh The lighter the cuff, the faster you move.

Tailor Four is normal nowadays, sir.

Stephen Hm. Tell you what, three on the left, four on the right.

Tailor Very good, sir. *(Jots in his notebook)*

Stephen Now, I dare say you'll be wondering why I asked you here.

Tailor Well I assumed you wanted a suit made.

Stephen Hm. Alan, do you know why I asked *you* here?

Hugh Nope.

Stephen Not even the teensiest hint of a suspicion?

Hugh None at all.

56

Stephen Good. *That*'s why I asked for you. That's *why* I asked for you. That's why *I* asked for *you*.

Hugh I don't follow.

Stephen You're an outsider, Alan, and that means I can trust you.

Tailor Excuse me, sir. Trousers.

Stephen Trousers? Oh yes, I think so. Got to have trousers. Look a complete arse without trousers.

Tailor Yes, sir. Did you envisage zip or button fly?

Stephen Hoo, tricky. Views, Alan?

Hugh Buttons are a dangerous luxury in my line of work. Personally, I'm a velcro man.

Stephen Really? Bit noisy, isn't it?

Hugh Noisy but fast. By the time they've heard your flies, it's a lifetime too late.

Stephen Right, velcro it is. Now Alan, I have a little theory that I'd like you to hear.

Hugh I'm listening.

Stephen The Department is rotten. Rotten to the core. Am I ringing any bells with you?

Hugh You're saying the Department is rotten?

Stephen It's a theory, Alan. Just a theory. Run with me, and let's see how it plays.

Hugh K.

Tailor One other thing, sir?

Stephen Yes?

Tailor Which side do you dress?

Stephen Er, nearest the window usually. Now Alan, I want you to cast your mind back to Berlin.

57

Hugh looks grim.

Stephen   Problem?

Hugh   You told me to draw a line after Berlin. Walk away and forget, you said.

Stephen   Of course. You had to get out in rather a hurry, didn't you?

Hugh   I can't remember.

Tailor   Ticket pocket, sir?

Stephen   Hm?

Tailor   On the waistcoat.

Stephen   Ticket pocket, ticket pocket, ticket pocket. I think not. Hermione and I don't seem to get out to the theatre as much as we used to these days. Seems a bit of a waste.

Hugh   Look, if you've hauled me all the way out here . . .

Stephen   Calm yourself, Alan. There's reason in my madness. Now tell me. What do you know of Carl Albert Beiderbeck?

Hugh   Beiderbeck. 5'11". Blue build, medium eyes. Father was a Romanian circus acrobat, did some courier work for the Soviets in the late fifties. Mother was a small business adviser for the Midland Bank in Altrincham. Small arms, big feet. Fluent at the violin. Distinguishing marks, a small mole in his garden.

Stephen   Ha. I'm impressed Alan.

Hugh   I've seen the file.

Stephen   Well then, you're one of the few people in the Department who has.

Hugh   Meaning?

58

Stephen	Meaning you're one of the few people in the Department who has.
Hugh	I see.
Stephen	The Beiderbeck file went walkies six weeks ago. Hasn't been seen since.
Hugh	I see. Hence your rotten apple theory.
Stephen	Noooo. Hence my rotten Department theory. I don't really have a rotten apple theory.
Hugh	Who drew the file last?
Stephen	That is what you're going to find out.
Tailor	Begging your pardon, sir . . .
Stephen	Oh no. You're not going to ask about turn-ups are you?
Tailor	No sir. About the Beiderbeck file.
Stephen	Yes?
Tailor	I was the last person to draw the file.
Hugh	You?
Stephen	Well I'll be rogered with a stiff wire brush . . .
Tailor	Mr Beiderbeck wanted a suit made. Said he was going on a trip, and where he was headed, no one knew how to cut cloth properly. He couldn't come in for a fitting, so I had to get his measurements from the file.
Stephen	Alan, are you thinking what I'm thinking?
Hugh	No.
Stephen	Ah.
Hugh	What sort of suit did Beiderbeck order from you?
Tailor	Three piece houndstooth worsted, zip fly, four button cuffs.

Stephen   Ticket pocket?

Tailor   Oh yes, sir. Mr Beiderbeck was a great one for the theatre.

Stephen   Was he? Was he by didgery-handpoo?

Tailor   Very flamboyant gentleman, Mr Beiderbeck. I often thought he'd have done well on the stage himself.

Stephen   You know what this means, don't you Alan?

Hugh   Berlin, sir?

Stephen   Precisely. We have to get that file back.

Tailor   Well I'll ask my wife to put it in a taxi, if you like sir?

Hugh   There's a Lufthansa flight in an hour.

Stephen   I'll ask Judy to book you on it.

Tailor   Well we're only up in Finsbury Park, sir.

Stephen   If that file should fall into the wrong hands . . .

Tailor   It's just sitting on the kitchen table . . .

Stephen   Or get tea spilt on it . . .

Tailor   Ah. Er . . . Which side do you keep your penis, sir?

Cut to the next sketch incredibly quickly.

VOX POP

Stephen   My wife and I have been going to Provence for years. Well before it was fashionable. We like to think that we discovered it. The French were amazed when we pointed it out. They'd simply never noticed it.

The Day I Forgot My Legs

Stephen addresses camera.

Stephen   I don't know if I ever told you about the day
I forgot my legs. I can't remember which day
it was: it was one of the ones that happened
in 1987, I can't remember which exactly, there
were so many. In particular there were quite a lot
of Tuesdays then, I remember, so I've a feeling it
might have been one of those. Anyway, I was on
my way into work with Sir Peter Thorneycroft, no
relation, one fresh June morning in early May and
we took the short cut across the fields. I stooped
to pick a buttercup, why people leave buttocks
lying around, I've no idea. The gentlest
breeze and mildest Camemberts were packed
in our hamper and all nature seemed to be
holding its breath. We made good time by taking a
back way across what was then the main Corpusty
to Saxmundham Road. I was just remarking to
Peter how still and peaceful everything was
when he suddenly agreed with me and said how he
thought everything was still and peaceful too.
You know how if you half-close your eyes you can't
see so well? I'd just discovered that it was equally
true if you half-opened them. I was pointing this
out when I suddenly noticed that I'd completely
forgotten my legs. We had to go back for them. The
moment was spoiled and three years later almost to
the decade, Margaret Thatcher was hounded from
office. I sometimes muse on what might have
happened if I had forgotten my ears as well. Never
go back, ladies and gentlemen. Never go back.

Firing

Stephen is sitting at a desk. Hugh knocks and enters.

Stephen Ah, Terry, thanks for dropping by.

Hugh No problem.

Stephen Good, good. You got my memo, I take it?

Hugh The one asking me to drop by?

Stephen Yeah.

Hugh Got it this morning.

Stephen Excellent, excellent.

Hugh You got mine, hopefully?

Stephen Yours? I don't think I did, no.

Hugh It's not important. Just said I would drop by.

Stephen Right. Probably in my in-tray. I dare say Carol will have taken care of it.

Hugh Right. How is Carol, by the way?

Stephen Er . . . How is Carol. Hold on a sec.

Stephen presses intercom buzzer.

Carol?

Carol *(Off)* Yes?

Stephen How are you?

Carol *(Off)* Fine, thank you.

Stephen She's fine.

Hugh Oh good.

Stephen I thought she was, but I don't have the paperwork in front of me. Anyway. Worth checking.

Hugh Absolutely.

Stephen Now Terry. I'd like if I may to go through a little recap of your career. You've been with us for nearly three years, am I right?

Hugh Seven, actually.

Stephen Seven, is it really? Seven years. Tscch. There was I thinking it was three, when all along it was seven. Well thanks for putting me right.

Hugh No trouble.

Stephen starts taking notes.

Stephen Now how would you describe your duties here in that time?

Hugh Well I suppose as personnel manager I guess it's been my job to look after the hiring and firing around here.

Stephen The hiring and . . .

Hugh Firing.

Stephen Firing. Hmm. *(Writing)* Two 'F's' in firing?

Hugh No, just one.

Stephen Just one. Firing. Yes of course it's one. One 'F' in firing. It would look silly with two. Now by firing, I take it that you don't mean rifles or anything like that? You mean firing in the sense of sacking, or dismissing an employee.

Hugh That's right. Although a rifle would be handy every now and then.

Stephen Would it? Oh my dear chap, you should have said.

Hugh No, not really.

63

Stephen You sure?

Hugh I've had to give courses of instruction to senior management.

Stephen In how to fire people. You've done wonders, Terry. The whole company is massively grateful to you for the guidance you've given in how to fire, sack or dismiss employees.

Hugh Well, I aim to please.

Stephen Ha. Aim to please, and fire to please.

Hugh Ha ha. Very good.

Stephen Thanks. Well now, Terry, I need your advice.

Hugh Fire away. Ha ha.

Stephen Ha ha ha. That's it exactly. I have to fire away. So Terry, let us suppose for a moment, that I wanted to fire someone.

Hugh Right. Well I advise directness and candour.

Stephen Two s's in directness. Directness and candour.

Hugh Start off with a brief recap of their career, how long they've held their present job . . .

Stephen Done that.

Hugh . . . and then tell them, as directly and candidly as you can, that they're fired.

Stephen Just like that?

Hugh Just like that.

Stephen So, sort of 'Terry, you're fired', you think would meet the case?

Hugh Absolutely.

Stephen Terry, you're fired.

Hugh That's it.

64

Stephen	Right. Good. Er . . . Terry?
Hugh	Yup.
Stephen	You're fired.
Hugh	That's perfect.
Stephen	Good, good. Terry, you are actually fired.
Hugh	Yeah, you only have to say it once.
Stephen	Oh do I? I don't have to repeat it?
Hugh	Best not to.
Stephen	So having said, 'Terry you're fired' you would ideally get up and walk out of the building?
Hugh	Sometimes.
Stephen	Sometimes?
Hugh	Sometimes I might break down in tears and beg you to take me back.
Stephen	Oh dear.
Hugh	I know.
Stephen	Well we don't want that.
Hugh	Other times, I would just go very quiet and nod.
Stephen	Well that's more the sort of thing I was hoping for, I must say.
Hugh	It varies a lot from case to case. Depends on the individual.
Stephen	Hmm. What about you?
Hugh	Me?
Stephen	Would you say that you were a crier, or a nodder?
Hugh	Well you never really know until it's happening.
Stephen	I see. I see.

Hugh	I think I'm a nodder.
Stephen	Right. Terry?
Hugh	Yes?
Stephen	You're fired.
Hugh	That's great.
Stephen	You're fired.
Hugh	No, just once.
Stephen	Mm. And if the person you want to fire, doesn't really take it seriously?
Hugh	That often happens.
Stephen	Does it?
Hugh	Thing to do is to look them right in the eyes and tell them.
Stephen	I see.

Stephen looks deep into Hugh's eyes.

Terry?

Hugh	Yes?
Stephen	You are . . . fired.
Hugh	Just like that, perfect.
Stephen	Good. Excellent. Thank you, Terry.
Hugh	So, is that all?
Stephen	No. There's one other thing. *(Searching through paper on his desk)* I'm having the most tremendous difficulty firing someone. I've followed your instruction to the letter, directness with two s's, candour, look them in the eye . . .
Hugh	And they can't take it on board, can't accept it's

66

them, give me their name and department, and I'll
take care of it for you.

Stephen   Would you Terry? That would be a great burden
off my shoulders.

Hugh   That's what I'm here for. Catch you later.

Stephen   Possibly Terry, possibly.

Hugh exits.

Stephen signs.

Hugh re-enters.

Hugh   You bastard.

Stephen   I thought you said you were a nodder.

VOX
POP

Hugh   I lost my sense of smell during
the Korean War. I was cycling down
Witford Street, just over there, and
I got knocked off by a GPO van.
Never smelt anything since.

Question of Sport

Question of Sport *studio. Hugh is Emlyn Hughes and Stephen is David Coleman.*

Stephen So, Emlyn, what happened next?

Hugh Well, the lad's gone through, he's gone through the door . . . and he's hit it, but it's gone right into the crowd, and so . . . he gets arrested. Bobby comes along and nicks him.

Stephen That's what you think happened next, is it?

Hugh Yeah. He's hit it, and been arrested.

Stephen So, you think he's hit it and then been arrested?

Hugh Yeah.

Stephen That is what you think actually happened?

Hugh Yeah.

Stephen Don't want to change your mind?

Hugh No, that's definitely what happened.

Stephen You are sure about that. You definitely think . . . that that is the right answer? He hits it into the crowd and then gets arrested . . .

Hugh Yeah.

Stephen . . . is what you think actually happened . . . next.

Hugh Yeah.

Stephen Well, Emlyn, I have to tell you that you are . . . righwroorigh . . .

Freeze frame: same happens again. We pull out from

68

the still to see another QoS *studio, and another David and Emlyn.*

Stephen   So, Emlyn, what happened next?

Hugh   Well, the lad's answered the question, and then he's got so pissed off because the other bloke wouldn't say whether the answer was right or not, that he's pulled out a gun and shot him.

Stephen   That's what you think happened is it?

Hugh   Yeah.

Stephen   You think that Emlyn shoots the host of the programme, because he takes so long to say whether the answer is right or not?

Hugh   Yeah?

Stephen   That is actually, what you think happened?

Hugh   Yeah.

Stephen   You think, that what you have just said is the right answer to the question?

Hugh   Yeah.

Stephen   Well, you are . . . righwrorigh . . .

Hugh shoots Stephen in the head.

. . . absolutely right.

VOX
POP

Hugh   I don't know much about pornography. But I know what I like.

Shoe Shop

Hugh   Morning.

Stephen   I beg your pardon?

Hugh   I said good morning.

Stephen   *(Calling)* Good morning to you sir. Mr Dalliard,
we have a gentleman in the shop. I have parried his
opening remark, and we are now having a pleasant
conversation. *(To Hugh)* Mr Dalliard will be joining
us as soon as is likely. Though of course, one *says*
good morning, does one not, Mr . . . ?

Hugh   Er. Pardoe.

Stephen   One *says* good morning Mr Jowett, but if you
would be delicious enough to pop your head out of
the door *(inexplicably impatient)* conveniently situated
just over there for God's sake! – is far from good. It
is very very win . . . try.

Hugh   Yes. Yes it is, isn't it?

Stephen   Very win . . .

Hugh   . . . try.

Stephen   That's right. Certainly. So. From win . . . triness
to you, young master Jowett. How may we serve?

Hugh   Yes. I was after a pair of shoes.

Stephen   Ah very well. I shall serve them first.

Hugh   No, no. I meant I am looking for a pair of shoes.

Stephen   To buy?

Hugh   To buy.

Stephen   Mr Dalliard. The gentleman wishes to buy a pair
of shoes. *(Pause)* Oh, what rotten decomposing luck.
Mr Dalliard tells me we have no shoes.

Hugh	I must say, you've got very good hearing.
Stephen	I beg your pardon?
Hugh	I didn't hear your Mr Dalliard at all.
Stephen	*My* Mr Dalliard?
Hugh	Yes, the fellow you . . .
Stephen	Oh sir, I've confused you.
Hugh	Have you?
Stephen	Indeed, yes. I should make it clearer than a Waterford bed-pan, that Mr Dalliard is most assuredly not *my* Mr Dalliard. He's *everybody's* Mr Dalliard. A gift to the nation, if you like. As much *my* Mr Dalliard as *your* Mr Dalliard, or, dare I say it, and I think I dare, Gary Lineker's Mr Dalliard.
Hugh	Gary Lineker?
Stephen	So it looks as if you've come to exactly the wrong place. I should advise you to turn around, leave by the door which is *(angry again)* still conveniently situated just over there for God's sake! *(Nice again)* Walk seventeen paces to your left and enter the shoe shop you will find next to a branch of Finlay's the tobacco people.
Hugh	This isn't a shoe shop?
Stephen	Good lord and lots else besides, no, Mr Jowett.
Hugh	Well, wh . . .
Stephen	This is a place where people come to meet privately and talk in an informal, intimate atmosphere with a view to enjoying a massage and several rounds of sexual intercourse.
Hugh	What?
Stephen	THIS IS A PLACE . . .
Hugh	You mean a brothel?

71

Stephen	I dislike the word brothel, Mr Jowett. I prefer to use the word brothels. Yes, this is a brothels.
Hugh	But . . . the shoes.
Stephen	Shoes?
Hugh	These – *(indicating the large shoes around the place)*
Stephen	Those are my prostitutes, Mr Jowett.
Hugh	Prostitutes. You mean people pay to have sex with those?
Stephen	Very much of course they pay, Colonel Jowett. I am not a charitable organisation, much though the evidence may point to my being reasonably tall.
Hugh	Lots of people?
Stephen	Ah. I fancy I detect a wrinkle of concern on your otherwise smooth and toboggonable brow. Business is not what it was, nor even what it is. It may not even be what it will be. We shall see. If it is. If it isn't, I may have to consider an early retirement. Mr Dalliard, I'm drivelling!
Hugh	Well, I mean really, having sex with shoes.
Stephen	Sir?
Hugh	It seems very . . .
Stephen	Very?
Hugh	Very. . .
Stephen	Very?
Hugh	Well, very . . .
Stephen	Well, very?
Hugh	Oh I don't know.
Stephen	Yes, it does, doesn't it? *Very* oh I don't know.
Hugh	I mean this . . . *(he picks up a large moccasin)*

72

Stephen	Fredericka is perhaps the most popular moccasin in this brothels, Professor Jowett, and I don't care who knows it.
Hugh	*(Feeling inside with his hand)* Well I grant you that the lining is very . . .
Stephen	Twenty pounds.
Hugh	I'm sorry.
Stephen	Master Anthony Jowett, you have just inserted your hand right inside Fredericka's most intimate interior partlets. You cannot be expected to do such things gratis.
Hugh	Yes but . . .
Stephen	Twenty pounds.
Hugh	And that's all I get for twenty pounds is it. A feel?
Stephen	No, no. If you would like to go into the copulatorium thither you may take Fredericka and an escort of your choice therein and sauce her to your heart's con . . .
Hugh	. . . tent, I see. Well, in that case, I suppose . . . *(He reviews the selection of shoes and holds up a small sandal)*
Stephen	*(Shocked)* Sir! It is more than my job's worth. If you want that kind of thing, I suggest you go to the Philippines.
Hugh	Ah, right. Well, I'll take Fredericka and . . . this one. *(He selects a Chelsea boot)*
Stephen	Very good, sir. Fredericka and Colin. Through there. You have half an hour.
Hugh	Er . . . Colin?
Stephen	I won't tell sir, discretion is my middle letter. *(Hugh exits. Stephen shouts off)* Mr Dalliard, we have a three way, see you at the peep-hole!

Get Well Card

Stephen enters a stationer's, general Sub Post Office, card shop sort of a place. He is an old man, from the north, with a voice not unlike a combination of Robb Wilton and Harry Worth. I don't know why, but there it is (as Harry Worth used to say). Hugh is a female assistant.

Hugh   Help you, chuck?

Stephen   Well dear, I don't know. I don't know as if you can help. Do you have any get well cards?

Hugh   Dozens. We've got dozens. Dozens we've got.

Stephen   Aye, well, that's all very high and dandy, but have you got one? You see, it's my daughter's twenty-first Friday week.

Hugh   You'll want a birthday card then, pet.

Stephen   I wish it were that simple. No, you see. Let me think. My wife. She's my second wife you see. The first drowned in a mixed salad in 1978. My second wife is a younger lady.

Hugh   Like myself.

Stephen   Like yourself. Very like yourself. Slightly heavier beard-line though. I've got a photo . . .

Hugh   Ooh, lovely.

Stephen   But it's of the Bolton Wanderers' reserve team playing away at Blackburn so it's of no use to you. Anyway, my second wife, she doesn't like younger ladies around you see. They remind her that she's getting on herself. And next Friday, when it's my daughter Amanda's twenty-first . . .

74

Hugh	That'll be her stepdaughter.
Stephen	My daughter by my first wife – she'll be jealous.
Hugh	It is never easy being a stepmother.
Stephen	She'll see her stepdaughter be all young on her twenty-first and she'll have one of her jealous spasms.
Hugh	They can be nasty, can spasms.
Stephen	Well that's right love. So I'd like to have a get well card good and ready.
Hugh	Well there's one here. It's got a message 'Sorry about the varicose veins, get well soon'.
Stephen	Well it's grand that. It's lovely. But I'm not sure as it's appropriate. Have they all got specific messages?
Hugh	Well they do these days. It's the acid rain, I think. Hold up chucker-pet, this is more like. 'Sorry to hear your teeth fell out in the Arndale Centre, All my love Thomas.'
Stephen	My, that is specific, isn't it?
Hugh	It *is* specific, doll, that's the charm.
Stephen	I see. I do see. Still not quite right though, is it?
Hugh	How about a nice printed poem? 'I'm right sorry to learn yer, Succumbed to another nasty hernia. You mustn't lift what you cannot carry, All the best, your grandson, Harry.'
Stephen	I'll take that one, on the off-chance.
Hugh	What off-chance, duck?
Stephen	Well on the off-chance I change my name from Fred to Harry and my grandmother comes back to life, and has another nasty hernia. You never know.
Hugh	It's as well to make sure. But I'm sure we've

got something that meets your particular case, petty-love. Ah, now. What's this? 'Where are your youthful years, your stepdaughter has 'em, That's why you had such a dreadful spasm, Hope you recover very quick, Your loving husband Frederick.' That's what you're after.

Stephen Oh, what a pity. I'm Alfred, you see. Not Frederick.

Hugh Now that's a shame.

Stephen Never mind I'd best forget it.

Hugh Well, you'd best take one of these from me then.

Stephen Hello. What's this. *(He reads)*
'Poor old Alfred life is hard,
You tried to buy a get well card
There wasn't one to meet your case
Ever so sorry, much love, Trace.'

Hugh That's me.

Stephen Well bless you chuck.

Hugh Least I could do, dove pot.

VOX
POP

Stephen All these so called chattering classes. Your Harold Pinters and your Lady Antonia Braggs and so on. They all earn good money and yet they claim to be socialists. Incredible. Only poor people should be allowed to be left-wing in my view. Anyway, if these people were real socialists they would give everything away. Oh no that's Christians who are supposed to do that isn't it? You'll have to forgive me, I'm mad.

76

'Photocopying My Genitals
With . . .'

*Hugh addresses the camera while standing behind a
large office photocopier.*

Hugh   Hello, I'm Tony Inchpractice, and welcome to
'Photocopying My Genitals With'. Tonight I shall be
'Photocopying My Genitals With' Sir Alan Beaverby,
one time Labour Employment Secretary, now an
active member of the International Orphans Trust.
Good evening, Sir Alan, thanks for coming on the
show.

Stephen   My pleasure, Tony. Good of you to have me.

Hugh   Now, Sir Alan, the equipment is ready . . .

Stephen   Hahaha.

Hugh   Hahaha, yes, so shall I go first?

Stephen   Yes, after you, Tony.

Hugh   Right.

*Hugh lifts up the cover of the photocopier, removing
his tackle: he then gently lowers the lid, all while
talking.*

Now, Sir Alan, you retired from politics last August
after a quarter of a century in the House of Commons,
in which you held a variety of Cabinet posts, was that
a particularly sad time for you?

Stephen   Oh yes, very sad indeed. Apart from anything else,
one makes so many friends in politics, and of course
I was very sorry to have to leave them behind, as it
were.

Hugh   Would you mind pressing the buttons for me?

Stephen   Oh yes, of course. Er . . . how many copies do
              we want?

Hugh   Well, one each for us, I think, and one for luck?

Stephen   Right you are.

*Stephen presses the relevant buttons and the machine
begins to whirr.*

Hugh   You had a particularly harrowing time in the late
              sixties, when it was alleged that you were involved
              in the Dobro property scandal. Were you at all tempted
              to leave politics then?

Stephen   It crossed my mind, Tony, obviously. But my
              wife was adamant that I should carry on, so I did.

Hugh   Do you still keep in touch with the political scene
              now?

Stephen   Oh yes, as much as I can. I'm still active in the
              constituency, and I like to drop into the visitors
              gallery at the Commons whenever I can.

Hugh   Right, Sir Alan, your turn.

Hugh removes himself from the machine.

Stephen   I say, would you mind if I did something slightly
              different?

Hugh   Not at all.

Stephen   It's just that I'd be much more interested in
              photocopying my bottom, if that's all right.

Hugh   Well I don't see why not. Can we do that? Yes,
              we can do that. Would you like me to hold anything?

Stephen   No, no. I'll just hop on here . . .

Stephen drops his trousers and sits on the photocopier.

There we go.

Hugh   Three copies?

Stephen   Well again, I don't want to go bucking the system and making a nuisance of myself, but would you mind doing a couple of hundred?

Hugh   A couple of hundred, wow.

Stephen   It's just that I do keep getting requests from charity auctions and that sort of thing, and it would be so useful to have something to send them.

Hugh   I quite understand. So . . . enjoying retirement?

Stephen   Enormously.

Hugh   Goodnight.

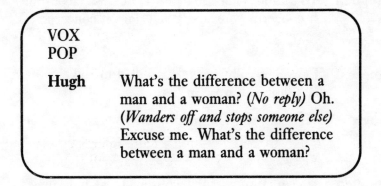

VOX
POP

Hugh   What's the difference between a man and a woman? (*No reply*) Oh. (*Wanders off and stops someone else*) Excuse me. What's the difference between a man and a woman?

My Ass

Stephen is seated at a large desk in American military uniform, smoking a huge cigar: a Stars and Stripes flag hangs behind him.

Stephen Jacobson! Get your ass in here right now!

Hugh enters, also in uniform, carrying a holdall.

Hugh Sir!

Stephen Jacobson, what the hell am I going to do with your ass?

Hugh My ass, sir?

Stephen Can you think of one goddamn reason why I shouldn't kick your ass all the way back to New Mexico?

Hugh Well, sir if this concerns . . .

Stephen You know what the hell it concerns, Jacobson. It concerns your ass! What does it concern?

Hugh My ass, sir.

Stephen Do you recall what it was I said to you the last time you were in here?

Hugh Well sir. You told me to move my ass, and haul my ass, and not to sit on my ass, because if I did, you would personally rearrange my ass.

Stephen Uh uh. Wrong, Mr Jacobson. I was not going to rearrange your ass – I was going to boil your ass in a bag, and have your ass for breakfast.

Hugh That's it, sir. Have my ass for breakfast.

Stephen	Read that sign, Jacobson.
	Hugh looks at a sign on Stephen's desk.
Hugh	'The buck stops at my ass.'
Stephen	See, that's why I have this star Jacobson. Because my ass is on the line.
Hugh	The bottom line . . . ?
Stephen	The bottom line.
Hugh	I understand.
Stephen	Well, I am glad you got your ass straight on that one. Now Jacobson, I've got myself a problem.
Hugh	A problem, sir?
Stephen	Yup. Seems that some goddamn college boy on the fifth floor wants a piece of my ass . . .
Hugh	Your ass, sir?
Stephen	You bet your ass, my ass. If I could just get my hands on this guy's ass, his ass is history.
Hugh	Whose ass would that be sir?
Stephen	The guy who's got his ass in my face, Jacobson.
Hugh	Sir?
Stephen	Yes, Jacobson?
Hugh	How does my ass fit into all of this?
Stephen	It's very simple, Jacobson. You are aware that your ass is mine?
Hugh	It is sir?
Stephen	Oh yes, your ass is mine, mister. The day you joined the army, you signed your ass over to me.
Hugh	I get it, sir.
Stephen	Oh you do, do you?

Hugh	This guy wants a piece of your ass, so you're thinking that, being as my ass is yours, maybe you could give him a piece of my ass as a way of saving your ass.
Stephen	Shut your ass, Jacobson. Nobody likes a smart Alec. Now boy . . .
Hugh	Sir?
Stephen	Got your ass with you?
Hugh	Yes sir.

Hugh plops the bag on the desk. Stephen looks into the bag.

Hugh	With respect, sir, don't jerk my ass around.
Stephen	Mm. Nice piece of ass.

VOX
POP

Hugh (*Holding a lead*) There's a lot of crap talked about pit bull terriers, really. They're great dogs. Absolutely great dogs. The pit bull terrier. You see Tyson here, he wouldn't hurt anyone unless . . . arrggh!

My Ass Critique

Late Show *type set.*
Graphic: The Not Quite Late Enough Show.

Hugh   With me to discuss that scene from Scorsese's new release *From Here to Just Over There,* is the critic, critic and critic Ray Daugh. Ray you've written countless, almost worthless books on the iconography of 'the bottom' in American films – in what context can we approach this piece?

Stephen   Not really, no. We knew already that 'the ass' has come to . . .

Hugh   By 'ass' you mean 'bottom'?

Stephen   Tremendously. You'll have to forgive my lapsing into jargon for a moment there . . .

Hugh   By 'jargon' you mean a series of specialist phrases, or better an 'argot' if you will, to describe a particular area of criticism?

Stephen   In some ways yes. The bottom has come to stand for the essence . . .

Hugh   The spirit?

Stephen   . . . the essence of the individual in modern American mythology . . .

Hugh   The contemporary single person living within a set of folkloric beliefs in Stateside North America.

Stephen   In my last book . . .

Hugh   A book being a work of thought or prose bound together between hard or soft covers and commonly sold in bookshops?

Stephen   Broadly . . . in my last book, *Backside Story: A History of the American Bottom* I devoted an entire chapter to the . . .

Hugh   A chapter meaning a sub-division in a book, of which there are perhaps twelve, fifteen, twenty, creating blocks of writing?

Stephen   Often . . . an entire chapter I devoted to the phrase 'my ass is on the line'. 'The line' being . . .

Hugh   I think we all know what a line is.

Stephen   In this case 'the line' being the vestigial notion of the frontier in American folklore. Partly – *(gesturing)* to put his bottom on the frontier – is still the goal of the modern American.

Hugh   *(Copying gesture)* By this you mean an utterly infuriating gesture guaranteed to put people's backs up in quite a major way.

Stephen   I hope so.

Hugh   Well, sadly the clock has . . .

Stephen   Large, circular timepiece . . .

Hugh   . . . beaten us once again.

Stephen   Flagellated, whipped us for at least a second time . . .

Hugh   So thank you . . .

Stephen   Expression of gratitude . . .

Hugh   Ray . . .

Stephen   Shaft, or beam of light . . .

Hugh   Very much.

Stephen   A lot.

Hugh   Pat.

Stephen   Small slab of butter.

84

News Report

Hugh is in a belted raincoat, addressing the camera with a microphone: behind him is an imposing building. He is a bit nervous: Stephen is the cameraman, hence we only hear his voice off.

Hugh   Ready?

Stephen   Yup.

Hugh   You don't mind that car being parked there? That's all right is it?

Stephen   Fine, we don't see it.

Hugh   OK. Right. *(Clears his throat)* The atmosphere outside Bristol Crown Court was tense this morning . . . sorry . . .

Stephen   What?

Hugh   Better just let these people through . . .

Stephen   What people?

Hugh   These people . . . Oh. Tsch. They've gone the other way. Huh. Looked as if they were going to come this . . .

Stephen   Ready whenever you are.

Hugh   Right. The atmosphere outside Bristol Crown Court was tense this afternoon as the defendants . . . oh damn. Ha ha ha.

Stephen   What?

Hugh   I said Plymouth Crown Court.

Stephen   No you didn't.

Hugh   Didn't I?

Stephen	You said Bristol.
Hugh	Did I? Tsch. Could have sworn I said . . . anyway. Ready?
Stephen	Ready.
Hugh	The atmosphere outside Bristol Crown Court was tense this afternoon . . .
Stephen	What is it now?
Hugh	Sorry. Frog in my throat. *(He does some very elaborate coughing)* That's better. Right. Shall we do it?
Stephen	Yes!
Hugh	I agree. Let's just go ahead and do it. In one. Ready?
Stephen	Jesus Christ.
Hugh	Right. The atmosphere outside Bristol Crown Court was . . . sorry, would you mind moving to one side . . . there were some kids staring at me, thanks very much. Right. This is it. Here we go.
Stephen	Arrgh.
Hugh	The atmosphere outside Bristol Crown Court was tense this afternoon, as the defendants . . . oh I don't believe it.
Stephen	WHAT IS IT NOW?
Hugh	Aeroplane.
Stephen	What!?
Hugh	Can't you hear it?
Stephen	NO!
Hugh	Aeroplane. Listen. I thought it was an aeroplane. Sounded like a DC10 actually . . .
Stephen	Can we get on with this?

Hugh	Yeah, hear hear. Let's do it right now. OK. The atmosphere outside Bristol . . . tell you what. I've just had a thought. Wouldn't it be better if we did this round the back, in case they come out that way . . .

Stephen Do this now, or I will kill you.

Hugh What?

Stephen I will kill you unless you do this now.

Hugh Oh look, hey, you can't expect me to work under these circumst . . .

The camera starts to move towards Hugh.

All right, all right. The atmosphere outside Bristol Crown Court was tense this afternoon as the defendants . . . oh my God!

Stephen What?

Hugh There they are!

Stephen Where?

Hugh Over there, coming out of that door!

The camera pans quickly round: nothing. Pans back: Hugh has vanished. Pans the other way: Hugh is disappearing down the street.

Stephen What a twat.

VOX
POP

Hugh   Computers? Bollocks, more like.

Patriotism

Stephen God save our gracious Queen,
Long live our noble Queen,
God save the Queen.
Send her victorious,
Happy and glorious,
Long to reign over us,
God save the Queen.

Now, some of the younger people watching me
here on this programme tonight might think that
there is something amusing or ridiculous in the
words of that grand old hymn, our own Great British
National anthem. I happen to find such people sick,
disgusting, degraded and enormously limp-making in
a sexual sense. There is nothing arousing at all about
people who can mock and sneer at simple love of
country, nothing to make the loins twitch and quiver
about the kind of hooligan who can despoil our flag.
The sort of cynical, atheistic, unpatriotic yoboiks who
hold nothing sacred have no power at all to bring
me to a proud stand. You're going to have to do
something a little bit more than repeat a few cheap
jibes about the land I love if you want me to thicken
and engorge with mounting excitement. In the old
days as soon as the national anthem was heard the
whole nation would rise stiffly to attention. Am I the
only one left? Goodnight.

AA

Stephen, Hugh and others are sitting around a large room. It is an AA session. Hugh is chairing the discussion. His chair is at the head, the others are grouped around him. He clears his throat.

Hugh   Peter, would you like to start?

Man   *(Stands)* My name is Peter Bales and I'm an alcoholic. I last had a drink two years, seven weeks and three days ago. *(Sits to sympathetic murmurs and congratulations.)*

Man 2   *(Stands)* My name is William Gerard. I'm an alcoholic. I haven't drunk for five months and six days. *(Sits)*

Woman 1   *(Stands)* My name is Andrea Mclean and I'm an alcoholic. I last had a drink two days ago. I'm sorry. *(Sits to sympathy)*

Hugh   OK Andrea, no problem. We'll talk about it later.

Camera has arrived at Stephen who appears to be reluctant to speak. He is shy and embarrassed.

Hugh   Would our new member like to speak?

Stephen   Um . . .

Hugh   I know it can be very hard; but everyone here at AA will tell you that the first thing to do is to face your problem. To give it a name.

Stephen   Yes, I see that.

Hugh   Until you can stand up and say it, we can't help you.

Stephen   Right.

89

Hugh　　I'm sure the others can confirm that AA is about confidence and about sharing. OK?

Stephen　Right. *(Deep breath)* My problem is basically that the starter motor seems to get stuck. Especially in cold weather.

　　　　　Pause.

Hugh　　Mm. Have you tried putting it in first gear and rocking it back and forwards?

Stephen　Yes. Yes I have.

Hugh　　We'll send someone round as soon as possible.

Stephen　Thank you.

Hugh　　*(Handing Stephen a hip flask)* Have a drink while you're waiting.

> VOX
> POP
>
> **Stephen**　Now when I was at school we had real schoolmasters. Not clever left-wing agitators in oh-so-smart Trotskyite sandals and Stalinist trousers. Proper, straight-down the-line honest-to-goodness schoolmasters. They didn't indoctrinate me with a lot of left-wing crap-trap. They indoctrinated me with a lot of *right*-wing crap-trap. They may have stroked my thighs slightly more than is considered fashionable these days, but they were proper schoolmasters.

Marmalade

*Stephen and Hugh are sitting at either end of a
long table, having breakfast. Hugh is a woman, Stephen
isn't.*

Hugh   Could you pass the marmalade, darling?

Stephen What?

Hugh   The marmalade, could you pass it?

Stephen You want me to arse the parlourmaid?

Hugh   No darling, there's a pot of marmalade at your
             elbow, I want you to pass it.

Stephen A potty marinade in my dildo, have you gone mad?

Hugh   Darling I want you to pass the marmalade.

Stephen *(Amazed)* You want me to fart the hit parade?

Hugh   Pass the marmalade.

Stephen Smile at Roy Hattersley? You want me to smile
             at Roy Hattersley?

Hugh   That doesn't sound anything like 'pass the mar-
             malade'.

Stephen Roy Hattersley hasn't found anyone to pass the
             marmalade? You're babbling, woman.

Hugh   No dear. I want *you* to pass the marmalade.

Stephen Roy Hattersley wants *me* to pass the marmalade?

Hugh   No, *I* do darling.

Stephen An eiderdown? I'm not going to pass Roy Hattersley
             an eiderdown.

Hugh   If you'll just listen.

Stephen   He can get his own damned eiderdowns like everyone else.

Hugh   The marmalade dear, can you pass it?

Stephen   Expecting people to pass him eiderdowns as if he was someone special. No one's ever passed me an eiderdown.

Hugh   Will you pass the marmalade?

Stephen   No I will not go to bed with Geoffrey Howe. Not at any price. I think you must be off your head.

Hugh gets up, walks down the table and picks up the marmalade.

Stephen buries his head in the paper.

Stephen   The Substantial Tide's Indebt smell by more quoits?

Hugh   No dear, the *Financial Times* Index fell by four points.

Stephen   Oh. Pass the marmalade will you?

VOX
POP

Hugh   We're slow but steady. You know, we get there in the end. (*Stopping a passer-by*) Excuse me madam. Does the name Jack the Ripper mean anything to you?

The Red Hat of Patferrick

*Violent violins. Organ music. Stephen in a deep leather
burgundy hide wing chair with dimpled buttons. He is
reading. He looks up.*

Stephen   Hello, I'm Gelliant Gutfright, your host on *The
Seventh Dimension*. Tonight's story is called 'The
Red Hat of Patferrick'. I must add a warning. The
BBC do not advise that you watch the unfolding of
this dark tale if you are in any way of an erotic
disposition.

He walks towards an office set.

Office life. Ha! It seems so ordinary, doesn't it?
So mundane. What is the worst that can happen in an
ordinary publisher's office? Susie loses the Tippex.
Carol forgets to fax that contract to Stuttgart. The
wrong manuscript is DHL-ed to San Francisco.
Nothing sinister about a modern office. Is there?
Is there? Or is there?

Jonathan Hadey. A nice guy. One of the world's
good scouts. Governor of his local primary school.
Rotarian. Chief High Coven Priest of the Amersham
and District Satanic Abuse Club. An ordinary,
decent British guy. Every day is much like the day
before for publisher Jonathan Hadey. Except today.
Except April the twenty-ninth of October. Oh yes,
except for today . . .

*Camera has been zooming in on Hugh, and Stephen's
last few words are over. The telephone on Hugh's desk
rings.*

Stephen	*(Over)* Louise is out of the office, flirting with Ted from marketing while she makes Jonathan's mid-morning coffee. He might as well answer the telephone himself for once.
Hugh	Hello?
Voice	*(Telephone distort)* I want to speak to Jonathan Hadey.
Hugh	This is him . . . he . . . him. I mean . . .
Voice	You have the Red Hat of Patferrick.
Hugh	The what?
Voice	Don't play games, Mr Hadey. You have just seven hours to return it to its rightful owners.
Hugh	Shall I put you through to marketing?

Phone click. Dialling tone.

Hugh stares into the phone. Puts it down slowly.

Louise enters with a coffee.

Louise	Sorry I took my time, Mr Hadey, but Ted from marketing was licking my breasts. Who was that?
Hugh	I don't know. A wrong number probably . . . except they asked for me. Something about a hat.
Louise	*(Slightly guilty, suspicious)* A hat?
Hugh	Yes, a hat from Portmerrick or something.
Louise	Not . . . Patferrick?
Hugh	Yes! That's it! The hat of Patferrick.
Louise	*(Terrified, but trying to hide it)* Did they say what . . . what . . . colour?
Hugh	The red hat I think they said.

94

Louise	*(Screams)* No! Not red! Please God not red. No, no, no, no!

She runs to the open window behind Hugh's desk and throws herself out.

Hugh rushes to the window and looks down.

Hugh	My God, Louise . . . oh sweet Jesus heaven, Louise why . . .
Louise	*(Off)* I can't explain Mr Hadey.
Hugh	But for the Lord's sake girl. Whatever it is, you can't stay down there.
Louise	If you don't mind Mr Hadey I will. For the time being.
Hugh	But . . .

Hugh is interrupted by a voice off behind him. It is the voice of Gerald Dandridge, his boss.

Dandridge	Hadey!
Hugh	*(Spinning round)* Mr Dandridge!
Dandridge	Can't have my editorial directors staring out of the window all day. Not got enough work to do?
Hugh	No, sir it's not that . . . it's . . .
Dandridge	Well, man . . . speak up.
Hugh	I'm afraid Louise is . . . behaving rather oddly.
Dandridge	Probably her time of the curse or whatever they call it. Give her the day off.
Hugh	Yes, that's probably it. Got rather upset about some sort of Hat. The Pink Hat of . . .
Dandridge	*(Gasping in fright and astonishment)* Pink hat? Did you say pink hat?

Hugh   *(Surprised)* Well . . .

Dandridge The hat of . . . the Pink Hat of *where*, man?

Hugh   Well it was some phone call . . .

Dandridge *(Grasping Hugh's collar)* In the name of mercy,
          Jonathan! THE PINK HAT OF *WHERE*??

Hugh   Well, I think he said Patferrick . . . does that sound
          right?

Dandridge *(Instantly relieved and relaxed)* Patferrick? Oh that's
          all right. The Pink Hat of Patferrick. Fine,
          my boy. Fine.

Hugh   Well come to think of it, it was red, the Red
          Hat of Patferrick, he said.

Dandridge *(Hugely loud scream)* No! Oh suffering hell,
          NO!!!! The Red Hat of Patferrick!!

          Dandridge runs to the window and jumps out.

Hugh   Sir! Mr Dandridge?

          Pause.

          Mr Dandridge? Sir?

Dandridge *(After a pause. Hissed whisper)* Go away!

Hugh   But what are you . . .

Louise   Please, Mr Hadey. Just leave us alone.

Dandridge Buzz off.

Hugh   Oh. Right.

          *Hugh backs away from the window, scratching his chin
          and very puzzled. The telephone rings very loudly in his
          ear.*

          (Answering it) Hello? . . . Police? . . . Yes, what is

96

it? My wife . . . what kind of accident? Oh my God . . . squashed! In heaven's name, what by? A hat? A *hat*? What kind of hat? Sort of maroony, burgundy-ish crimson. Damn it man, you mean red. If it's red say so. A red hat . . . from the dust on the brim it could only come from one place, you say? Don't tell me, I already know. Patferrick. My God, it was the Red Hat of Patferrick.

He drops the telephone and buries his head in his arms.

Louise enters with a coffee and shakes him on the shoulder.

Louise   Wake up, Mr Hadey. It's your coffee.

Hugh   What . . . I . . . the pat . . . the hat . . . the redferrick of hatpat . . . I . . . oh.

Louise   Dreaming again, Mr Hadey. I don't know.

Hugh   But it was so . . . so *real*. *(Laughing)* What's the matter with me? I think I need a holiday.

Louise   Oh there's a man on his way up to see you. Says he's bringing 'The Red Hat of . . .' somewhere or other.

Hugh   NO!!! Oh my Christing hell-god no! The red hat of where? Speak, girl.

Louise   Well Pat-something, I think he said.

Hugh   Oh God, no. The Red Hat of Patferrick! No.

Hugh runs and jumps out of the window. Louise clutches her cheeks and screams.

Enter Stephen as Gelliant Gutfright. A bundle of papers under his arm.

Stephen   Something wrong, my dear?

Louise   It's Mr Hadey, he just . . . twenty-three floors up and he just . . . oh! *(She shudders)*

97

Stephen   Ah. Well. I had better take The Red Hat of Patferrick somewhere else, hadn't I?

Louise   The Red Hat . . . that's why Mr Hadey jumped. What is it?

Stephen   Oh just a manuscript of a story my dear. A wholly improbable tale. It concerns a young publisher who has a dream about a hat, and when he awakes . . . but it is *(turns and stares into the camera)* nothing but fancy. It could never really happen. Could it? Could it? Or could it? Perhaps it could. Or could it? Goodnight.

VOX
POP

Stephen   I've found that young people are no longer enticed into church simply on the promise of guitars and a little folk music. We have to move with the times. We've started showing leather and bondage films in St Barnabas's and the results have been very good. We were packed last Sunday. Mostly Young Conservatives, but it's a start.

Balls

Stephen enters a bookshop. Hugh is the assistant.
Stephen stares at Hugh for a long time.

Hugh   Help you?

Stephen   *(Holding up a book)* Did you write this?

Hugh   *(Examining book) Jane Eyre.* No, that was Charlotte Brontë as a matter of fact.

Stephen   Right. Well I'd like to see her then please.

Hugh   I'm afraid she's no longer with us.

Stephen   Oh? Indeed? I can hardly say I'm surprised. Where can I get in touch with her?

Hugh   No, no. I mean 'no longer with us' in the sense of 'dead'.

Stephen   Dead?

Hugh   Quite dead.

Stephen   When did she die exactly?

Hugh   Um . . . 1855 I believe I'm right in saying.

Stephen   Let me see, 1855, that's five minutes to seven, isn't it?

Hugh   I'm sorry. I mean '1855' in the sense of the year '1855'. Was there some problem?

Stephen   Well you'll have to do I suppose, since you sold me the book. I want my money back.

Hugh   Do you mind me asking why?

Stephen   I'll tell you why. Because this book is balls, that's why. It is complete balls.

Hugh   I'm afraid I really can't agree with you there.

Stephen   Oh can't you? Well listen to this then . . . *(riffles through book and selects a passage)* 'I mounted into the window-seat: gathering up my feet, I sat cross-legged, like a Turk.' I mean ???? It's just balls.

Hugh   Balls in what sense?

Stephen   Balls in the sense of balls. I mean 'window-seat'? What window-seat? This is on the first page. Window seat. Where is this window seat, hm? What's it doing? And what Turk? I've never seen a Turk mount a window-seat. Simply balls. Nothing but balls.

Hugh   Well I think you're supposed to imagine it.

Stephen   Ho? All right, then, all right then: what about this . . . um . . . chapter thirty-eight . . . 'Reader, I married him.' Now if that isn't balls, kindly fax me an explanation of what is. 'Reader'? What reader? Or are you supposed to imagine this reader as well?

Hugh   No, that's you. It's addressed to you, the reader of the book.

Stephen   OH BALLS. How could she know me? You just told me the stupid tart died at five to seven.

Hugh   Well not you specifically. I mean whoever is reading it at the time. Jane Eyre is telling you that she married Mr Rochester.

Stephen   Jane Eyre is a made-up character! Kyor! She didn't exist.

Hugh   No but she writes the story. She is the 'I' of the story.

Stephen   MAKE YOUR FRIGGING MIND UP. You just told me Charlotte Brontë wrote the story.

Hugh   She did . . . but . . .

Stephen   Well you're clearly as confused as I am. It's just balls and you know it. Complete balls. I want my money back. I want to read a book that doesn't go

on about window-seats you've never even heard of
and then has some mad bitch who's supposed to be
dead calling you 'reader' all the time.

Hugh   What about this ... proving very popular.

Hugh hands Stephen a book.

Stephen What's this?

Hugh   *The Invalid* by Myra Penworthy Fennerweave.

Stephen Any good?

Hugh   Excellent.

Stephen starts to read.

Stephen 'Talbot entered the room in a feverish haste,
bearing his precious cargo before him like a votive
offering. Elizabeth lay back on her bed, her face pale
and pinched. "Richard is that you?" she moaned
plaintively.' Oh this is just complete BALLS! Balls,
balls, balls.

Hugh   It's not actually. It's true. It actually happened.

Stephen Oh double balls and bollocks.

VOX
POP

Hugh   I just wish they hadn't called it the
Common Market. Is that snobbish
of me? I mean why not the *Nice*
Market. It would be so much nicer.

Mental Health

Hugh addresses the camera.

Hugh   Ladies and gentlemen, I'm extremely lucky to have
been born physically healthy, physically whole. I have
two eyes, two arms, two legs, four nipples, I'm physically normal and I give thanks for that every single
day. However, I do have a mental problem. I suffer
from what psychiatrists call a split personality. No I
don't. I've had this for some time now, no I haven't,
but recently it seems to have got worse. How could it
get worse, if it was never there? At the suggestion of
my psychiatrist, God what a fraud he is, I have given
my other personality a name. I call him Anthony.
Yes, what do you want? Now Anthony is not like
me. You can say that again. Anthony likes different
music, books, films, he likes double pleats on his
trousers, where I prefer single, and if it were up to
him he would drive a Citroen GX. They happen to be
extremely stylish cars. But perhaps Anthony's biggest
problem is that he suffers from a split personality. I
bloody do not! Anthony's other half, as it were, is
called Nathaniel, and he claims to be Welsh. What do
you mean claim, I am Welsh, I just don't happen to
live there at the moment.

Spaghetti

Hugh and Stephen in vests are sitting at a table eating spaghetti, with huge napkins tied round their necks. At the sink is a largish Italian mamma.

Stephen I gotta ask you something.

Hugh Go 'head.

Stephen You sleepin' with my wife?

Hugh What?

Stephen I said are you . . .

Hugh I heard what you said.

Stephen So, you gonna . . .

Hugh What the hell kind of a question is that?

Stephen You gonna answer?

Hugh Hell no.

Stephen Hell no?

Hugh Hell no. It's a dumb question.

Stephen Are you sleeping with my wife is a dumb question?

Hugh You're damn right.

Stephen So?

Hugh So what?

Stephen Are you sleeping with . . .

Hugh Don't ask me that. Stop asking me that dumb question.

Stephen That means yes.

Hugh	What the hell means yes? Stop asking me dumb questions means yes? What the hell is the matter with you?
Stephen	You haven't answered the question. I asked you a question, you haven't answered it.
Hugh	For Chrissake, I'm eatin' dinner. I'm sittin' here eatin' dinner, and you start with these dumb questions.
Stephen	If you're sleepin' with my wife . . .
Hugh	What? What the hell you gonna do?
Stephen	I'll kill you.
Hugh	You'll kill me?
Stephen	Yeah.
Hugh	You'll kill your own brother?
Stephen	Yeah.
Hugh	Yeah, well relax. I ain't sleepin' with your wife.
Stephen	You prove that?
Hugh	Prove what?
Stephen	You prove you ain't sleepin' with my wife?
Hugh	How the hell'm I gonna prove that to you? Uh? What would be nice maybe is if you believe me. You know? You trust me when I tell you something, instead of askin' a lot of dumb questions.
Stephen	OK.
Hugh	OK what?
Stephen	I believe you.
Hugh	You believe me?
Stephen	I believe you.
Hugh	Well thank you. Can I eat my dinner now?

Stephen	Sure.
Hugh	OK.
Stephen	You sleepin' with my sister?
Hugh	What?
Stephen	Are you sleepin' with . . .
Hugh	Wait a minute, wait a minute.
Stephen	What?
Hugh	You're my brother, right?
Stephen	Right.
Hugh	So your sister is my sister.
Stephen	Waddya mean?
Hugh	Waddya mean waddya mean? You're my brother and so your sister is also my sister, we have the same sister, you and me.
Stephen	So?
Hugh	So? Jesus, you're askin' me if I'm sleepin' with my own sister?
Stephen	Are you?
Hugh	Am I . . . what the hell is the matter with you?
Stephen	Are you sleepin' with your sister?
Hugh	What the hell am I doin', bustin' my balls, sittin' here listenin' to this?
Stephen	You're eatin' spaghetti.
Hugh	Spaghetti bullshit.
Stephen	Bolognese.
Hugh	I come here to eat my dinner, and I'm gettin' all this bullshit for what?
Stephen	For . . .

Hugh   You shut your mouth. All right? Just shut your mouth. Sleepin' with my own sister, Jesus.

Stephen   You sleepin' with my mother?

Hugh   That's it. One more word out of you . . .

Stephen   And what?

Hugh   You know what. You and your dumb bullshit questions.

Stephen   Whose dumb bullshit questions?

Hugh   Hey, mamma. You hear him? You hear all this bullshit he's givin' me?

Stephen   What bullshit? I ask you a question is all.

Mamma   *(English – to camera)* Both my boys just adore New Ragazzo Sauce.

Stephen   You sleepin' with my brother?

VOX
POP

Stephen   Allergies? Well, I'm not good on strawberries, come out in a bit of a rash. The worst one though is Marmite. Only got to smell the stuff and I start voting Conservative.

Countdown to Hell

We are in the Countdown *studio. Stephen is Richard Whiteley. Hugh is Hugh.*

Stephen Right . . . so . . . er . . . right. And . . . right . . . so Simon, I think . . . right . . . it's your choice, I think.

Hugh *(Wetly)* Consonant please, Carol.

A piece of totty puts up a consonant and says its name.

Girl Right. Consonant. 'B'.

Hugh Vowel please.

Girl 'O'.

Hugh Consonant please, Carol.

Girl 'L'.

Hugh Another consonant please.

Girl And that's 'L' again.

Hugh Vowel please, Carol.

Girl Another 'O'.

Hugh Consonant please.

Girl 'C'.

Hugh Another consonant please.

Girl 'S'.

Hugh And another consonant please.

Girl 'K'.

Stephen All right . . . right . . . so . . . right . . . right . . . your countdown starts . . . now.

Music, clock ticking etc. as is.

The thirty seconds are up.

Stephen   Right . . . so . . . Simon, how did you get on?

Hugh   Just four I'm afraid.

Stephen   Four, just four. Right, so, Liz, how about you.

Liz   Four as well.

Stephen   Right, four too. So four each there. Very interesting. Four each. What was your four Simon?

Hugh   Lobs.

Stephen   Lobs. So, lobs. Right. Lobs. Meaning 'lobs' I suppose. Lobs. Right well let me 'lob' it over to you Liz and ask what you got for your four?

Liz   Look.

Stephen   Look. Look. I think we can allow that. No need to 'look that one up' in our dictionary. What did our guardian of the dictionary find? Anything better?

Gyles   *(For it is he)* Well now, as a celebrity rather than a member of the public, I naturally did rather better and came up with 'books' for five, or 'blocks' for six or there is an eight actually.

Stephen   An eight . . . right . . . an eight . . . well that's very exciting . . . an eight . . . and what's your eight?

Gyles   Sloblock.

Stephen   Sloblock. Sloblock. So, sloblock. And what does sloblock mean, exactly?

Gyles   Basically, and I'm indebted to Myra Perks of East Hell for this jumper, by the way . . . basically sloblock means balls, the things we keep in our scrotums, or by extension something that is rubbish or a pile of

108

nonsense. 'Oh that's a load of sloblock' you might say.

Stephen Right well let's hope no one thinks this programme is 'sloblock'. Now ... right ... so then ... right ... it's time for our Conundrum. Thirty seconds to solve it and here it comes ... now.

The conundrum appears. Clock ticks etc. The conundrum is the word 'pathetic'.

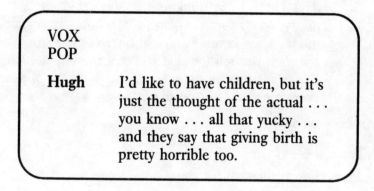

VOX
POP

Hugh I'd like to have children, but it's just the thought of the actual ... you know ... all that yucky ... and they say that giving birth is pretty horrible too.

The New Cause

*A garden shed: Hugh is in a cardigan trying to
mend a lawnmower. Stephen appears in abrupt sort of
blazer and stands behind him. Eventually Hugh notices
him and jumps.*

Hugh Good heavens Jack, you gave me such a fright.
Good Lord. There I was trying to mend the old
lawnmower, bloody old thing, well of course it's not
old, it's quite a new lawnmower.

Stephen Hello Neddy.

Hugh Well hello, Jack. Sorry. I was wittering rather just
now. It's just that, well, you know . . . lawnmower's
bust, and . . . How are you Jack?

Stephen Well, thank you Neddy.

Hugh Well? Oh that is good news. That's quite made my
day. There I was thinking that the world was a
pretty bloody sort of a place, where you can pay good
money for a lawnmower that doesn't even work . . .
but then you tell me that you're well, and suddenly
things seem to be not so bad after all. Sort of puts
everything into perspective . . .

Stephen Neddy?

Hugh Jack.

Stephen I've a question for you.

Hugh Oh good.

Stephen I'd be grateful if you could furnish me with an
honest answer.

Hugh Furnish you, Jack? 'Course I'll furnish you. You
ask away, and leave the furnishing to me.

Stephen	Good.

Stephen has picked up a Stanley knife. He works the blade in and out.

Hugh	Ha. Clever little toy that, isn't it. Stanley knife. It's a sort of knife made by a feller called Stanley. First name or second name, I'm not sure. I could find out for you, Jack, if you're interested? Make some inquiries, as it were . . .
Stephen	Ingenious.
Hugh	D'you like it, Jack? Well for heaven's sake you keep it, old sport. Present from me.
Stephen	That's very kind of you Neddy.

Stephen puts the knife into his pocket.

Hugh	Not at all, Jack. Plenty more where that came from.
Stephen	Neddy . . .
Hugh	Still here, Jack.
Stephen	How would you like to be Prime Minister?
Hugh	Ha.
Stephen	Well?
Hugh	Sort of a trick question, is it Jack?
Stephen	Not at all.
Hugh	Not at all. I see. How would I like to be Prime Minister? Hm. Fancy a cup of tea, Jack?
Stephen	When you've furnished me with an answer, Neddy, a cup of tea would be most agreeable, thank you.
Hugh	Prime Minister. Lord. Well, I suppose it would be rather fun to be Prime Minister, Jack, yes. Riding around in big motor cars. Policemen saluting you,

and all that. Yes, I expect it would be very interesting work.

Stephen You'd like to be Prime Minister?

Hugh Well, yes, Jack. I expect there are worse jobs hahahahaha.

Stephen What about your wife?

Hugh Oh. I wouldn't like to be my wife, Jack, no. I mean . . .

Stephen How would your wife take to your being Prime Minister?

Hugh Oh I see. Er, well. I'll pop in and ask her, if you like. Won't be a sec.

Stephen I want your opinion, Neddy. As you know, I represent a group of people.

Hugh Yes, I know that, Jack. Yes, jolly fine people too, I've no doubt.

Stephen People who are, shall we say, concerned about the direction in which this country is headed.

Hugh Right.

Stephen We feel, as a group of concerned people, that the current Prime Minister won't do.

Hugh Won't do.

Stephen Won't do.

Hugh Won't do what, Jack?

Stephen Won't do, Neddy.

Hugh Oh I get you.

Stephen Do you?

Hugh No.

Stephen We feel that a change is needed, if disaster is to

	be averted, and we would like you to be the next Prime Minister.
Hugh	Crikey.
Stephen	Will you do it, Neddy? For England?
Hugh	Jack. Jack, old sport. Let me say first of all, that I really am deeply touched by the offer. Deeply touched. Thing is . . . Jack, can I tell you something?
Stephen	By all means, Neddy.
Hugh	Jack, when I was at school, I used to play cricket for the third eleven. No bloody good, of course, went in number eight. I was number seven once, when Proby had his appendix out, but otherwise well down the order . . .
Stephen	Is this relevant, Neddy?
Hugh	Well I think so, Jack, yes. You see, there was this one match, we played them every year, a match against Trenton House. Bit of a needle match, to be honest, Jack, you know what boys are like. Well anyway, this one year, they turned up without an umpire, and the captain told me to get out there and call the shots as it were. And the thing is, Jack . . .
Stephen	Yes?
Hugh	I couldn't do it.
Stephen	What do you mean couldn't do it?
Hugh	I mean I just couldn't do it. Responsibility, you see, Jack. I couldn't cope with the decisions. 'Howzat' they would scream in my face, and I just went into a sort of dreadful funk . . . gave one chap out before he'd even left the pavilion. What I'm saying, Jack, is that I'm a follower, if you know what I mean. Not a leader.
Stephen	Precisely, Neddy.

113

Hugh	Precisely, yes, Jack.
Stephen	You are precisely the man we need.
Hugh	Oh lor.
Stephen	Well, Neddy? Will you do it?
Hugh	Will I do it? Good heavens, Jack, of course I'll do it. Yes. Anything for my old pal Jack. I just . . .
Stephen	Excellent. Congratulations Neddy. The country is in safe hands, I know it.
Hugh	Oh good. Right, so I'll start being Prime Minister . . .
Stephen	Whenever you're ready, Neddy.
Hugh	Ready, Neddy, very good. Ha. One thing?
Stephen	Yes?
Hugh	All right with you if I just get this lawnmower up and running before I start? Won't take a moment.

Cut to 'Neddy PM'

VOX
POP

Stephen	Secret vices? I don't know. Rather too fond of chocolate Hob Nobs. My wife tells me I overdo the heroin. Otherwise, not really.

Neddy PM

A known and loved newsreader addresses the camera.

Newsreader The House of Commons sat in stunned silence as the Prime Minister, Mr John . . . damn, I've got it here somewhere, *(flicks through the pages of his script)* Major, that's it, Mr John Major announced his intention to resign, saying he wanted to spend more time with his collection of miniature fire engines. His replacement, a Mr Neddy Muldoon of Orchard Lane, St Neots, has been elected unopposed by the Parliamentary Conservative Party.

Cut to a news conference: Hugh addressing the press. Stephen stands slightly to one side.

Hugh Good heavens. Not a bad turnout, eh Jack?

Reporter 1 Mr Muldoon?

Hugh Yes, over here. I'm Muldoon.

Reporter 1 Mr Muldoon, what is your position on Europe? Do you see yourself as a federalist?

Hugh Oh, er . . . crikey. Federalist is as federalist does, that's always been my watchword.

Reporter 1 Does that mean you'll be advocating the German model in future discussions?

Hugh Er . . . *(to Stephen)* Jack, a boy from Trenton House is screaming 'Howzat' in my face . . .

Stephen *(Sotto voce)* I believe very strongly in the notion of peace through strength . . .

Hugh So do I.

Reporter 1 You do what?

Hugh I believe in what Jack just said. Peace through strength.

Stephen And if it becomes necessary . . .

Hugh If it should, at any time, in the future, become necessary . . .

Stephen To protect the interests of this country . . .

Hugh To protect, in a manner of speaking after a fashion, the interests of this country . . .

Stephen We will not hesitate to invade Poland . . .

Hugh We will not hesitate to invade . . . excuse me for a moment, everyone. *(To Stephen)* Jack, you sure that's not pitching it a little strong?

Stephen It's what we agreed.

Hugh We?

Stephen Your supporters, Neddy. We agreed.

Hugh But Jack, I'm not altogether sure that I can . . .

Stephen produces the Stanley knife.

Hello, I see you've still got the knife I gave you. Doing all right is it? Useful?

Stephen Extremely useful, Neddy, thank you.

Reporter 1 Mr Muldoon, did you say that you were prepared to invade somewhere?

Hugh No no. Crikey no. No, little misunderstanding, that's all. No, I've always thought that the best way to work these sorts of things out is to sit round a table – although you could also sit along the side of a table, it doesn't have to be a round table – and just have a bit of an old chat and a head scratch.

116

Stephen stabs Hugh: shouting and commotion. Hugh falls to the ground and looks up at Stephen.

	Jack?
Stephen	Yes, Neddy?
Hugh	Someone's gone and stuck a knife in me.
Stephen	The police are after them now, Neddy.
Hugh	Jack?
Stephen	Yes Neddy?
Hugh	I want you to have my lawnmower.

VOX
POP

Stephen I had a *blue* hat once but a dog ate it up, shredded it to bits he did. I went to him and said 'Look here this dog has eaten my hat.' He said, 'I don't bloody care.' So I said, 'I don't like your attitude,' he said 'It's not my 'at 'e chewed, it's *your* 'at 'e chewed.' My uncle used to tell me that in the bath before he was arrested.

My Dear Boy

Hugh in spectacles and bulging anorak is ringing the doorbell of a prosperous-looking London house. It is answered by Stephen, who is fat (yes, yes, get on with it, we know that) and swathed in chinoiserie and camperie. Possibly a tasselled smoking cap. As he opens the door he regards Hugh with pleasure.

Stephen   My dear boy! Come in, come in, come in, come in, come in, come in, come in, come in!

Hugh looks surprised.

(Looking down at the floor) Don't mind Clothilda, she gets excited by strangers.

Stephen scoops up a blue Persian cat and presses against the open door to allow Hugh to pass through.

Hugh   This is 42 Cheyne Gardens?

Stephen   Come through to the atelier, my dear, and let me mix you something devilish of my own devising. A little thick cream, a suspicion of parfait amour, a whisper of orgeat, garnished with sprig of hyssop and, of course, a cocktail cherry. I call it my Moroccan Sunrise. It has caused, in its time, my dear, many a son of Morocco to rise . . . oh, I must stop myself, really I must. Please pay me no attention; Clothilda here will tell you that I am no better than I should be, won't you Clotty dear? I don't believe I caught your name?

They are in a Chelsea studio. It is littered with tigerskin rugs, louche art, bronzes, statuettes, paintings etc.

Hugh   Nigel Carter.

Stephen   Nigel Carter. Nigel Carter. There's a breath of something fine and ripe in that name, something impossibly noble and yet thrillingly rotten. Sit, Nigel Carter. Sit, sit, sit.

Stephen pushes Hugh gently on to a seat which is part of a double chair.

It's called a lover's seat. I picked it up in San Gimigniano in 1963. That and so much else besides. You may keep your clothes on for the moment while I weave my magic with the cocktail shaker. Clothilda shall amuse you with stories of the gorgeous east.

Hugh   It's about the advertisement in this month's *Model Aeroplanes*.

Stephen   Such a stimulating read. I never miss a copy. You have the bluest eyes, has anyone ever told you that? It was for eyes of such a hyacinthine blue that Apollo languished long ago on sunbleached Delos.

Hugh   Mm. Yes. *(Takes out a cutting and reads)* 'Highest prices paid for all models. Apply Simbold Cleobury, 42 Cheyne Gardens, SW3.' That is you, isn't it?

Stephen   It is I. My parents christened me Donald, a name entirely without hope. Do you know, I think I'm going to give you two cocktail cherries? One for each of your blue eyes. I usually pay models thirty pounds a sitting. Does that seem fair, my dear?

Hugh   I've got a Sopwith Camel, full RFC markings, scale one twentieth. I brought a photograph.

Stephen   A camel?

Hugh   It's quite old, but in very good condition.

Stephen	Heavens! And where do you keep it?
Hugh	In my room at home. In Greenford.

Stephen drops into the other seat next to Hugh.

Stephen	(*Giving Hugh his cocktail*) And they dare to claim, Nigel Carter, that the age of romance is dead. (*As Hugh sips*) I think you will agree that it is the hyssop that makes all the difference. (*Into Hugh's ear*) I love hyssop, don't you?
Hugh	Very tasty.
Stephen	What is the name of this camel who lives with you in Greenford?
Hugh	Well, Sopwith.
Stephen	Sopwith! Too heavenly. Perhaps I shall paint you astride this Sopwith, Nigel. It is not impossible. But first I shall have you sprawled naked on the tiger-skin, firelight dancing on your shivering thighs.
Hugh	Erm . . .
Stephen	Have you modelled before?
Hugh	Oh, all my life. Well, since I was four.
Stephen	Mercy, Nigel. Mercy. Since you were four?
Hugh	My grandfather started me off.
Stephen	So often the way.
Hugh	We both ended up covered in glue.
Stephen	Nigel, you amaze me.
Hugh	It was a Fokker.
Stephen	It sounds it, Nigel. In glue you say? You may fear no such extravagances from me. Perhaps a little light rubbing with oil to bring out your flesh tones, Nigel, but no more.

Hugh   Would you like to see my Jumbo?

Stephen   Nigel, I would like to see your Jumbo very much indeed.

Hugh shows Stephen a photograph.

(Looking at it) Nigel, that is a photograph of a large jet aeroplane.

Hugh   *(Staring down at the photo for a moment)* Oh, I'm sorry, I don't know how that got in there. *(Rifles through)* Here we are.

Stephen   My, that *is* a jumbo, isn't it? Now then, clothes off and on to the tiger-skin with you.

Hugh   *(Stripping)* Righto.

VOX
POP

Stephen   It's less than a year since they ditched her and already she's forgotten – consigned to the dustbin of history. She personally liberated all of Eastern Europe, but she's forgotten. That's how grateful we are to Margaret . . . Margaret . . . Datchett was it?

Horrormen

Stephen and Hugh are seated at a table in a restaurant, holding large menus. Rather bookish; spectacles, tweeds etc. All four of their eyes are closed all the time, in a revolting, condescending sort of a way.

Stephen How nice. How absolutely delightful.

Hugh Charming. Quite charming. A charming restaurant.

Stephen A charming as you say restaurant.

Hugh Quite delightful.

Stephen I think one of my most favourite quite delightful restaurants.

Hugh I agree. I agree. I do. I really do agree.

A waitress approaches.

Waitress Are you ready to order?

Stephen and Hugh cock their heads.

Hugh Did you say something?

Stephen No.

Hugh I thought I heard . . .

Stephen I rather think it may have been a member of the restaurant staff.

Hugh Ah.

Stephen and Hugh reach into their pockets and pull out pairs of half-moon spectacles, put them on, and peer at the waitress.

Hugh	Aahh.
Waitress	Are you ready to order?
Hugh	I will have the melon, followed by the roast lamb.
Waitress	Melon, lamb. And you, sir?
Stephen	I will have the *soupe de poisson*, and the roast lamb also.
Waitress	Fish soup. Lamb.
Stephen	I'm so sorry.
Waitress	Yes?
Stephen	What did you say just then?
Waitress	Fish soup, lamb.
Stephen	Mmm. Perhaps I didn't make myself absolutely clear. I would *actually* like the *soupe de poisson*.
Waitress	*Soupe de poisson* is fish soup.
Stephen	Oh dear.
Hugh	Oh deary me.
Stephen	Was I speaking too quickly for you?
Hugh	You seem to be a little confused.
Stephen	I asked for *soupe de poisson*.
Hugh	*Soupe de poisson*.
Waitress	*Soupe de poisson* is fish soup.
Stephen	No. No.
Hugh	No no no no.
Stephen	I obviously lost you. *Soupe de poisson* is *soupe de poisson*.
Hugh	D'you see?

Stephen   One thing cannot be another thing. And when you advertise *soupe de poisson*, and I order *soupe de poisson*, it means, to put it very simply, that I would like you to bring me *soupe de poisson*.

Hugh   And some mineral water.

Waitress   Mineral water.

Stephen   Thank you.

Hugh   Thank you very much indeed.

Waitress exits. Stephen and Hugh return their spectacles to their pockets, and close their eyes again.

Stephen   What a charming restaurant.

Hugh   Absolutely delightful.

Waitress returns and puts a bottle of mineral water on the table.

Waitress   Mineral water.

Stephen   Oh dear.

Hugh   Oh waitress?

Stephen and Hugh don their spectacles again.

Stephen   Waitress?

Waitress   Yes?

Hugh   Can you remember what it was that I asked for? I think I saw you write it down, did you write it down?

Waitress   Yes, Mineral water.

Hugh   Bravo.

Stephen   Excellent, well done.

124

Hugh	But you have brought us a bottle of mineral water.
Stephen	Do you see? *(Pointing to the bottle)* These are called bottles.
Hugh	We asked for mineral water.
Stephen	Mineral water. Just as you carefully wrote down on your small pad.
Waitress	How much mineral water?
Hugh	Some.
Stephen	Some mineral water is how much we asked for I believe.
Hugh	Some.
Waitress	Some?
Stephen	But we can check precisely what it was we asked for. We always tape our conversations against just such a contingency.

Stephen rewinds a cassette.

Tape	'Man: Get out the pair of you, you snotty wankers . . .'
Stephen	Ah, no. That was the restaurant we were in yesterday.
Hugh	A delightful restaurant it was too.
Stephen	Quite delightful. Here we are.

Fast forwards.

Tape	'Hugh: And some mineral water. Waitress: Mineral water?'
Hugh	You see?
Stephen	Some.
Hugh	No mention of bottles.

Waitress	Shall I bring it in a jug?
Stephen	My suggestion is that you should bring us mineral water in a jug when we have asked for mineral water in a jug, until then, perhaps you would be so kind as to bring us some mineral water.
Hugh	All right?
Stephen	Thank you.

Exit waitress.

Hugh	What a delightful restaurant.
Stephen	Quite delightful.

Waitress enters with a pipette. She carefully squeezes a drop in front of each of them.

Hugh	Thank you.
Stephen	Delightful.
Hugh	I wonder, my dear, is there a gents' nearby. I'm rather desperate for a pee.
Waitress	Well . . . there is one, but it was out of order earlier on. I'll just check.

Waitress disappears.

Stephen	Charming waitress, do you see?
Hugh	This is right. Simply charming.

Waitress enters with a small green pea, which she places in front of Hugh.

	Um . . .
Stephen	Er . . .
Hugh	You really must excuse my stupidity, but . . .

Waitress takes tape recorder.

Waitress You asked for it. Listen.

Tape 'Hugh: I'm rather desperate for a pee . . .'

Hugh Ah . . .

Stephen Err . . .

> VOX
> POP
>
> **Hugh** People often ask what we keep
> under our helmets. Well, I'll show
> you. (*Takes off his helmet and looks
> very pleased with himself – puts his
> hand on top of his head and feels
> around*) Hold up, some bastard's
> nicked it.

Tahitian Kitchen

Music and titles. Typical cookery programme. Beautifully presented. Stephen is dressed as Elizabeth Martin, a television cook.

Stephen   Good morning, I'm Elizabeth Martin and welcome to this week's Tahitian Kitchen. Last week if you can be bothered to remember, we looked at presentation and garnishing of main dishes, Tahitian style. We covered the range of exotic and tasty herbs and spices that characterise this all too bloody often neglected cuisine. This week, I'm thinking particularly of those who might be on a tighter budget and who would like to prepare Tahitian dishes without stretching their sodding pockets too much. So I'm going to show you what you can do with some of the rarer off-cuts of meat, lights and offal, which while they may not sound appetising are, when properly prepared, as tempting, nutritious and arsingly well worth eating as any of the dearer cuts.

We see on her chopping board a number of bowls with heaps of spices and so on. There are also some parcels of meat wrapped in greaseproof paper.

Now I know a lot of people are funny about eating ears, eyes, brains, noses and so on, but with a little care I think you'll find out that they can be worth the trouble. I have two young ears here, for instance, which I have salted slightly and marinaded overnight.

She pulls out two human ears.

It is important that they are young, these are taken from an Anglia television local journalist, whom I slaughtered two days ago. Freshness is the most important factor with ears. What I'm going to do is combine them with the sweetbreads, or testicles *(she produces them)* and the fingers *(brings up the fingers)* in a provençale sauce of tomato and garlic.

She blends them together.

If you want to add feet and toes I would urge you to remember that smaller is tastier. These are from a Welsh articled clerk, Welsh feet are preferable if you can find them at this time of year. It's a good idea to hang the carcass upside-down for at least five hours just after killing. The toes are ideal as finger-treats or appetising dips.

She shows a bowl of toes, lightly grilled.

Care to have a try, Michael?

Hugh comes on from another part of the set.

Hugh   I'm game for anything, Elizabeth!

Stephen   *(Rather violently)* Don't I know it. There you are, this is a simple barbecue sauce.

Hugh dips the toes into a sauce.

Hugh   I must say. Rather delicious.

Stephen   And they won't break the bank either.

Hugh   *(To camera. In announcer mode.)* And talking of breaking the bank, Sue has been investigating . . .

Devil's Music

DJ intro

Gary Davies introduces 'The Bishop & The War-lord'.

Gary Woo! Get seriously down to that. Well now it's time to crank it up and tune it in, with some back to back fat beat, and have ourselves a rocking good time and no messing with the Bishop and the Warlord! Give me at least five!

'The Bishop & The Warlord'

'The Bishop & The Warlord' in performance. Stephen is dressed as a bishop, but with one leather cut-off glove. Hugh is fairly standard heavy metallurgist. Long hair, leather waistcoat, chains etc. Stephen sings from a pulpit, Hugh accompanies.

My baby turns some heads
When she walks in through the door
She's got red ruby lips
And legs down to the floor
She walks just like a wildcat
And she sings just like a dream
She's the greatest thing
That you've ever seen
Yes I need the heat of your loving, baby
You've got to burn with your desire
Start smoking at the edges
Set yourself on fire
You're mine mine mine mine mine
My baby is mine.

Courtroom Scene

A TV monitor, showing the last few bars of the song as played on Top of the Pops. *Pull out to see that we are in an American courtroom. Stephen is in the dock, as the bishop. Hugh is the prosecuting attorney. Clerks, stenographer etc. scattered around. Seated next to Hugh is a woman covered in bandages. Hugh switches off the monitor and addresses the court.*

Hugh   'Set yourself on fire'. Four words, your honour. Four innocent words. Every bit as common in our language as 'freedom' or 'vitamin-enriched'. But play those words backwards, and what do you have? 'Erif no flesruoy tes'. But that isn't enough. These people are smarter than that, because if you play 'Erif no flesruoy tes' backwards, you have 'Set yourself on fire'. A clear, explicitious and unambigualistical instruction to my client, which she obeyed, to pour a can of gasoline over herself, and set light to it, causing untold physical and mental traumatisation.

Judge   Let's get this straight, Mr Sanchez. Your client listened to the song . . .

Hugh   'Grease My Gristle, Blow My Whistle'.

Judge   Hm. Catchy title. And as a result, she set fire to herself?

Hugh   Precisely, your honour.

Judge   I see. As a matter of interest, did she also grease her gristle and blow her whistle?

Hugh   She certainly did, your Honour, causing herself grievous internal bruisality. That case comes to trial next month.

Judge   I see. Any other cases pending?

Hugh   Yes, your Honour. We have a suit of seven hundred million dollars against the group Queen, who caused

	my client to suffer a broken jaw, by urging her to become 'champion of the world'.
Judge	In what?
Hugh	Light middleweight boxing. Four hundred million against Frankie Goes To Hollywood, for instructioning her to Relax And Not Do It.
Judge	Relax and not do what?
Hugh	Relax and not apply the brakes of her automobile at a T-junction. And finally, nine hundred million against Jason Donovan.
Judge	For what?
Hugh	We haven't decided yet, your Honour.
Judge	I see. Three billion dollars. That's a pretty substantial figure, Counsellor.
Hugh	Well, to be honest, my wife and I are hoping to buy a little place down South, for weekends, space for the kids, you know.
Judge	Really. What's it called?
Hugh	Paraguay.
Judge	That's nice. Now, do you have any witnesses?
Hugh	I call the defendant, the self-styled clergyman of cool, the Bishop of Attleboro.

Stephen as the bishop takes the stand.

Judge	Take the book in your right hand and say after me. I have no objection . . .
Stephen	I have no objection . . .
Judge	. . . to this trial being televised . . .
Stephen	. . . to this trial being televised . . .
Judge	. . . and subsequently being made . . .

Stephen	. . . and subsequently being made . . .
Judge	. . . into a motion picture, book, or stage musical so help me God.
Stephen	. . . into a motion picture, book, or stage musical so help me God.
Hugh	What is your name, sir?
Stephen	My name is William . . .
Hugh	Just answer the question yes or no, please. What is your name?
Stephen	Yes.
Hugh	Yes?
Stephen	Yes.
Hugh	That is your real name?
Stephen	No.
Hugh	No is your real name?
Stephen	No.
Hugh	No is not your real name?
Defence	Objection your Honour. Counsel is badgering the witness.
Judge	Hmm. Are you badgering the witness, Mr Sanchez.
Hugh	Certainly not, your Honour.
Judge	Good.
Hugh	I am, possibly, weazelling the witness, and I certainly hope to squirrel him with my next question, but I am not badgering him.
Judge	Mr Sanchez you're dicking me around.
Hugh	No sir.
Judge	Good. Proceed.

Defence   But . . .

Judge   Your objection is overstained, Counsellor.

Hugh   Now then, Mr Yes, you are the lead singer of the
              Heavy Metal band The Bishop And The Warlord?

Stephen   That is substantially correct.

Hugh   Substantially?

Stephen   Well of course, being a bishop, I also have a great
              deal of work to do within my own diocese, as well
              as attending the Council of Synod meetings, which
              means that I can only devote limited time to the
              band, but in essence you are correct.

Hugh   In essence I am correct, I see. And when you look
              upon the poor, wretched figure of my client now, Mr
              Yes, an innocent victim of your handiwork, how do
              you feel?

Defence   Your honour, I really must stand up and make
              some pretence of earning my fee.

Judge   Nice work, Counsellor.

Hugh   I say again, how do you feel?

Stephen   Well I'm most awfully sorry.

Hugh   Awfully sorry?

Stephen   Well it simply never crossed my mind that people
              could be told what to do so easily. I mean on my
              second album we wrote a song called 'Bake Me A
              Love Soufflé' . . . if I thought that people would
              actually . . .

              Hugh's client whispers to Hugh. Hugh produces a cake.

Hugh   One love soufflé, baked by my client sadly not
              at any personal injury to herself.

Judge   Mr Yes, in the face of this evidence, I really

134

have no choice but to find for the plaintiff. Have you anything to say before I name the figure?

Stephen   Well, perhaps just one thing, your honour . . .

Judge   Yes?

Stephen   Perhaps I might put it this way. One two three . . .

Hugh   Objection!

Stephen starts to sing.

Stephen   Woman! *(Crashing chords)*
Get out of my face!
Woman!
Woman drop your case.
Don't press those charges
Pay all my legal costs
You know that this case
Is as good as lost.

Forget the whole thing ever happened
And get yourself out of my life
Woman woman woman
Get out of my face.

Pause: woman in bandages whispers to Hugh.

Hugh   Your honour, it appears my client no longer wishes to proceed with her claim against Mr Yes, she wishes to pay all legal costs, to drop the case, and *(she whispers again)* she would also like permission to get out of his face.

Judge   Such permission is so engranted, Mr Sanchez. Case dismissulated. Now, what next?

Hugh   The state would like to call Mr Tony Inchpractice.

Woodland Voles

*Stephen is at his horrible house, answering the door.
He wears a cardigan with leather patches. He smokes a
pipe which has a stitched leather bowl holder. He opens
the door. Hugh stands without. He is dressed in similar
fashion. These are people with whom John Major would
have a great deal in common. Hugh is holding a hosepipe
reel.*

Stephen John!

Hugh Afternoon, John. I'm returning the hosepipe you
so kindly lent me.

Stephen Decent. Very decent. In you come, for heaven's sake.

Hugh Thankee.

Stephen I was just rearranging my collection. I don't know
if you've ever seen it.

Hugh Collection? Now there's a thing. What do you collect
exactly?

Stephen Well, it ain't stamps.

Hugh It ain't stamps. Coins, perhaps?

Stephen It ain't coins.

Hugh You find me intrigued, John.

They are walking into John's den.

Stephen Follow me into the rumpus den, John and all
will be revealed.

Hugh Lead on, lead on.

Inside the rumpus den there is a large collection

of plates with woodland creatures painted on them.
There are statuettes called 'Spirit of the Dance' and
glass figurines of robins. You have never seen such a
disgusting collection in all your life. It is spotlit and the
joy of Stephen's life.

Hugh   My word, John. My word, my heavens, my goodness.

Stephen   The plates are mostly the work of the artist Elizabeth
              Bridwell, ARA; one of the leading artists of today.

Hugh   *(Examining a plate)* I can see that she is one
              of the leading artists of today at a glance, John.

Stephen   She captures the spirit of woodland creatures in a
              variety of heritage series that you will want to keep
              for ever as a lasting joy and investment.

Hugh   Investment, John?

Stephen   For surely sure investment, John. Only a very
              limited edition of these is produced; ensuring rarity
              and individuality.

Hugh   *(Holding a saucer)* I am bound to say, John 'what
              a marvellous thing to possess'.

Stephen   The mischievious expression on that hedgehog's
              busy, enquiring little face as he snouts for black-
              berries is beautifully rendered and brings vividly to
              life the atmosphere of our heritage native woodlands.
              I bought a hundred of those.

Hugh   A hundred, John? I am gobsmacked. Simply
              gobsmacked.

Stephen   I instantly destroyed ninety-nine. In this way I
              have increased the rarity of this beautiful object
              considerably. Only forty-nine others exist.

Hugh   And where are they?

Stephen   In the hands of other connoisseurs, I must assume.

Hugh   Connoisseurs who also read the *Mail on Sunday*?

Stephen	In a nutshell.
Hugh	John, if you could track down these other tasteful readers of the *Mail on Sunday* and offer to acquire their saucers of the busy enquiring mischievous . . .
Stephen	*(Correcting him)* Mischievious.
Hugh	Mischievious, I do beg your pardon. If, as I say, you could acquire the remainder of these heirloom heritage pieces you would be sitting on the only mischievious hedgehog left in the world.
Stephen	Such is my ambition, John. Who knows what this saucer would be worth should that be the case?
Hugh	When you think, John, of the amounts fetched by paintings by Picasso which do not have a tithe of the character, saucy mischieviousness and enquiring business of this little heritage hedgehog . . .
Stephen	It's quite a thought, John. And that is just one saucer. There is a series of statuettes here in frosted dance entitled 'Spirit of the Dance' by John Petty C.R.A.P.
Hugh	John, they seem to crystallise in lovingly ground glass the movement, grace and gossamer freedom of a great ballerina.
Stephen	That they do, John. In spades. I bought two hundred of each in the series and . . .
Hugh	Destroyed one hundred and ninety-nine of them?
Stephen	Precisely.
Hugh	*(Very serious)* John.
Stephen	Yes?
Hugh	I do hope you are properly insured. There are international art thieves around who . . . if they

	got so much as a whisper of what a trove you have in this rumpus den . . . well . . .
Stephen	I know, John. Believe me I know. I'm well protected, believe you I.
Hugh	I do believe you I, John. I do. Tell me a thing.
Stephen	Gladdingly.
Hugh	What does Joanie make of these. She paints, I believe?
Stephen	Ah now. Now. Joanie is rendered speechless. I sometimes find her in here staring at these *objets* with her arm sort of flung up in front of her face.
Hugh	As if unable to comprehend such talent.
Stephen	Exactly. I think she comes in to draw inspiration. Sometimes though she can't bring herself to look at them at all.
Hugh	As if dazzled.
Stephen	As if dazzled. I'll call her in. *(Calling off)* Oh Joanie.
Joan	*(Off)* What?
Stephen	Could you come in a second, my love?
Hugh	Is she at work at the moment?
Stephen	She is, yes.

Enter Joanie. She is still holding her palette and is obviously still at work. She enters the room sideways, as if trying to avert her gaze from the collection. Stephen and Hugh catch each other's eyes and mouth the word 'dazzled' to each other with triumphant confirmation.

Joan	Yes?
Stephen	You remember John, don't you Joanie?
Joan	Oh. Hello.
Stephen	We were talking about the collection.

Joan emits a little squeak.

Hugh   You're a painter yourself, of course, Joanie. You must marvel at this kind of artistry.

Joan starts to make little retching noises.

All the more so when you consider the rarity of these pieces.

Joan   Yes. *(An idea begins to dawn)* As a matter of fact John, I was going to tell you . . .

Stephen Yes?

Joan   I tracked down a man in Carshalton who has a collection exactly the same as yours.

Stephen No!

Joan   Yup. Piece for piece.

Stephen If only he would sell . . .

Joan   He will! I've ordered the whole collection: it's on its way here.

Stephen Marvellous. That is marvellous.

Hugh   Oh, congratulations.

Stephen All I have to do is destroy it and this will be worth even more.

Joan   Or of course . . .

Stephen Yes?

Joan   *(Trying to be casual)* You could destroy this lot and keep the one that's on its way.

Hugh   True.

Stephen Well, there's no need. These are in place.

Hugh   Be fun though wouldn't it?

140

Joan   *(Almost hysterical)* Yes! Think what fun it would be.

Stephen   All right. Let's do it.

Joan, like a savage animal, unleashes herself on the collection. Hugh joins in. Stephen too, slightly puzzled by the incredible ferocity of Joan and Hugh's attack. Soon it is all in pieces. Joan is frenzied with joy.

(A little doubtful) Well. There we are. Can't wait for the new set to arrive.

Hugh   Congratulations.

Joan   Thank you.

Stephen   This calls for a drink I think. Fancy a gin and ton, John?

Hugh   Hoo, why not?

Stephen   Coming up.

Exit Stephen.

Joan waits for him to go and then falls into Hugh's arms.

Joan   Thank you, John. Thank you a million times over.

Hugh   Think nothing of it. Sometimes a public duty can be a private pleasure. But for God's sake cancel that subscription to the *Mail on Sunday*.

Joan   I have.

VOX
POP

Stephen   Used to be this chap at my school called Richard Braine. You'll never guess our nickname for him. We used to call him Rick Brain. Oh no, that can't be right.

Flying a Light Aircraft with ...

Hugh and Stephen are standing in front of a light aeroplane.

Hugh   Hello and welcome to 'Flying A Light Aeroplane Without Having Had Any Formal Instruction With ...'. Today I'm going to be Flying A Light Aeroplane Without Having Had Any Formal Instruction With Sir Peter Winstanton, former Chairman of the National Trust, and now Maître De Danse at the Galliard Ballet Company. Hello Sir Peter.

Stephen   Good afternoon Johnny.

Hugh   Mmm. My name isn't Johnny.

Stephen   Never said it was.

Hugh   Right now, Sir Peter, you've never flown an aeroplane before?

Stephen   Never flown in my life, Johnny, no.

Hugh   And you've never had any lessons?

Stephen   Oh I've had lessons, maths, geography ...

Hugh   But not in flying?

Stephen   No.

Hugh   And I've never flown before. Is this something you've always wanted to do?

Stephen   Not particularly. So when you rang up I just leapt at the chance.

Hugh   Right.

Hugh and Stephen start to climb into the aeroplane.

Now can I begin, Sir Peter, by asking you about your early influences. Your parents died when you were very young, and you were brought up by your aunt in a boarding house on the South Coast.

Stephen That's right, Johnny, yes. Did a lot of shrimping as a kid.

Hugh Shrimping?

Stephen You know, roll up your trousers, get out there with a net and a box of sandwiches, got to watch the tide though.

Hugh Have you?

Stephen Not now. When you're shrimping. Got to make sure you don't get caught out by the tide, because Johnny?

Hugh Yes?

Stephen It waits for no man . . . hahahahaha.

Stephen is now fiddling with the controls of the aeroplane.

Now what do we do here?

Hugh I'm afraid I haven't the faintest idea.

Stephen Oh well, let's see.

Pushes and pulls at various levers.

Hugh So yours must have been rather a lonely upbringing.

Stephen Oh good heavens no.

Hugh Good heavens no?

Stephen Good heavens no. Very happy time. Got to know lots of people. It was a brothel, you see.

Hugh What was?

Stephen The boarding house that my aunt ran was, in fact, a brothel.

143

Hugh	Really?
Stephen	Lots of people coming in and out at all hours of the day and night. It really was . . .

The engine suddenly fires and the propeller turns.

	Hello. That was a bit of luck.
Hugh	Well done.
Stephen	Ha. Something had to happen eventually.
Hugh	But presumably you can't have got to know many people of your own age through the brothel?
Stephen	Well no, but I became very friendly with members of the local council. The deputy chairman taught me to play bridge, as a matter of fact. He was a county player himself, and a marvellous teacher.

He lets the brakes off and the aeroplane trundles forwards.

	Huh. Look out. Seems like we're off.
Hugh	I really am very impressed by the way you're managing. Were you mechanically minded as a child?
Stephen	Good God no. Couldn't open a tin of beans without an instruction book.
Hugh	*(Shouting back to camera)* Next week, I shall be In an Intensive Care Unit With . . . Peter Trenton, star of *Home And Away*. B' bye.

> VOX
> POP
>
> | | |
> |---|---|
> | **Hugh** | Well they said Enoch Powell was mad, of course . . . Oh look, there's John the Baptist floating upside down past Dewhurst's. |

Cocktail Ending 2

*Hugh and Stephen address the camera at the end of
the show. They are in black tie and Hugh is sitting at
the piano.*

Stephen   Well that's just about it for this week.

Hugh   That's right. The clock has once again . . .

Stephen   Oh be quiet. So it's goodnight from me . . .

Hugh   And it's goodnight from me . . .

Stephen   And it's goodnight from me. We're going to leave
you with tonight's recipe. This is for 'A Mug Of
Horlicks'. You'll need some Horlicks, some milk, a
teaspoon and a mug.

Hugh   Huh, will I do?

Stephen   I meant mug in the sense of a drinking vessel.

Hugh   Right.

Stephen   You will also need an idiot to hit on the head
with your teaspoon.

Hugh   Huh, will I do?

Stephen   Admirably. *(Hits Hugh on the head with teaspoon)*
And one two three, kick. Hit it Mr Laurie, if you'd
be so very kind.

*Hugh strikes up a jazzy sort of riff while Stephen
footles around with a pan of milk and a camping gas
stove. Credits, if there are any.*

A BIT MORE
Fry & Laurie

To Bob Holness

The authors would like to make public their immense feelings of gratitude towards Roger Ordish, Nick Symons and Jon Canter who produced, produced and script-edited 'A Bit of Fry & Laurie' Series 2 respectively. It would be no exaggeration to say that their contributions towards the programme were quite useful.

S.F. & H.L.
St James's Club, Antigua
July 1991

Introduction

Stephen   Well, Hugh.

Hugh   Well, Stephen.

Stephen   Here we are again.

Hugh   More or less.

Stephen   More or less?

Hugh   Last time, if you remember, we were between MAPS and BIOGRAPHIES on the other side, but now they've changed the whole bookshop round.

Stephen   I think I prefer it here.

Hugh   Oh so do I.

Stephen   You get a nice view of the till and the fire exit, and we're only a short stroll away from the Leisure Interest section.

Hugh   I wouldn't want to go back, certainly.

Stephen   But anyway, Hugh, here we are again, with another collection of comedic ensketchments to thrill, tease and sexually arouse our reading public.

Hugh   More or less.

Stephen   More or less, yes. Wasn't it Big Ron Atkinson who said 'you can sexually arouse some of the people all of the time, and all of the people some of the time, but if you want to sexually arouse all of the people all of the time, you've got your work cut out to a certain extent'?

Hugh   No.

Stephen   Tsk. I'm thinking of Abba.

Hugh	Not wishing to interrupt or anything of that sort, but isn't it about time we rolled up our sleeves and got down to the job of introducing the ladies and gentlemen to this book?
Stephen	Haven't they met?
Hugh	Don't think so.
Stephen	I'm so sorry. I could have sworn they were both at the Hendersons' last New Year's Eve.
Hugh	What a night that was.
Stephen	Well, early evening.
Hugh	Yes. What an early evening that was.
Stephen	Well anyway, ladies and gentlemen, this is the book. Book, say hello to the ladies and gentlemen.
	Slight Pause.
Hugh	They seem to have hit it off remarkably well.
Stephen	Oh, I think it's going swimmingly.
Hugh	Well if you'll excuse me, I think I'll just nip to the lavatory.
Stephen	Hugh?
Hugh	Yes?
Stephen	We're in the lavatory.
Hugh	Of course we are. Tsk.
Stephen	You were thinking of Abba.
Hugh	Must have been.
Stephen	Hugh, my old china, I've a question for you.
Hugh	Off you go.
Stephen	Have I gone mad, or were we supposed to use this introduction as a way of issuing a warning?
Hugh	You've gone mad.

Stephen   If I have indeed gone mad, it's the sort of madness in which I have moments of achingly lucid sanity. Here's one now.

Hugh   Steady. Don't waste it.

Stephen   I seem to remember being given some advice by our solicitors.

Hugh   You're quite right. We were advised, by our solicitors, to write out a cheque to our solicitors.

Stephen   Made payable to bearer, if memory serves.

Hugh   Memory has served an ace in this instance, Stephen. We were asked to write out a cheque and advised that it was our duty to warn the potential purchaser of this book, this book with which they are already making such fast friends . . .

Stephen   Fast, but within the speed limit.

Hugh   Just.

Stephen   Just.

Hugh   It was our duty, I think I was saying . . .

Stephen   . . . before you were so attractively interrupted.

Hugh   . . . to warn the reader that these sketches are for external application only.

Stephen   On no account are they to be swallowed.

Hugh   Or performed in public without written permission from the publishers, unless and until you are the only human being left alive on the planet Earth.

Stephen   Which, in case you're starting to get alarmed, is an unlikely set of circumstances, and not one you would expect to come across every day of the week.

Hugh   But that's what you pay these legal johnnies for – covering angles that the rest of us wouldn't think of.

Stephen	A humbling thought, Hugh. A humbling thought.
Hugh	Any other duties we have to discharge, before the ladies and gentlemen ask this book back to their place for a cup of Horlicks and a snog?
Stephen	Not really, except for heaven's sake make sure you've actually got some Horlicks.
Hugh	Oh. That can be embarrassing, can't it?
Stephen	Always have the wherewithal to back up your story. There's nothing worse than an idle boast.
Hugh	Wasn't it the Swedish pop group Abba who said 'a man who claims to have Horlicks when he hasn't, is no man at all – and certainly wouldn't be welcome at Sheffield Wednesday'?
Stephen	No.
Hugh	Oh.
Stephen	It was G.K. Chesterton.
Hugh	B'bye.
Stephen	B'bye.

VOX
POP

Stephen I think they should call it industrial *in*action, hahaha, if you ask me, hahaha.

Dammit 1

Stephen and Hugh are pacing the boardroom.

Stephen   Dammit Peter.

Hugh   John?

Stephen   Dammit four times round the car park and back in for another dammit.

Hugh   Do I get the feeling that something's on your mind, John?

Stephen   Come on, Peter, you know what the hell I'm talking about.

Hugh   At a guess I'd say that this had something to do with the DDL Enterprises takeover bid?

Stephen   You know it's funny, Peter. Four years. Four hard years I've put into building up this Health Club. And now I'm supposed to stand by and let a bunch of wet-arsed college kids take it all away from me.

Hugh   I know, John.

Stephen   If only Marjorie hadn't left us the way she did . . .

Hugh   Marjorie? Hell John, you can't go blaming yourself for that. You and Marjorie had . . .

Stephen   Had what, Peter? A marriage that was nothing more than a bad joke, and not even a very good one?

Hugh   You made some mistakes, John, that's all. You and Marjorie had different ideas about where the company was headed. End of story.

Stephen   But dammit, Marjorie was good, Peter.

Hugh	A good wife, or a good business partner?
Stephen	Is there a difference, Peter?
Hugh	I hope so, John.
Stephen	And now, while we're up to our arses in a major takeover scrap, she's sunning herself in the South of France.
Hugh	South of Wales actually, John.
Stephen	Well, wherever the blue-rinsed hell she is. Oh what a damned fool I've been.
Hugh	John, listen to me, this is no time for you to start feeling sorry for yourself.
Stephen	But dammit all sideways, Peter . . .
Hugh	John. Do something for me. Take a look out of this window.
Stephen	What is this, Peter? Some sort of game?
Hugh	No game, John. Look out there and tell me what you see.
Stephen	I see a car park.
Hugh	Well that's funny, John. Because the last time you looked out of that window, you saw an idea. Don't you remember?
Stephen	Yes. I remember.
Hugh	I thought so.
Stephen	I remember thinking that that would be the best place for the car park.
Hugh	Dammit John, I'm talking about the big idea. The dream that you and I shared. The dream of a health club that would put Uttoxeter on the goddamned map once and for all.
Stephen	Yeah, well maybe . . .

156

Hugh	Maybe? Maybe? I don't believe I'm hearing this. What the hell's happened to the old John?
Stephen	We pulled it down when we built the car park.
Hugh	Dammit John, you're not hearing me.
Stephen	Peter I . . .
Hugh	Don't Peter I me! We've got *that* close. And you're going to lie down and just walk away.
Stephen	Peter, don't hassle me. I'm tired.
Hugh	Tired be damned!
Stephen	A man's got to know when he's licked, Peter. And I know the feeling. I've been licked before.
Hugh	The Lord's Saints preserve us.
Stephen	Did I ever tell you about the time Marjorie licked me? Licked me good and proper? Well I've got the same feeling now, Peter, and it's sore. Maybe it's time to move on.
Hugh	John. I'm going to tell you what I see out of this window.
Stephen	Is this another one of your games, Peter?
Hugh	Same game, John. Different rules. *(Looking out)* I see Tom and Sally and Debbie . . .
Stephen	I thought Sally was off with the flu . . .
Hugh	Exactly, John! Exactly! But she's come in today because she believes in you! God knows why! She believes in what you're trying to do here in Uttoxeter. And you're going to just turn your back on those kids? You're going to walk away from . . . dammit, I make no apology, a vision?
Stephen	Dammit Peter, maybe you're right.
Hugh	You're damn right maybe I'm right.

Stephen	Damn, double damn, and an extra pint of damn for the weekend.
Hugh	Daaaaamn!
Stephen	Right, Peter.
Hugh	Damn?
Stephen	Get a fax over to Cliff at Harlinson's. Extraordinary General Meeting, 3.00p.m. today. Call Janet, and see if we can pull Martin in from . . . where the hell is Martin?
Hugh	High Wycombe.
Stephen	And get Sarah in here. We've got an agenda to work up.
Hugh	Welcome back to the fight, John. Sorry if I was a little rough on you back there.
Stephen	Hell, Peter, I deserved it. I was a damned fool.
Hugh	And if Marjorie calls . . . ?
Stephen	If Marjorie calls . . . *(Pause)* Tell her I'm busy.
Both	DAAAAAAMN!!!

VOX
POP

Hugh	Moira Stewart . . . and Jill Gascoigne . . . neither of them wrote back. Can you believe these people? I mean how much trouble can it be to just bung a pair of stockings in the post?

Dinner With Digby

*Kensington dinner party set. Candles, tablecloth, fruit,
epergne etc. At the head of the table, dinner-jacketed,
is Susan Digby, played by Stephen. Hugh, similarly
DJ-ed, plays Jeremy James Duff, a poncy John
Julius Norwich type, there is also Leslie Crith of the
Independent.*

*Camera is on Stephen, who is talking, but studio sound
isn't up yet.*

Captions   Susan Digby with dinner guests

*Camera pans along the table to Hugh, lips also moving
wordlessly.*

Jeremy James Duff, travel-writer, broadcaster and
journalist

Pan/track along to Leslie.

Leslie Crith, the *Independent.*

Stephen   . . . and similarly louche places. But Jeremy, I must
tell you. I was in Venice last year.

Hugh   Ah, *la serenissima!*

Stephen   That's right. You probably know more than anyone
else in the world about Venice.

Hugh   The Queen of the Adriatic.

Stephen   Is only one of the things you've been called. I was
walking across the Rialto, returning from a walk
that took in Santa Maria della Salute and San
Giorgio Romano . . .

Leslie   Along the Giudecca?

159

Stephen	Along the Giudecca, and I think I'm right in saying that I counted no less that seventy-nine backpackers . . .
Leslie	Backpackers, oh dear lord.
Stephen	. . . who were 'doing', as I believe they say, the Accademia.
Hugh	Ugh, ugh, ugh, ugh. Tourists, you see.
Stephen	And I remember thinking, they're taking away our Venice.
Hugh	Our Venice is being taken away from us. It's crawling with Germans.
Leslie	And Italians.
Stephen	Our Venice is sinking under their weight, not just physically, but the beauty, Jeremy, the grandeur of our Venice is sinking under the blue nylon of their wind-cheaters, their Cola-Coca cans, their eternal flashlight photo-cameras.
Leslie	And that monstrous tinny noise that emanates from their Sony Walkmans.

Hugh and Stephen are baffled.

Stephen	Their . . . ?
Hugh	Erm?
Stephen	Oh you mean those personal stereophonic discothèques?
Hugh	Stop it, stop it, stop it at once.
Stephen	If only . . .
Hugh	Ah, yes well now you see, I have campaigned for years now to have tourists banned from Venice.
Stephen	Have you? Have you?
Hugh	I have, I have. It sounds very harsh, very cruel, very . . .

Stephen	Déglanté?
Hugh	Very déglanté, thank you. But I'm sure it's the only way.
Stephen	Ng, ng, ng, ng.
Leslie	Who was it, who was it, who said '*He* is a tourist, *you* are a holidaymaker but *I* am a traveller?'
Hugh	Oh, was it Humbert Wolfe?
Stephen	It was Cocteau, surely?
Hugh	It doesn't sound very Cocteau.
Stephen	But then Cocteau never did, which is how you can always tell it's Cocteau.
Hugh	True, true. Trouché!
Leslie	Of course it's not just Venice is it?
Hugh	It's not just Venezia, Venedig, Veneeess, not by a very long stroke.
Leslie	Our whole world is being stained.
Stephen/Hugh	Stained, stained.
Stephen	Eheu fugaces! O tempora, o mores, Jeremy.
Hugh	Yes indeed.
Leslie	I blame television. I'm sorry but I do.
Hugh	(*Pained at the thought*) Ah . . . ah, ah, television. That fearful Mervyn Bragg.
Stephen	Mervyn Bragg, stop it, don't, shush, now please, really. If I had my way with Mervyn Bragg . . .
Hugh	No one would be in the least surprised.
	Lots of laughter.
Leslie	This is most awfully good Tarte Citron.

Stephen/Hugh
Er . . . ?

Leslie Tarte Citron.

Stephen Oh, the lemon pie. Thank you. I always say I could never really be friends with someone who didn't love lemon pie.

Hugh Susan, don't be sly, did you make it yourself?

Stephen Let's just say I made it to the shops in time to buy it.

Hugh/Leslie
Marks & Spencer?

Stephen Who else, but M & S?

Hugh M & S!

Leslie M & S! M et S. They are simply amazing aren't they?

Hugh And have you tried their new boxer shorts?

Stephen No I haven't, I haven't, I haven't.

Leslie I have. Delicious.

Hugh And their dips! Oh bless me, their dips.

Leslie In my local one there's a really marvellous school.

Stephen A primary school?

Leslie Oh yes. Both mine and my husband's children go there.

Stephen Mine's just opened a hospital section.

Hugh Have they? Have they really?

Stephen Oh yes, you can go in and have minor operations, everything.

Hugh In the one just round the corner from me they sell weaponry.

Stephen Is that right?

Hugh   Oh it is. Quite right.

Leslie   Mine too.

Hugh   I bought an F1-11 there last week . . . so *fresh* . . . I
              swear it was made that day . . .

              Fading out.

Stephen   And of course if you're unhappy, you can always go
              back and change it . . .

VOX
POP

Hugh   *(Holding up plate)* See this? You
              could eat your dinner off this.

Commentators

Hugh and Stephen are two rather doddery old commentators.

Stephen   As we look down now, on this glorious July afternoon . . . what a splendid sight it is, Peter.

Hugh   It's an absolute picture, isn't it? The sun beating down . . .

Stephen   Beautiful day . . .

Hugh   The crowds . . . not a seat to be had anywhere . . .

Stephen   Packed house . . .

Hugh   Absolutely packed . . . and the grass looking so lovely . . .

Stephen   Green as anything.

Hugh   Green as you like. Absolutely as green as could be . . .

Stephen   Grass has never looked greener . . . The groundsman Arthur . . .

Hugh   Alan.

Stephen   Is it? Alan Dixon. Alan Dixon has done a marvellous job . . .

Hugh   Marvellous job, he really has. What a scene.

Stephen   Marvellous scene . . .

Hugh   Oh I say there's a bus.

Stephen   Yes, look there's a beautiful old English . . . what is that? Number 29?

164

Hugh	It's a 29 bus, yes.
Stephen	A beautiful English 29 bus, yes, what a marvellous scene. Grass, sun, bus, marvellous.
Hugh	Yes, that bus making its way now along the Garboldisham road.
Stephen	Garboldisham, beautiful village that is . . .
Hugh	Absolutely delightful village . . .
Stephen	Garboldisham. What a lovely name.
Hugh	Lovely name. Lovely English name.
Stephen	Hello, there are some people getting off the bus . . .
Hugh	Look out . . .
Stephen	They're off to enjoy their good old English strawberries and cream . . .
Hugh	Oh English, yes, watch out for those German strawberries . . .
Stephen	Not the same . . .
Hugh	Not the same thing at all . . . English strawberries and cream . . . 29 bus going down the Garboldisham road . . .
Stephen	Grass . . .
Hugh	Cream . . .

They begin to gather momentum in some sort of unpleasant sexual exchange of fruity things.

Stephen	Garboldisham . . .
Hugh	Crowds . . .
Stephen	The South Downs . . .
Hugh	Malvern hills rolling like a . . .
Stephen	Motor cars . . . leather gloves . . .

Hugh	A quarter pound of Mrs Faversham's extra strong peppermints . . .
Stephen	Ovaltine . . .
Hugh	Wellington boots . . .
Stephen	Cream . . .
Hugh	Heaps of cream . . . cream and lawnmowers . . .
Stephen	Summer holidays in Cromer . . .
Hugh	Vaulting over a stile in a country lane . . .
Stephen	Catching sticklebacks in an old tin can . . .
Hugh	'Honestly nanny, I never touched them . . .'
Stephen	Piano lessons with Mrs Duckworth . . .
Hugh	Father's hands on the steering wheel . . .
Stephen	Sit up straight!
Hugh	Going faster and faster . . .
Stephen	Locked in the cupboard for being rude to Mrs Howlett . . .
Hugh	Take the Wolseley for a run . . .
Stephen	England . . . Elgar . . . Malvern Hills.
Hugh	Bath Olivers. Play the game . . . elbows off the table.
Stephen	Who's a brave soldier then? Nanny's hands all steamy and starched.
Hugh	England! England and cream . . .
Stephen	Custard cream . . .
Hugh	Strawberries and cream . . .
Stephen	Strawberries and English cream . . .

Hugh	Take the B road to Petersfield. England.
	(Shouting now)
Stephen	Creamy England!
Hugh	England!
Stephen	Cream!
Hugh	The roast cream of old England.
Stephen	Oh.
Hugh	Oh I say.
	A post-coital interlude.
Stephen	And here comes Nigel Lawson now . . .

VOX
POP

Stephen   A challenge for her? Yes I've got a challenge for her. Why doesn't she see if she can bleeding well BLEEP herself. For charity obviously.

First Kiss

Hugh   My first kiss. I suppose everyone can remember their first kiss. Nothing quite lives up to it, does it? I was eleven years old I remember and my great-uncle had come to stay for a few weeks on parole. We used to play a game where I would sit on his lap and he would pretend to be a train. Then one day . . .

Stephen comes on.

Stephen   Hugh, Hugh, what are you saying?

Hugh   I was telling the ladies and gentlemen about my first kiss.

Stephen   Yes, but Hugh, this is a delicate area, I really don't think –

Hugh   We agreed that 'A Bit More Fry & Laurie' was going to be an arena for the expression of all kinds of ideas and experiences that wouldn't normally find their way on to television, didn't we?

Stephen   We did, we did agree.

Hugh   So my surprise at feeling a tongue suddenly . . .

Stephen   Hugh, there are valid arenas and valid arenas. This is not one of them.

Hugh   But I want that experience to be understood, it may help others to know that they're not the first to feel that wet . . .

Stephen   Hugh. Believe me this is a whole can of worms you're opening here, and if there is one single taboo left, one unmentionable subject not fit for comic treatment, you've just mentioned it.

Hugh	But surely there's nothing so very odd about it. There I was, on my great-uncle's lap and in came Lucy.
Stephen	Lucy.
Hugh	Yes, Lucy.
Stephen	And how old was Lucy?
Hugh	Oh, twelve I think. And I kissed her.
Stephen	You kissed her.
Hugh	Yes.
Stephen	You've done this deliberately haven't you?
Hugh	Done what?
Stephen	You set it up to make it sound as if –
Hugh	As if what?
Stephen	Never mind. Get on with it.
Hugh	All right. So I kissed Lucy, and was very surprised to feel her tongue pop out. It was my first real snog and I loved it. You can imagine that I fell in love instantly. Sadly the next year Lucy developed distemper and had to be put down.
Stephen	Doh.

VOX
POP

Stephen   (*As woman*) Well, I was born
           Mary Patterson, but then I
           married and naturally took my
           husband's name, so now I'm Neil
           Patterson.

Brainstorm

Five people around a table: flimsies, photographs, graphics etc. The people are Stephen, a copy-writer, Hugh a ditto, Fee, an imponderably stupid graphic artist, Rhiannon an aggressive producer, and Dick, another copy-writer.

Stephen   *(Standing and stretching)* All right. Before we crack off on this new campaign, I'd like you all to get to know each other. Rhiannon, you must all know, worked on that draught-excluder commercial, the one with the young guy in the American leather jacket, driving around in an old pink Cadillac.

Rhiannon   Hi, everyone.

Hugh   Hiya. That was a great television commercial. Made me weep.

Rhiannon   Thanks.

Fee   That was really beautiful work actually. Because I saw it.

Stephen   Fee of course was the power behind that brilliant campaign for Total Protein Concept Balance System shampoo, the one with . . . how did it go? It had a guy in an American leather jacket, driving round in a . . .?

Fee   . . . an old pink Cadillac. Hi.

Rhiannon   That was bitchingly good.

Hugh   World class, world class.

Stephen   Jake, obviously, came up with the commercial for Dong Jeans, which had a guy in an American leather jacket driving round in a . . . what was it, Jake?

170

Hugh	It was an old blue Cadillac.
Rhiannon	Incredible.
Fee	Genius.
Stephen	I hardly need say that Jake's ideas tend to be a little bit off the wall.
Hugh	Yeah, I'm crazy.
Stephen	And joining us from an out of town agency is Dick. Dick's just come from working on that fabulous commercial for 'Pretension' by Calvin Klein . . .
Dick	Er . . . no . . . that wasn't me.
Stephen	Oh . . . they've sent us another Dick, have they? Well what was the last thing you worked on, Dick?
Dick	I wrote an advertisement for Tideyman's Carpets.
Stephen	Yeah?
Dick	It had a picture of lots of carpets, and a voice said 'Tideyman's Carpets, sale now on'.
	Slightly embarrassed silence.
Stephen	Great stuff.
Hugh	Yeah, fantastic.
Stephen	So we have a team here with one hell of a proven track record. Drinks anyone?
Hugh	Jack Daniels.
Rhiannon	Jack Daniels suits me.
Stephen	Bourbons for everyone then, yeah?
Dick	A Fanta for me, please.
	Stephen is at the fridge.
Stephen	OK. Floor's yours, Jake.

171

Hugh rises; he's a gum-chewing cockney whizz.

Hugh   What we've got here, people, is a big campaign for a new bank account. The Nexus Bank Account.

Stephen   I want to stress new here. New means different. That means *different* advertising.

Fee   Different.

Hugh   Different.

Stephen   Different.

Rhiannon   I want it on record that I think this should be different.

Stephen   Point taken.

Fee   Can I butt in here?

Stephen   Sure, Fee.

Fee   Thanks.

Stephen   All right. So let's brainstorm it. Let's find a hook, a peg, an angle, a line, a channel . . . what is it that's going to *sell* this bank account?

Rhiannon   What's going to sell that guts and kidneys out of it?

They all start clicking their fingers, clapping their hands. All except Dick that is, who sits there slightly surprised by their behaviour.

Hugh   Right well. How about . . . how about . . . a guy.

Rhiannon   Young?

Hugh   A young guy, thanks darling, he's wearing . . . I dunno . . . what?

Fee   Sweatshirt?

Rhiannon   Jeans?

Dick   A cardigan?

Hugh	No wait . . . What about an American leather jacket?
	They whoop and emote.
Stephen	An American leather jacket!
Rhiannon	Jake I hate you!
Fee	That's brilliant. That's really brilliant because people wear those.
Dick	Um . . .
Stephen	Yes, Dick?
Dick	It's not very different.
	Silence.
Stephen	Maybe Dick's right.
Hugh	Hell I'm not married to the idea.
Fee	It always worried me, I must say.
Rhiannon	I always hated the bastard.
Stephen	OK. Clean slate, everybody. Let's start afresh from scratch one.
Hugh	What about a Canadian leather jacket . . .
Stephen	Suede . . .
Rhiannon	That's it! A Canadian suede leather jacket. And . . . *(She's got an idea coming)* and . . .
Hugh	Yeah?
Rhiannon	*(It dawns on her)* HE'S DRIVING AN OLD CAR!!!!
Fee	An *old* car! He's driving an *old* car!
Hugh	An old Jaguar!
Stephen	What about *(Thumps the table)* a Cadillac. He's driving a sodding old pink Cadillac!

Thunderous applause and cheering.

Rhiannon   Something.

Stephen   Perfect. Amazing work. Right, well. Lunch everyone?

They make as if to go.

Dick   That's it, is it?

Hugh   I see what Dick's getting at. We need something else as well.

Stephen   Okay, let's run with Dick's something else as well idea for the moment. The young guy has got to have something else as well.

People start getting up and looking at things.

Hugh   *(Picking up a coffee cup)* Something aspirational ... Coffee ...?

Stephen   Bigger!

Rhiannon   *(Picking up a stapler)* A stapler?

Stephen   Bigger than that!

Fee   A telephone? They can be quite big. I've seen.

Stephen   Much bigger!!

Hugh   Wait a minute ...

Stephen   Jake's got something ...

Rhiannon   What have you got, Jake?

Hugh   A baby. The guy's got a baby.

Stephen   New man, caring, tender, Jake I love you!

Fee   That's brilliant because people have those. A really huge baby.

Rhiannon   A really huge American baby.

Stephen   Wearing ...?

174

All	An American leather jacket!!!
Stephen	So what are we saying? What are we saying about Nexus here? We're saying . . .
Hugh	We're saying 'this bank account is so good it will virtually make you American'.
Dick	Why are we saying that?
Hugh	Well, um . . . we're saying that . . . we're saying that because . . . we're saying that . . . Problem, Dick? Objection?
Dick	Well why does everything have to be American? Why couldn't it be an English leather jacket?
Hugh	Oh dear.
Stephen	Dick, I'm sensing you're not with us on this. You have another idea?
Dick	Well, I have worked something out as a matter of fact.
Fee	We're all ears.
Rhiannon	We are. Nothing but ears.
Stephen	I'm just one huge ear, Dick.
Dick	Um . . . *(Reading)* 'The Nexus bank Account. It offers the same rate of interest as every other young person's account and comes with a perfectly normal plastic card. You may find it quite useful.'

Stephen grabs Dick's notepad.

Stephen	Dick, Dick, Dick.

Stephen hands notepad to Hugh.

The anti-ad. Dick, you've got something there.

Hugh	Christ, I'm beginning to see what you mean! 'The Nexus Bank Account. It's not so bad really.'

Rhiannon   Sen-Christing-sational.

Fee   You're so clever, Dick. Because that's a really good idea.

Hugh   You've cracked it, Dick.

Rhiannon   Dick's cracked the son of a bastard.

Stephen   Dick's cracked it!!

Fee   Dick, you're a star.

Dick   Well, looks like the Fantas are on me then.

VOX POP

Stephen   *(Showing the places on his body)* They cut me right round that way to see if they could find anything. Then they had a dig about down here. Still nothing. So they poked this thing up my . . . you know . . . had a look up there. Nothing. I'm going through the red channel next time.

Spies/Pigeons

Hugh knocks and enters the spies' office. It is empty, but the window is open.

Hugh   Morning Control, I was just. . . . oh.

He looks round the office, disappointed. He is about to leave when the phone on Control's desk starts ringing; Hugh is unsure about answering it, but eventually does.

Hello, this is the Secret Service. . . . No, I'm afraid Control's not here at the moment, who is this please? Oh hello Mrs Control . . . No it's rather strange. I just popped into Control's office to see if he'd like a cup of coffee, because it's nearly eleven o'clock, and there's no one here . . . I can't think where he can have got to. I agree with you, Mrs Control, that he'll probably turn up. Bye bye.

He hangs up, just as Stephen enters.

Stephen   Hello Tony.

Hugh   Control, there you are. I was beginning to worry.

Stephen   Oh?

Hugh   Mrs Control has just been on the telephone, and between me and Mrs Control, neither of us seemed to know where you were.

Stephen   Ah. Well let me explain, Tony. But let me first ask whether you notice anything unusual about the office?

Hugh   Let's see. The only thing that struck me about it was that you weren't in it, Control. Apart from that . . .

Stephen	What about the window, Tony?
Hugh	The window, of course! The window always used to be slightly further to the left!
Stephen	Not quite, Tony.
Hugh	Oh. It was a bit of a guess, actually.
Stephen	No, the window is in the same place that it's always been. I know we talked about moving it, and you very kindly looked into the feasibility of the whole thing, but after a while I had to make the difficult decision that that particular game just wasn't worth the candle.
Hugh	Yes, and after you'd made that decision, I remember you talked at some length about what you saw as the loneliness of command.
Stephen	That's right, Tony. No, what's unusual about the window is that it's open.
Hugh	You're right, Control. Is this in some way connected to your not having been in the office earlier on?
Stephen	Yes, Tony, it is. You see, I fell out of the window.
Hugh	Control, I can only say how sorry I am, and ask whether you were hurt in any way.
Stephen	To my surprise, Tony, I am in fact not hurt at all.
Hugh	Well that is something of a blessing anyway.
Stephen	Yes, you're right.
Hugh	Because one of the other things about being Control, I've always thought, is that your office is on the sixth floor, so that in the event of something like this happening, you have got slightly further to fall than if you were in the Record department which is located on the first floor of this building.

Stephen	Very similar thoughts were going through my mind, Tony, as I travelled towards the pavement with gathering speed.
Hugh	But how did this whole sorry business come about, Control?
Stephen	Tony, I've a confession to make. One of the things I like to do before you very kindly bring me my morning coffee is feed the pigeons who perch on my window sill.
Hugh	Control, I can't say I'm surprised. There had been some rumour in the canteen to that effect.
Stephen	Well then, I'm glad to be able to silence those wagging tongues one way or another. I do feed the pigeons, and it was while I was doing this that I fell out of the window.
Hugh	Control, I think I can picture the scene. There you were, at the open window, so engrossed in what you were doing that you neglected not to fall out of the window. Am I fairly near the mark?
Stephen	Spot on, Tony.
Hugh	I thought so. And I'll tell you another thing that has resulted from this whole adventure.
Stephen	What's that?
Hugh	It's after 11 o'clock and you've not had your coffee.
Stephen	You're right. Huh. It never rains but it pours, eh Tony?
Hugh	Yes, Control, but quite often it rains and pours at the same time.
Stephen	Yes. Well on your way to the coffee-making area, could you ask Valerie to pop out and apologise to an old lady who was selling flowers outside the main entrance.

Hugh	I'll certainly do that, Control. Did she happen to be the unlucky one who broke your fall?
Stephen	No. She was fortunate in that respect, Tony. But she might be a little upset that her young grandson did.
Hugh	Fair enough, Control. Tell you what then. She might welcome a cup of coffee too!
Stephen	Good thinking, Tony. B-bye!
Hugh	B-bye.

VOX
POP

Hugh	Both of them. Stark naked and at it like knives. BBC 1 at seven o'clock in the evening. It was disgusting. I don't know what that David Attenborough thinks he's about.

Society

A sitting room. A doorbell rings. A woman gets up and answers the door to Stephen and Hugh. Most of the way through Hugh is repeating everything Stephen says, a fraction of a second later.

Stephen Morning.

Hugh Morning.

Stephen We're from the Westminster Society . . .

Hugh Society . . .

Stephen We wondered if we could come in and talk to you about our aims, and the possibility of you joining us.

Hugh . . . joining us, possibly, who knows?

Woman Well . . .

Stephen Thank you . . .

Hugh So much.

Stephen I'm Mr Willis. And this is Mr Barraclough.

Hugh Barraclough . . .

Stephen No relation, in case you're wondering.

Woman Sorry?

Stephen We're not related to each other, in case you thought we were.

Woman Well why should you be?

Stephen Well we shouldn't, that's what I'm saying. We shouldn't be related and we're not. Hence the totally different names.

181

Woman	So, what can I do for you?
Stephen	As I say, my colleague and I are thinking of founding this society . . .
Hugh	Society . . .
Stephen	Would you be interested in joining us?
Hugh	. . . perhaps joining us?
Woman	And what is this society for?
Stephen	It's . . .
Hugh	Well . . .

They look at each other.

Stephen	Well obviously this is one of the things we need to look at . . .
Hugh	Look at it very carefully indeed . . .
Stephen	And I think you've already shown that you would be a very useful member . . .
Hugh	Useful member of the society.
Woman	But you said you had some aims.
Stephen	I don't think we did.
Hugh	. . . did say that, we may have done . . .
Woman	But when I answered the door, you said could you come in and talk about the aims of your society.

They look uncomfortable.

Stephen	Well that's a matter of opinion . . .
Hugh	Subjective opinion, really . . .
Woman	Well all right, but what is the point of this society? I mean you've got to have a point, otherwise . . . there's no point.
Stephen	Hmm. That's a good point.

182

Hugh	Well made . . .
Woman	I mean are you going to collect postage stamps?
Stephen	Yes.
Hugh	Definitely. Collect postage stamps.
Woman	Or are you going to practise Highland dancing?
Stephen	Yes. Stamps and Highland dancing are very high on the society's agenda.
Hugh	Hardly anything higher on the agenda than those two.
Woman	Or talk about Roman ruins in Shropshire?
Stephen	Definitely that.
Hugh	That's even higher on the agenda. That's right up at the top.
Woman	But you don't know?
Stephen	Know what?
Hugh	Know what, precisely?
Woman	You don't know for certain what the society is going to be for?
Stephen	Well, we have made one or two notes . . .
Hugh	Just one or two . . .
Woman	Yes?
Stephen	But unfortunately, not to do with the society.
Hugh	On a completely separate matter.
Stephen	However, to answer your question in the spirit in which it was asked . . .
Hugh	In that very selfsame spirit . . .
Stephen	My view is that the society should be run in the interests of its members.

Hugh	Brilliant. That's my view too. Members.
Stephen	But you see, until we have some members, we don't really have any interests.
Hugh	You might say that our hands are tied . . .
Stephen	So. Will you help us?
Woman	Can I make a suggestion?
Stephen	Of course. Suggestions.
Hugh	Eureka. Suggestions.
Stephen	Tuesdays and Thursdays could be suggestion evenings.
Woman	No, can I make a suggestion now. And that is that you come back when you've decided what this society is supposed to be for. I can't stand here talking all day.
Stephen	Now there's an idea.
Hugh	Definitely an idea there.
Stephen	A society for people who can't stand here talking all day.
Hugh	All day and all night.
Stephen	I think that would be a very popular society. . . .
Hugh	Flock to join that society . . .
Stephen	When you think of all the people who knock on your door.
Hugh	Knock on your bell . . .
Stephen	Jehovah's witnesses . . .
Hugh	Witnesses to the Jehovah's incident . . .
Stephen	Charity collectors . . . estate agents . . . small boys wanting their ball back . . .

184

Hugh	The ball which accidentally went over the fence back . . .
Stephen	Could we interest you in joining that society?
Woman	I'm going to shut the door now.
Stephen	Excellent.
Woman	What?
Stephen	Shutting the door indicates a definite interest in joining a society for people who can't stand here talking all day . . .
Hugh	Total commitment to the society.

She slams the door. Cut to a shot of them outside the door.

Stephen	Well that's one member for our society, then . . .
Hugh	One member for definite member . . .
Stephen	Shall we try next door?
Hugh	Next door, why not?

VOX
POP

Stephen	He just picked me up and slapped me. Really hard. I cried and cried, but he wouldn't take any notice. Then he put a plastic tag round my wrist, cut my umbilical cord and put me in a cot. It was awful.

Introducing My Grandfather To . . .

Hugh in studio with an old man and Stephen.

Hugh   Hello and welcome to 'Introducing My Grandfather To'. Tonight I shall be Introducing My Grandfather To the novelist and corporate accountant Sir Benton Asher. Good evening Sir Benton.

Stephen   Good evening.

Hugh   May I introduce you to my grandfather? Grandfather, this is Sir Benton Asher.

Stephen   *(Shaking hands with old man)* How do you do?

Old Man   Yes.

Hugh   Next week I shall be introducing my grandfather to Desmond Lynham. Until then, goodnight.

VOX
POP

Hugh   Everyone looks on me as the local historian. But it's amazing what a fascinating history Solihull does in fact have. But the odd thing is that I am the only person, so far as I know, to find it even remotely interesting.

Combat Games

Stephen rings the doorbell of a semi, dressed in an anorak and sensible hat. The door swings open, but there is no one there. Stephen enters hesitantly.

Stephen   Hello? Hello? Yoo hoo? Anyone at ho . . .

Hugh springs out, hanging upside down, dressed in camouflage gear with a headband and khaki greasepaint all over his face: he is holding a gun.

Oh good afternoon.

Hugh   In a combat situation you would be dead meat, mister.

Stephen   Sorry?

Hugh   If you'd have been some sort of gook, I would have burned you away and had your arse for breakfast.

Stephen   Oh. Right.

Hugh   You're not a gook, though, are you?

Stephen   I hope not.

Hugh   No. Gooks don't wear anoraks, as far as I can ascertain. Pass friend.

Stephen   Thank you. Are you anything to do with Martin Wilson's Recreational Wargames Limited?

Hugh   Indeed. I am he.

Stephen   Who?

Hugh   I am Colonel 'Mad' Martin Wilson, and Recreational Wargames are very much my business.

Stephen	Oh good. I'm interested in taking part in one of these combat games.
Hugh	Well, you've come to the right place. This is what I call the game zone.
Stephen	I see. This is where the combat games take place, is it?
Hugh	That is correct, my friend. Trust no one and nothing. The game zone is full of surprises.
Stephen	Yes. The first surprise is, it's your front room.
Hugh	A front room equipped for war. This, for example, is an anti-personnel magazine rack.
Stephen	Is it?
Hugh	No. But you couldn't possibly have known that.
Stephen	Is this what we're going to play with?
Hugh	Please do not aim your weapon unless you intend to discharge it, and then only if in a full combat situation.
Stephen	It's a water pistol.
Hugh	Yes. Loaded with live water.
Stephen	Righty ho.
Hugh	I will count to ten, and you will secrete yourself somewhere in the game zone, preferably in a potential ambush position. I will then come after you in what I choose to call a search and destroy mission.
Stephen	Crikey.
Hugh	And remember, the first rule of the game zone is, there are no rules. And the second rule is, don't go into the kitchen. It's out of bounds.
Stephen	Understood.
Hugh	Right, the game time begins . . .

188

A woman enters from the kitchen.

Woman   Do you want some tea, Martin? Oh good afternoon.

Stephen   Hello.

Woman   I was just making some tea for my husband. Would you fancy a cup?

Stephen   Oh that'd be very nice. Thank you.

Woman   Won't be a minute.

She goes back into the kitchen.

Stephen   That's very kind of her.

Hugh   Coo. You really are dead meat. Never trust civilians.

Stephen   But she's your wife, isn't she?

Hugh   She said she was my wife. But she could easily be a gook, for all you know.

Stephen   Well surely gooks don't wear aprons, do they?

Hugh   Never mind.

Stephen   Cooks do.

Hugh   All right. Game time begins. One. Two. Three. Four . . .

Stephen tiptoes out of the room.

Five. Six. Seven. Eight, nine, ten seconds of game time have elapsed.

Hugh opens his eyes and looks round the room: then he suddenly drops on to the floor and starts to move around the room in a series of somersaults and ridiculous combat poses. Eventually he is forced to give up.

(*Calling out*) Right. Congratulations, my friend. You are the first person ever to have outwitted Colonel

'Mad' Martin Wilson in a game situation. Hello?
Tscch. Honestly. That chap is dead meat.

Mrs Wilson enters with a tray of tea things.

Woman   There you are dear.

Hugh   Thank you dear.

Woman   Where's your friend?

Hugh   Friend? He is the enemy, dear.

Woman   Well doesn't he want his tea, then?

Hugh   Well he might do.

Hugh is standing by the window: Stephen opens it from the outside and sticks his pistol through at Hugh's head.

Stephen   We meet again, Colonel.

Woman   Your tea's ready.

Stephen   Oh thanks very much.

Hugh   You went outside the game zone. You broke the rules.

Stephen   In combat there are no rules. Except survival.

Hugh   All right then.

Hugh drops his water pistol.

Stephen   That's better. Now then. Very slowly reach out and pass me my cup of tea. By the handle, Colonel.

Hugh   Very well.

Hugh makes as if to do so, but grabs his wife round the neck, holding a large knife to her neck.

One false move and the woman gets it.

Stephen   Oh come come, Colonel.

Hugh   I mean it. Drop your weapon.

Stephen   How do I know that she isn't a gook?

Hugh	She's not a gook.
Woman	I'm not a gook.
Hugh	There you are. So come on. Throw down your weapon.
Stephen	No. I call your bluff, Colonel.
Hugh	I'm serious.
Stephen	Off you go then.

Hugh suddenly cuts her throat: lots of blood: she falls to the floor.

Er . . . looks like you've killed your wife.

Hugh	It's only a game. *(Pause)* Isn't it?

VOX
POP

Stephen	I'm not really interested in clothes. Not really. As long as they get me from A to B.

Small Talk

Stephen addresses the loyal audience.

Stephen When I was nine, oh fewer years ago now than
I care to remember, hum, hum! my mother told
me that in this life one could either be an elf or
a pixie. What she meant by that, I fully suppose
you may be able all too readily to guess. But her
remarks set me thinking and from that moment
on I purposed to be worthy of her admonitions
and advisalments. I suppose I can look back
on my whole life as a kind of quest, a search, a
hunt, an interrogation if you like. Yesterday was
my birthday, I won't tell you which, because I
hate you, and I celebrated it in fine style, in the
company of a cold bottle of Chablis and a couple
of prostitutes. I suppose in a sense my quest has
come full circle, OR RATHER, my hunt is over
and I can rest now. Goodnight.

VOX
POP

Stephen Well I personally think that
the nineties will be the decade
in which masturbation really
takes off.

Dammit 2

Hugh and Stephen are in an office. Hugh is finishing a phone conversation.

Hugh	Right. Much obliged for your time, Keith.
	Puts phone down.
	Dammit.
Stephen	What?
Hugh	It's pretty much as we feared, John.
Stephen	Yeah?
Hugh	Only a whole heap worse.
Stephen	Suppose you start from the beginning.
Hugh	Not much to say. Seems that twenty minutes ago, our time, Derwent Enterprises went into liquidation.
Stephen	What?
Hugh	Keith called a couple of hours ago from Helsinki.
Stephen	But that was Keith just now, wasn't it?
Hugh	Yeah, just now our time. But he called a couple of hours ago his time.
Stephen	I see. And he called to say that Derwent has gone under?
Hugh	That's right.
Stephen	Damn!
Hugh	Damn it to damnation!

Stephen	Damn, blast, and two extra slices of buttered damn. Who else knows about it?
Hugh	It'll be all round town before you can say 'Hell and double-blast, dammit to Hades twice.'
Stephen	Hell and double-blast, dammit to Hades ...

The phone rings. Hugh picks it up.

Hugh	Yes.

He hangs up.

Derek knows.

Stephen	Dammit.
Hugh	If they pull on their options ... Christ it doesn't bear thinking about. This whole health club could go belly up.
Stephen	Right. I want to know who's behind them, I want to know who's pulling the strings, I want to know WHAT IN HELL'S NAME IS GOING ON.
Hugh	John, I do believe you're scared.
Stephen	You're damned right I'm scared, Peter. I sense Marjorie's hand in this.
Hugh	Marjorie?
Stephen	I never told you this, Peter, but when Marjorie left me I settled a block of shares on her and the boy.
Hugh	Shares in the health club? Were you out of your goddammed mind?
Stephen	In the club, no. I knew I couldn't trust her there. But I gave her shares in D-Tec.
Hugh	And you think ...
Stephen	Think? I don't think anything. There isn't time to think. There's only time to act.

194

Hugh	But is Marjorie really capable of pulling a scrimshaw trick like this?
Stephen	*(Bitter laugh)* Marjorie? She would float her own grandmother as a holding corporation, and strip her clean of preference stock if she thought it would hurt me.
	Stephen picks up a framed photo of Marjorie and her son.
	Three pints of damn and a chaser of hellblast!!
Hugh	What about the boy, John?
Stephen	The boy's Dennis, Peter.
Hugh	No. What about the boy. . . . John.
Stephen	Leave the boy out of this, Peter. He's only a boy.
Hugh	Something I've always wondered, John.
Stephen	Yeah?
Hugh	How come the boy has been living with Marjorie since the divorce?
Stephen	Hih. The court ruled that I was violent and unstable, an unfit father.
Hugh	You, John? That's a damned laugh. If they had seen the way you've parented this company . . .
Stephen	Well, Marjorie told this story . . . one night I came home, I was tired, there was something about the way she looked at me, I sensed a mocking, a sneering . . . I dunno, anyway I flipped . . . emptied a bowl of trifle over her pretty little head.
Hugh	And she got custody.
Stephen	Very.
Hugh	John, it must hurt, not being able to watch Dennis grow up.

Stephen	Hurt? No. He's nothing to me now.
Hugh	Oh yeah, John? So how come every year on his birthday you take him down to London to see *Phantom of the Opera?*
Stephen	I do that because I hate him.
Hugh	Fair enough.
Stephen	But I give Marjorie due warning . . . if she wants a fight, then by God she's going to get one!
Hugh	And the prize, John?
Stephen	As big as they get, Peter. The entire leisure market in the Uttoxeter catchment area goes to the winner. No strings attached.

Picks up photo of Marjorie.

Why can't you leave me alone?

Hugh	John, what was it you once said to me about perspective?
Stephen	Er . . . I seem to remember asking you how it was spelt. . . .
Hugh	No no, after that.
Stephen	What are you saying to me, Peter?
Hugh	I'm saying, John, I'm saying, I'm saying . . . dammit I'm saying *I'm* here, Marjorie's a hundred and fifty miles away her time, if we can't fight this bastard son of a mongrel bitch then we aren't the team who weathered the Babylex crisis and came up smelling of roses. That's what I'm saying.
Stephen	Peter, you're right. Call Ipswich now, your time and tell them Derwent Enterprises or no Derwent Enterprises this Health Club is in business and stays in business.
Hugh	And if Marjorie should call?

196

Stephen   Marjorie? Never heard of her.

Hugh   Dammit John, I love you when you're flying.

Stephen speaks into an intercom.

Stephen   Sarah, bring in a pot of hot strong coffee and a dozen memo pads. *(Intercom off)* Now, let's get the hell out of here before they arrive.

VOX
POP

Hugh   I don't really believe in all this fuss about clouds of radioactive dust. It'll all blow over before long, I'm sure of it.

197

Flushed Grollings

The set is one of those warehousey sort of places, where the merchandise is behind the assistant who wears a brown warehouse coat. Lots of blue plastic trays with pro-ey looking bits and pieces.

Stephen enters with a list.

Hugh   Help you, sir?

Stephen   Um, a dozen grollings please.

Hugh   Flushed or galvanised?

Stephen   Flushed.

Hugh   Right. That be it?

Stephen   A copper flange-pipe, braced, two jubilees, seven nipples . . .

Hugh   Greased?

Stephen   Greased nipples, yeah. Five olive-spantles, jigged and onioned.

Hugh   Twelve or seventeen mill?

Stephen   Twelve. Metre of fleeling wire, coaxial, twenty UJ's and a parping couplet.

Hugh   Male or female?

Stephen   Male. No, second thoughts, one of each.

Hugh   Do you want the parping couplet standing proud?

Stephen   No, embarrassed I think.

Hugh   An embarrassed parping couplet. That it?

Stephen	Two rolls of spowling tape.
Hugh	Double-sided?
Stephen	Do they do single-sided?
Hugh	Only in Viennese lengths.
Stephen	Better go with double then. Six sheets of gruddock paper.
Hugh	Parkinised?
Stephen	No.
Hugh	Right.
Stephen	Nearly there. Four felching pens and a bevelled spill-trunion.
Hugh	Only got one felching pen left. Got some frotting pencils though.
Stephen	Will they do?
Hugh	Well, you know the thrush-plate?
Stephen	Yeah.
Hugh	You can use a frotting pencil on that, rude to the look-out valve on the fumpspoke and you can cut out the felching altogether. As long as you rim the satchel-arm properly first.
Stephen	Right. Four frotting pencils then.
Hugh	So, that's it, is it?
Stephen	Yup.
Hugh	You've already got a clip-jawed double lock brace have you?
Stephen	Do you reckon I'll need one?
Hugh	Well, are you going straight or curved?
Stephen	Straight, then curved.

Hugh   Ah. Well you should be all right then, as long as you remember to suck the clenching pin tight to the arc thrust.

Stephen slaps Hugh in the face.

Stephen   How dare you.

Hugh   Sorry.

VOX
POP

Stephen   *(As woman)* I had shares in Gas, Electricity, Water, the lot. But then the government sold them all.

Rosina

Stephen is in the drawing room of a stately home. He plays an old aristocratic dowager called Rosina, Lady Madding.

Stephen I live here alone in what, when I was a girl, used to be called the Dower House. I suppose I am technically a dowager, though my son Rufus, the fourth earl, is not yet married. I love the country, it's very peaceful here. I am surrounded by photographs of my past. On the piano I have a photograph of myself dancing with David, the Prince of Wales – later of course Edward the Eighth and subsequent Duke of Windsor. David was a very bad dancer, always trod on one's toes and I remember he once crushed the metatarsal bones in the foot of a girlfriend of mine – discreet lesbianism was fashionable at the time.
Here's a photograph of Noël Coward – darling Noël as we always called him. He was a very witty man, you know – it's a side of him not many people are perhaps aware of. I recall an occasion when I came onto the dance-floor of Mario's in Greek Street wearing a very daring frock, very low-cut, a frock that revealed more of my décolletage than was then considered proper – now of course I dare say it would raise nothing more than an eyebrow – but at the time it was very wicked. I came onto the floor and darling Noël came up to me and said 'Rosina,' – he always used to call me Rosina – it is my name, you must understand. 'Rosina,' he said in that voice of his, 'Rosina, where did you find such an alluringly high-cut body?' This was Noël's little way, you see. The portrait above the fireplace was made

when I was in Paris – Claude my husband was
Ambassador in the late 20s and I used to hold
very literary parties at the embassy – Plum and
Duff Cooper, Scott and Garrett Fitzgerald,
darling Geoffrey Chaucer of course, Adolf Hitler
and Unity Mitford, Gertrude Stein and Alice
B. Topless, Radclyffe Hall and Angela Brazil –
they could always be relied upon to attend. And
of course O. Henry James Joyce Carey Grant. I
remember F.E. Smith, later Lord Birkenhead
of course, *(Pointing, but we stay on Stephen)* that's
his picture there, just below the dartboard,
F.E. used to say 'All the world and his live-in
lover go to Rosina's parties' which pleased me
very much. Later when Claude and I went to
India to take up the Vice-regency I met Gandhi
with whom I used to play French cricket – he
was awfully good at cricket, as a matter of fact,
Claude always used to say 'what the loin-cloth
trade gained, the wicket-keeping trade lost.'
Pandit Nehru was very impressive too, though if
Edwina Mountbatten is to be believed his length
was too variable for him ever to enter the ranks
of Indian leg-spin immortals. The large bronze
statue of the nude male which stands on top of
the synthesizer is of Herbert Morrison the Cabinet
Minister. I use it to hang my bracelets on when
I'm playing at the keyboard now. I spend a lot of
time here in this room, remembering the past.
Silly Poles Hartley, L.P. Hartley, you know, once
said that the past is a foreign country, but I don't
agree. The food was better for a start, and the
people didn't *smell*. People often tell me I was
one of a spoilt generation, rich, beautiful, idle,
parasitical. It is true that I had every conceivable
luxury lavished upon me during my life, met
many famous and influential people, saw many
exciting places and never did anything more
taxing than organise large house-parties. But

you know, despite that, if I had my time over again I wouldn't change a thing. Regrets? A few. I shouldn't have let dear T.E. Lawrence borrow my motorbicycle. I'm tired now. Let me rest.

VOX
POP

Hugh   Now Kenneth Baker, it seems to me, is a perfect argument for why one should always try and kill Kenneth Baker.

Rhodes Boysons

Caption	'The Rhodes Boysons Hour'
	Stephen and Hugh are both dressed and made-up to look like Rhodes Boyson the popular and absurd Conservative member of parliament.
Stephen	Hello there, I am Rhodes Boyson.
Hugh	Good evening. My name is Rhodes Boyson.
Stephen	We are the Rhodes Boysons. And this is our hour.
Hugh	This is very much our hour. An hour in which phrases . . .
Stephen	Certainly phrases . . . phrases yes, certainly.
Hugh	Phrases like 'centres of excellence' will be much in evidence.
Stephen	You will find, in this our hour, that phrases comparable to, congruent with and exigent under, 'centres of excellence' will be, to some extent, utilised.
Hugh	And by a centre of excellence we mean . . .
Stephen	We mean, primarily . . .
Hugh	Primarily that is . . .
Stephen	A centre that is . . .
Hugh	By and large.
Stephen	By-ly and large-ly.
Hugh	Excellent. In some regard.
Stephen	In some regard or other.
Hugh	In some, or other, regard.

Stephen	That is what we mean when we say 'centre of excellence'. I hope that's cleared that one up.
Hugh	Absolutely. Another phrase meaning 'centre of excellence' might be 'school that is quite good'.
Stephen	That is substantially correct in essence. A centre of excellence is a school that is quite good. But the phrase 'school that is quite good' doesn't sound nearly as . . .
Hugh	Ludicrous?
Stephen	Nearly as . . .
Hugh	Pompous?
Stephen	The phrase 'school that is quite good' doesn't sound as ludicrous or pompous as the phrase 'centre of excellence'.
Hugh	And for that reason . . .
Stephen	And that reason alone.
Hugh	We will be using the phrase 'centre of excellence' throughout our hour.
Stephen	Our hour.
Hugh	Another word that can't be stressed enough is 'standards'.
Stephen	Standards as in 'standards of excellence', moral standards, standards of accountability.
Hugh	I like that one. Standards of accountability.
Stephen	Rolls off the tongue, doesn't it? Standards of accountability.
Hugh	So for the time being, we'll leave you with those two. 'Centres of excellence'.
Stephen	That's centres of excellence.
Hugh	And 'Standards of accountability'.

Stephen   Standards of accountability. Ooh, I do like that one. I shall be using that in bed tonight. Standards of accountability. Lovely.

Hugh   Really quite lovely.

Stephen   Perfectly lovely.

Hugh   So until the next time, it's goodbye from Rhodes Boyson.

Stephen   And it's goodbye from Rhodes Boyson.

Both   Goodbye.

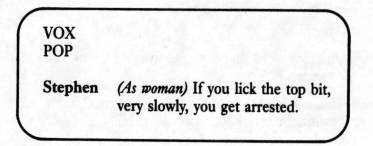

VOX
POP

Stephen   *(As woman)* If you lick the top bit, very slowly, you get arrested.

Major Donaldson

A German castle. Stephen, as Major Donaldson, is slumped over a desk. Hugh is looking at a painting on the wall, his back turned towards Stephen.

Stephen stirs to some kind of consciousness.

Hugh   *(Still not looking at Stephen)* Ah, we return to some form of consciousness, Major.

Stephen   Who . . . whirr . . .

Hugh   You must forgive the rough methods of my colleagues. They are barbarians, barbarians. No finesse, it grieves me to say.

Stephen   Where the hell am I?

Hugh is inspecting another painting.

Hugh   You admire Matisse, Major? Such bold strokes of the brush, such masterly control. What were you doing so far in front of your lines, Major? What was the nature of your operation?

Stephen   Donaldson, Eric, Major. Serial number 46589320.

Hugh   Come, come, Major Donaldson, you can do better than that, you know. Really so much better.

Stephen   That's all you'll get out of me.

Hugh   *(Still hasn't faced Stephen)* Such a pity our two nations were ever at war. We have a great deal in common you know. *(Swings round)* Tell me please when exactly is planned your invasion of France?

Stephen   *(Looking down)* Do you think I know and do you think if I *did* know *(He looks up)* I'd . . . tell . . . you . . . oh my God!

207

Hugh	Yes what is the matter please?
Stephen	You . . . I can't believe it!
Hugh	You are not believing what, please?
Stephen	You! You're so . . . so beautiful!
Hugh	What are you saying?
Stephen	I can't . . . this is . . . oh my God, this is it! Who'd've believed it? Here? Now? You're just the most fantastic, the loveliest creature I've ever set eyes on.
Hugh	Don't play games with me, Major Donaldson. I'm not very good at them.
Stephen	Games? Games? This is no game! This is the reallest thing that's ever happened to me. I just don't . . . where the hell have you been all my life, you fabulous darling?
Hugh	Now look . . .
Stephen	Oh God there's so much I want to know . . . your name, I don't even know what he's called . . . God, we've so much lost time to make up for.

Stephen turns round a name card on Hugh's desk.
It reads in Gothic upper case 'Oberleutnant Friedrich
von Stoltz'.

Friedrich! Yes, Friedrich! it suits you.

Hugh	Have you taken leave of your senses?
Stephen	Yes! Yes, Friedie, I have! For the first time in my life I have taken leave of my senses, and I love it! Did anyone ever tell you you have the sweetest, silliest little nose . . . and the biggest bluest eyes?

Hugh turns angrily away.

Hugh	I give you one last warning, Major Donaldson!

Stephen	Get that arse! That has got to be the cutest little bum *ever!*
Hugh	*(Furious by now)* No, now this is enough! Enough you hear?! Perhaps you are trying on me some of your English senses of humour, but I tell you . . .
Stephen	And the accent, it's just so *dreamy!*
Hugh	WHEN IS PLANNED THE INVASION?
Stephen	Oh, who cares about the stupid little invasion, Friedrich honey-puss? July the third, three beach-heads on Normandy codenamed Omaha, Utah and Nebraska, I think. But what does that matter? What matters is that we've found each other.
Hugh	Normandy?
Stephen	Normandy. Now, don't you think that deserves a kiss?
Hugh	Well, maybe just a little one.

VOX
POP

Stephen   There was a very famous
writer once, I can't actually
remember who it was, but
he was once asked by a hotel
porter for his name, and he said
'G.K. Chesterton'. I think it
might have been Oscar Wilde.

Spies/Pulse

Hugh enters Control's office. Stephen appears to be taking his own pulse.

Hugh Hello, Control. *(No reply)* Control? Are you all right? You appear to be taking your pulse.

Stephen I am a Russian spy, Tony. That's what I am.

Hugh I beg your pardon?

Stephen I plan to overthrow the Queen.

Hugh Control, this is a bit of a surprise. All the more so because you're actually the head of British Intelligence.

Stephen I aim to undermine the entire Western way of life.

Hugh Mmm. Before you do that, I'll go and telephone the relevant authorities. And as a precaution, please don't open any more letters.

Stephen No, it's all right Murchison. I'm not really a Russian spy.

Hugh Now Control. You mustn't say that just to spare me the paperwork.

Stephen No honestly, Tony, I'm really not a Russian spy. And you were right, by the way. I was taking my pulse.

Hugh I thought as much. Because you were gripping your wrist lightly but firmly and counting to yourself.

Stephen You see, our American counterparts have invented a new machine called a lie-detector, that lets you know you when people are telling you fibs.

210

Hugh	Surely that would be rather useful for people in our line of work, Control?
Stephen	Exactly, Tony. The machine works on the well-known scientific principle that when someone's telling you a fib, their pulse speeds up.
Hugh	Gosh, Control, how incredibly ingenious but at the same time how quite simple.
Stephen	Sadly however, these machines are rather expensive to buy.
Hugh	Oh dear. Our American counterparts do often seem to have lots more money to spend than we do, don't they, Control?
Stephen	Yes, but what they have in money, I like to think we make up for in British know-how.
Hugh	I'm not quite following, Control.
Stephen	Well, Tony, at a fraction of the cost I have come up with this lie-detector.
	Indicates (stop-watch).
Hugh	A stop-watch, of course! It cuts out the need for expensive and cumbersome equipment.
Stephen	When I told you I was a Russian spy, I was telling a deliberate fib.
Hugh	Ah. You wanted to see if your pulse got faster?
Stephen	That's right.
Hugh	Did it?
Stephen	No.
Hugh	Oh dear. If your pulse didn't speed up, that must mean . . .
Stephen	Yes. When I said I was a Russian spy, I must have been telling the truth.

Hugh	Mm. So on the very first try of this technique you've discovered that you, the Head of British Intelligence, are a Soviet agent.
Stephen	That's right. And Tony?
Hugh	Control?
Stephen	The £9.50 that it cost me to buy that stop-watch turns out to have been money well-spent.
Hugh	Gosh, Control. The implications of your discovery are considerable.
Stephen	Aren't they, Murchison? The Minister will be ever so pleased.
Hugh	Mmm. Don't you think we ought to test the technique again, just to make sure?
Stephen	Good idea. We don't want to go round boasting that we've discovered that I'm a top level Russian spy unless we're absolutely certain.
Hugh	My thoughts exactly, Control.
Stephen	All right, Tony, you tell me a fib, and I'll see if your pulse goes up.

Stephen takes Hugh's pulse.

| Hugh | Hmm. Let's see if I can think of something that isn't true. Oh yes, I know. My name is Susan Donovan. |

Pause. Stephen counts and then withdraws his hand.

Stephen	Well, that seems to prove it.
Hugh	Really?
Stephen	Yes, Susan, really.
Hugh	Mm. *(Pause)* Control?
Stephen	Yes, Susan?
Hugh	Why don't we go back to our old way?

Stephen	You mean . . .?
Hugh	Yes. The good old British Secret Service method of finding out if someone is telling you a fib or not.
Stephen	All right. You first. Is your name Tony Murchison?
Hugh	*(Holding up hand)* Yes. Cub's Honour.
Stephen	My turn.
Hugh	Are you a Russian spy?
Stephen	I am not a Russian spy, cross my heart and hope to die.
Hugh	Phew!
Stephen	Glad we're all sorted out again.
Hugh	Me too! You know what, Control?
Stephen	What, Tony?
Hugh	I'm going to bring you a cup of nice coffee now . . .
	Makes to leave. Stops and smiles at Control.
	. . . and that's the truth!
Stephen	Boh!

VOX
POP

Stephen	*(As woman)* I've always loved that story.

213

Anal Retention

Hugh is on a couch. Stephen sits beside him.

Stephen So, Mr Sedelmayer, you believe yourself to be
anally retentive?

Hugh Not half.

Stephen Not half. No, I imagine not half. Now
anal retentiveness is a complex condition,
Mr Sedelmayer. What gave you the idea that you
were suffering from this problem?

Hugh A book.

Stephen A book? Well, well, well, well, well. A book on
psychiatry?

Hugh First World War Biplanes.

Stephen First World War Biplanes. It was a book on First
World War Biplanes that led you to believe that
you were anally retentive?

Hugh That's right.

Stephen Mm. I must say I can't pretend to understand you
– not without going to Drama School and taking
an expensive course of lessons in how to pretend
to understand someone.

Hugh Well it's like this. I'd just come in from the garden
for a cup of tea and . . .

Stephen Please, Mr Sedelmayer, I'm not a machine.

Hugh I beg your pardon?

Stephen A little slower, if you please.

Hugh Oh right. I sat down on this chair . . .

Stephen	Well, get on with it.
Hugh	Right. I sat down on this chair.
Stephen	This chair?
Hugh	No, no. The chair in my kitchen. And as I sat down, I noticed that on the chair was this book all about First World War Biplanes and I sat down and had a cup of tea, nice cup of tea, very nice, the tea wasn't the problem, no sir, the problem was that when I got up I noticed that the book wasn't there.
Stephen	Yes?
Hugh	It wasn't anywhere, you see. It had vanished. That's when I realised that I'd retained it.
Stephen	You'd retained it.
Hugh	Correct.
Stephen	Anally?
Hugh	Of course anally. Of course. What other explanation could there be?
Stephen	You tell me, Mr Sedelmayer.
Hugh	No.
Stephen	All right. Now this chair. Describe it to me.
Hugh	Oh you know, a chair. A kiitchen chair. Made in Hungary.
Stephen	A Hungarian kitchen chair. My oh my. And where is this chair now?
	Pause.
	Where is this chair now?
Hugh	Isn't it obvious? I sat down again, you see, because I was shocked by the disappearance of the book on First World War Biplanes, and when I got up . . .

215

Stephen	No chair?
Hugh	Vanished. Gone.
Stephen	Retained . . . by you . . .
Hugh	Anally.
Stephen	Anally. Yes. I see. So the disappearance of a book on First World War Biplanes and a Hungarian kitchen chair have forced you to the conclusion . . .
Hugh	Oh they're not all.
Stephen	Oh lordy Belgrano. You mean there's more?
Hugh	Much more. Look out of the window.
Stephen	Mr Sedelmayer, I am a man of science, I haven't time to look out of windows.
Hugh	Please.
Stephen	Very well.
Hugh	I came here today by car.
Stephen	Yes?
Hugh	I've never been one for public transport. Too many germs. I came here today in a blue Vauxhall Carlton, purchased from Howden, the Used Car Dealers, for a pretty sum . . .
Stephen	On the Bardon Road?
Hugh	That's it. Big place, with a lot of cars. They're dear, mind, but they give you peace of mind.
Stephen	And you can't put a price on that.
Hugh	Well, £6,299 was the price they managed to put on it.
Stephen	Right, yes. Good, excellent. So you came in your Carlton, parked . . .

Hugh	Exactly. I parked, got out of the vehicle, turned round to effect the security procedure . . .
Stephen	To wit . . . ?
Hugh	To wit, locking the door . . . and what do you think met my gaze?
Stephen	Nothing?
Hugh	You've got it in one. The blue Vauxhall Carlton had, in effect, been retained by me.
Stephen	I see.
Hugh	So I suppose what I'm asking in my stumbling, hopeless fashion is, what can I do?
Stephen	Well it wouldn't hurt to take the bus just once . . .
Hugh	No, no, no. You misunderstand me for comic effect. I mean what am I to do about my anal retentiveness?
Stephen	Well now, Mr Sedelmayer, I could lie to you. It would be ridiculously easy just to tell you a lot of lies . . . in fact that's what I think I'll do. You're fine, Mr Sedelmayer, you've got absolutely nothing to worry about.
Hugh	Goodness me, that's a relief.
Stephen	And if you're worried about your car –
Hugh	Not particularly, it was insured.
Stephen	Oh that's all right then. I was going to suggest a couple of pints of kaolin and morphine and a bowl of prunes, but if it's insured . . .

Over To You

Stephen plays Colin Essdale, a drama producer, Hugh plays a complaining woman called Mary Barratt. The presenter is called Elspeth.

Hugh   Well I thought it was disgusting. The whole thing was disgusting.

Elspeth   Yes, did . . .

Hugh   There was no warning of what was in store, none whatever . . .

Elspeth   To be fair, the . . .

Hugh   And for goodness sake what about my children? No thought was given to this at all.

Elspeth   Did your children see the . . .?

Hugh   No they didn't. They didn't see it. But only thanks to the purest good fortune that they don't happen to have been born yet, otherwise I dread to think what damage may have been caused. It was simply disgusting.

Elspeth   Yes, the . . .

Hugh   Simply disgusting.

Pause. Elspeth thinks that Hugh has stopped.

Elspeth   Turning to you Mr . . .

Hugh   Simply disgusting.

Elspeth   Mm. Colin Essdale, as the producer, what do . . .?

Stephen   *(Nodding caringly)* Mm. Mm. Mm. Mm. This is obviously difficult . . . mm . . . perhaps it would help if I explained that I couldn't give a flying toss about Mrs Barratt or her feeble views.

Elspeth	Er, well the . . .
Hugh	I beg your pardon?
Stephen	Now, if you don't mind, or even if you do . . . I have only an estimated 45 years left on this planet and I don't propose to waste a further second of them talking to a confused old gasbag like you.
Elspeth	Well, on the other hand . . .
Stephen	*(Unhooks tie-mike à la John Nott)* So, I'm off to see a colleague about making a programme which I fully hope will irritate you and your half-wit friends even more than the last one. Bye!
	Exit Stephen.
Elspeth	So, Mrs Barratt are you satisfied with what you've heard?
Hugh	Well not really, no.
Elspeth	Tough. *(Shouting off)* A last word from you, Mr Essdale?
	Stephen re-enters with drink.
Stephen	Pim-hole.

VOX POP

Hugh The people of Berlin are doing very exciting things with the city at the moment. Basically they had this idea of just knocking it through into one.

219

Grandfather's Things

Stephen I was just sorting through my grandfather's old
hairdriers the other day, when I came across this,
wedged in the filter of an old Pifco Easy Tress
Ultramatic.

Holds up a small piece of paper.

It's a letter addressed to my grandfather from
the then Minister of Housing, Ernest Dalloway,
later of course Lord Dalloway of Spalding. I'll
read it to you, if I may. 'Your letter to the Home
Secretary has been passed on to me, as Minister in
charge of urban development. I dream of covering
your upturned face with a thousand burning
kisses . . .' and there's a bit more like that . . .
but, oh yes here we are . . . this is the good bit,
'I would direct your attention to Section 17 of the
Housing Act (Urban) 1916, paragraph 5: "Where
a local authority has given no other sanction," you
furious ball of shining beauty, blah, blah blah, "the
entitlement to grants under the scheme will come
mandatorily into operation," please, please let me
stroke your thigh. I hope this answers your enquiry
in the matter of 14 Stanshall Avenue, I yearn to
drink clarified butter from your armpits, etc etc
etc Ernest Dalloway.' Fascinating little glimpse of
history, there, I think.

Stunts

Stephen   Ladies and gentlemen, many of you have expressed the worry that some of what Hugh and I do in this show is physically very dangerous, and have asked whether or not we ever use stuntmen in the performance of our sketches.

Hugh   Well the answer is basically that Stephen and I do all our own stunts.

Stephen   All our own stunts.

Hugh   Every single one.

Stephen   And almost none of our own acting.

Hugh   That's right. It's not widely known, but acting is in fact an incredibly dangerous thing to do . . .

Stephen   Incredibly dangerous, and for insurance reasons we have been forbidden from delivering all but the simplest lines.

Cut to Stephen and Hugh 'in performance' while their voices continue off . . .

Hugh   *(Voice-over)* Take for example this sketch, that we're about to record now. It's called 'The Adventures Of Colin The Serving Hatch', and it begins with me diving through a plate-glass window, with my bottom on fire.

Hugh dives through a window, trousers ablaze.

Stephen   *(Voice-over)* Those of you who are doing this sketch for A-Level will know that the next thing is for me to smash Hugh in the face with a cricket bat . . .

Hugh   *(Voice-over)* Whereupon I crash through a wall and fall on to some iron railings.

In vision, the relevant actions can be seen. Somebody
shouts 'cut' and Stephen steps in and addresses
the camera.

Stephen   Now comes the really dangerous bit – the
first line. And to do this line, we've drafted in
Alan Witheridge, who has almost twenty years
experience of delivering lines like this one. Alan
is going to 'double' for Hugh at this point in the
sketch, and say the line 'I'm so sorry, I thought
you were my brother.'

We can see Alan preparing for the line. Kneepads etc.
Stephen goes over to interview him.

Alan, how's it going?

Alan   Fine thanks, Stephen. Just putting the final
touches to the preparation.

Stephen   Are you nervous at a time like this?

Alan   Not nervous, no. If you've done your homework,
which I think I have, there should be no problem.
Anyway, we'll see.

Stephen   Well Alan, the very best of luck.

Alan takes up his position in the set. A voice shouts
'stand by'.

(Voice-over) Just to remind you that Alan is now
going to try and say the line, 'I'm so sorry I
thought you were my brother.' Fingers crossed.

A voice shouts 'action' and Alan begins.

Alan   I'm so sorry, I thought . . .

Alan explodes and people run in with fire extinguishers.

Stephen   Well, a lucky escape for Hugh there.

222

Wrong directions

Hugh   Good evening and welcome to 'Realising I've Given The Wrong Directions To'. Tonight I shall be Realising I've Given The Wrong Directions to Rabbi Michael Leibovitz. Sadly, Rabbi Leibovitz is unable to be with us tonight. Till next time, bye bye.

VOX
POP

Stephen   Margaret Thatcher is the best thing that's ever happened to this country.

Mountaineer

A hotel bar at the foot of Ben Enormous. Stephen is the bartender, with a ludicrously long beard, Hugh is a git.

Hugh	Oh she's beautiful, isn't she?
Stephen	She?
Hugh	The mountain.
Stephen	Ah.
Hugh	I always think of the mountain as 'she'. To me, the mountain will always be 'she'.
Stephen	I know what you mean.
Hugh	Do you? Yes, I think perhaps you do.
Stephen	But to me, you see, the mountain is an 'it'.
Hugh	An 'it'.
Stephen	'It', yes. To me, the mountain has always had an 'itty' sort of quality.
Hugh	Interesting.
Stephen	I think of my wife as a 'she'.
Hugh	Is that right?
Stephen	Oh yes. I always think of my wife as being a woman. Does that sound mad?
Hugh	Mad? No, it's not mad. Your wife as a woman. Interesting.
Stephen	Well, romantic, perhaps. You married?
Hugh	Yes indeed. Oh yes. Marriage is a wonderful thing. It's upstairs at the moment. It's a bit tired after the journey.
Stephen	'It'?

224

Hugh	My wife.
Stephen	Oh I see. I thought you meant the mountain. I thought you meant the mountain was upstairs.
Hugh	No no no.
Stephen	So are you going to be climbing tomorrow?
Hugh	Oh yes. I shall be up her face tomorrow morning, first thing.
Stephen	With your wife?
Hugh	Oh no. It's never really enjoyed climbing. It doesn't like heights, you see. Mind you, neither do I.
Stephen	Then why do you climb? That sounds very odd. It sounds very strange indeed.
Hugh	It is strange, it's mad really. I can't think why I married it. That's why I climb mountains, I suppose. To get away from it.
Stephen	And of course you're so beautiful.
Hugh	I beg your pardon?
Stephen	You are so ravishingly lovely.
Hugh	Well that's very kind of you I'm sure.
Stephen	Wales, that is. I always think of Wales as a 'you'. Don't know why.
Hugh	Oh, I understand. Yes, you certainly are lovely, aren't you?
Stephen	Oh yes. What a great country you are.
	Drifting through the window we hear a lilting Welsh hymn.
Hugh	Ah. You hear that? What a beautiful hymn.
Stephen	Ah. You think of that as a him, do you? That's funny, because I'd call that a 'they'. To me, that's a beautifully sung 'they'.

Hugh	Ah, it's pure poetry, isn't it?
Stephen	Your wife? Your wife is poetry?
Hugh	No, the hymn is poetry.
Stephen	Well I don't know. I don't think they is poetry. I always think that poetry is poetry.
Hugh	You're talking now of Dylan Thomas.
Stephen	Dylan Thomas, yes . . . or any of the other great poets, like . . .
Hugh	Dylan Thomas.
Stephen	Yes and . . . er . . .
Hugh	Dylan Thomas.
Stephen	Coal black . . .
Hugh	Black as black . . .
Stephen	Slow black . . .
Hugh	Black . . .
Stephen	Black . . . Aye.
Hugh	I?
Stephen	Yes. I always think of aye as yes. Yes, there's no doubt about it, we're very, very lucky.
Hugh	We?
Stephen	The Welsh. I always think of the Welsh as 'we'. A great stream of we.
Hugh	Yes, a huge reservoir of we, I know what you mean.
Stephen	Oh Wales, you're so lovely.
Hugh	You certainly are. I'd live there if the bastards didn't keep burning down my holiday cottage.

Dammit 3

Hugh is on the phone in the boardroom. Stephen enters and throws off his coat. Hugh nods a greeting.

Hugh	*(Looking at his watch)* Dammit to blue-rinsed Hades!
Stephen	Problem, Peter?
Hugh	*(Hangs up)* Yeah. This watch keeps losing time, John. It was a birthday gift from Nancy and I haven't the heart to tell her that it keeps time about as well as a Rangoon stevedore. So tell me John, how did the meeting go?
Stephen	I don't know how the meeting went, Peter.
Hugh	I don't understand, John.
Stephen	It's very simple, Peter. I didn't go.
Hugh	You didn't go, John? I understand even less ...
Stephen	Would it help if I told you that Marjorie was at the meeting, Peter?
Hugh	Marjorie?
Stephen	Check. With her two lap-poodles, Dexter and O'Neill.
Hugh	What the deuce was that hell-bitch Marjorie doing there?
Stephen	Marjorie is a majority stockholder in Barraclough Leisure, Peter. She's entitled to attend any damned meeting she chooses.
Hugh	Oh come on, John. Marjorie holds stock in just about every major leisure corporation in the Uttoxeter *Yellow Pages*. Are you telling me ...?

Stephen	I don't know what I'm telling you, Peter. But I decided there and then that if Marjorie and I were going to war, it would be on the ground of my choosing . . .
Hugh	But dammit, John . . .
Stephen	Wait a minute, I haven't finished.
Hugh	Sorry, John.
Stephen	It would be on the ground of my choosing . . . Peter.
Hugh	Right. But there's something else on your mind. In can tell. I've seen that look before.
Stephen	I was just thinking, how old's the boy now?
Hugh	The boy? Where does he come into this?
Stephen	Half that Barraclough stock is his, remember?
Hugh	You mean . . .?
Stephen	I mean, Peter, the boy's old enough to think for himself. If he's anything like his father he'll have a mind of his own.
Hugh	You're his father John.
Stephen	No Peter. As a matter of record, I'm not.
Hugh	This is a story I've not heard.
Stephen	*(Pouring himself a drink and staring into the distance)* It was while I was working every hour that God sent and plenty more on top of that, making something of this health club, wheeling, dealing, bobbing, weaving, ducking and diving through every centimetre of red tape the local Uttoxeter bureaucrats could tie me up with, hustling, breaking my DAMNED ARSE to set this company on the right road.
Hugh	And Marjorie wanted children.

228

Stephen	That's right. The business was just starting to turn the corner, and there was Marjorie, asking me to throw away ten minutes of my life in order to have a child. I just couldn't do that.
Hugh	I understand, but I don't understand.
Stephen	Simple. I did what any good businessman would have done in my place. I delegated. Put Tim on the case.
Hugh	Tim ...
Stephen	Luckily he was able to fit it in. The rest, as they say, is damned history. Tim is the boy's father.
Hugh	Not strictly true, John.
Stephen	Peter? You have some input on this?
Hugh	I swear to you John, I had no idea where the brief originated, but Tim came to me one night saying that he'd bitten off more than he could chew, and could I get him out of a jam.
Stephen	Don't tell me ...
Hugh	I'm afraid so, John. Tim delegated the delegating.
Stephen	Damn his arse! Are you telling me that you're the boy's father, Peter?
Hugh	Not as simple as that, I'm afraid. I was up to my neck with Nancy at the time. Strung out on a wire trying to set up finance for her Vegetable Boutique.
Stephen	So you delegated?
Hugh	I had no choice, John. Things were happening so fast you had to run just to keep moving.
Stephen	Come on, Peter. Who did you dump this one on?
Hugh	You're not going to like it, John.
Stephen	No ... you can't mean? Marjorie?

Hugh	That's right. Marjorie. Who else could I have turned to, John?
Stephen	So Marjorie is the boy's father? That is sick.
Hugh	No no no. It gets a little bit complicated here, John. Marjorie was hustling some deal out Peterborough way, on the road day and night . . .
Stephen	Marjorie delegated? I can't believe this. Who to?
Hugh	The boy, John.
Stephen	To the boy? The boy is his own father?
Hugh	That's right. The boy is his own father.
Stephen	Seven types of executive damn with a free hellblast!
Hugh	But John, maybe this can still work for us. Maybe we can bring pressure to bear on the boy by appealing to his father.
Stephen	Get the boy to persuade himself to vote our way, you mean?
Hugh	It might work.
Stephen	What can we lose?
Both	Daamn!!

VOX
POP

Hugh   I don't think so.

Michael Jackson

Hugh is sitting in a chat show swivel chair, addressing the camera.

Hugh	Ladies and gentlemen, this is a genuinely exciting moment for me. We're extremely honoured to have on the show tonight one of those very rare performers – a man who perhaps more than any other can lay claim to the title 'superstar'. Ladies and gentlemen, will you please welcome, Michael Jackson.

Applause and music: 'Bad'. Stephen enters, shakes hands with Hugh and sits down.

	Michael, thank you very much indeed for coming on the show.
Stephen	Pleasure.
Hugh	I know you must be frantically busy . . .
Stephen	Things are a bit hectic at the moment, yes.
Hugh	I believe you're about to start work on a new album?
Stephen	A new album, that's right. It's absolutely brand new. Even the little hole in the middle is new.
Hugh	I love these clothes, by the way.
Stephen	Oh thank you, yes. This is a plain Irish Thornproof, very hard wearing, I've had it for some time actually.
Hugh	I bet thousands of kids all over the world are trying to copy this look right now.

Stephen	Well haha . . . perhaps.
Hugh	Now Michael, you've been in the music business for . . . well most of your life . . .
Stephen	Just about, yes.
Hugh	Right, and of course 'Thriller' has sold more copies than any other record, you're without doubt the biggest star of this or perhaps any generation. Have you ever wondered what your life would have been like if none of this had ever happened?
Stephen	Yes. Yes, I do. There's no way of knowing this, obviously, but I sometimes think if all this hadn't happened, my life would have been very different indeed.
Hugh	Really?
Stephen	Well I think so, yes. It's so hard to know, of course.
Hugh	Now Michael, I have to ask you this. There has been some speculation over the years that you have, with the aid of plastic surgery, set about altering your appearance.
Stephen	Well I don't really pay any attention to that. That's just newspapers, you know . . .
Hugh	So you absolutely deny it?
Stephen	Well I don't think it's even worth denying. All it boils down to is people being jealous of my success. People will say anything.
Hugh	Yes. We've got a picture of you here, when you were with the Jackson Five – you'd just signed to Motown, I believe . . .

Cut to eight-year-old Michael Jackson.

You do look a bit different . . .

232

Stephen	I was eight years old, for heaven's sake. I mean of course I've changed. We've all changed.
Hugh	Absolutely. Well, Michael, I hope that's answered your critics. Now I believe you're actually going to do a song for us now from the new album?
Stephen	That's right. This song is called 'Move It On Out Girl'.
Hugh	Ladies and gentlemen – 'Move It On Out Girl' – Michael Jackson!

Stephen walks over to 'performance area' and starts grooving to the intro. He somehow gets on to an exercise treadmill to do the walking on the spot. He apparently sings.

Stephen	Move it on out girl, Don't leave it where it is, girl, Put it somewhere else, girl, Don't move it on in.

If you move it on in, girl,
I might have to find another girl,
Who'll give me less trouble girl,
Who'll move it on out . . .

Stephen does a groovy dance break, during which Hugh comes over and interrupts the song.

Sorry, is there a problem?

Hugh	No no, Michael, that was very enjoyable. It's just that I couldn't help noticing that you were miming.
Stephen	No I wasn't.
Hugh	Yes you were.
Stephen	No I wasn't.

From now on we begin to notice that Stephen is actually miming his answers to Hugh's questions.

Hugh   I mean I'm sorry, but you see I just think that this is so disappointing. It's almost impossible for the kids to see an artist doing a live performance nowadays . . .

Stephen Look, I know some people do it, but I promise you that miming is simply not the Michael Jackson way. Atishoo!

Visually, Stephen's sneeze is about five seconds after we hear it.

Hugh   *(To camera)* It's tragic when stars don't live up to your expectations.

VOX
POP

Stephen No, I was joking. She's as mad as a house.

Sponsored Sketch

This is shot entirely from a low level. All we see are bare legs, from the knee down.

Stephen	*(Kissing the guests)* Tom, Irene, welcome!
Hugh	Dick, thanks for inviting us.
Selina	First all-naked party I've been to for years.
Stephen	Yes, well we thought it would make a change.
Hugh	Saves the problem of having to decide what to wear anyway!
Stephen	Right!

They find this really amusing.

Selina	Nice carpet . . . is it a Tideyman's?
Stephen	Now how on earth could you tell that?
Hugh	Well I suppose it was the modern, up-to-the-minute design wasn't it darling?
Selina	And the practicability.
Stephen	I'm surprised how large your breasts are, Irene.
Selina	Why thank you. And I must say you have a very amusingly shaped . . .
Hugh	*(Interrupting)* . . . Dick, I believe I'm also right in saying that it repels stains and resists spills.
Stephen	The carpet, I hope you mean! Yes, that's right. Nothing soaks into a Tideyman's.
Hugh	I expect we'll be putting that to the test before the evening's out.
Stephen	Rather. Let me stroke your thighs, Irene.

Selina	Thanks. I have to say it's a great colour. What would you call this colour, exactly?
Stephen	Well, flesh-coloured, I suppose.
Hugh	I think Irene was referring to the Tideyman's actually.
Stephen	Oh right.
Selina	No I wasn't.
Hugh	Oh.
Selina	It's a sort of purple, really, isn't it?
Hugh	But come to think of it, what made you choose this colour of Tideyman's?
Stephen	Well it was quite difficult at first, because they had so many to choose from, but with the aid of their highly trained sales staff we finally came to the right decision.
Hugh	Seems to me you made the right decision right at the beginning.
Stephen	Oh?
Hugh	By going to Tideyman's in the first place.
Stephen	Right! Dip?
Selina	Yes, it does rather, doesn't it.

VOX
POP

Hugh   We took the caravan down to
Dorset this year, and pushed it
over a cliff.

236

Shoplifting

Stephen is sitting at a desk in a dingy office. Hugh and a woman enter. Hugh is a supermarket security guard, she is a housewife.

Hugh	Come on, in you go.
Woman	There's no need to push. I can walk.
Stephen	Ah. Tango Four, is it?
Hugh	Sorry to bother you, Mr Turner. It looks like we've got a ten twenty-three on our hands.
Woman	Will you let go of my arm?
Stephen	A ten twenty-three, oh dear.
Woman	You have absolutely no right to keep me here.
Stephen	Won't you have a seat, Mrs . . .?
Hugh	Target responds to the name of King, sir.
Stephen	All right, Tango Four, let's have your report.
Hugh	Sir. As per your briefing instructions, I was positioned in aisle number three, between breakfast cereals and bread, operating a mobile figure of eight pattern around frozen vegetables.
Stephen	Textbook stuff, Tango Four.
Hugh	Thank you, sir. I then observed the target loitering opposite the Coco Pops.
Woman	Look, I have to pick up my children at four o'clock, so if you . . .
Stephen	What's your name. son?
Hugh	Lewis, sir. Oliver Lewis.

237

Stephen	This your first taste of action?
Hugh	Yes, sir.
Stephen	Quite a feeling, isn't it?
Hugh	Oh yes, sir. Quite a feeling.
Stephen	I remember my first ten twenty-three. 1968. Still had me bum fluff.
Woman	Look, I'm sorry to interrupt, but my children are waiting for me at school . . .
Stephen	My advice to you, Mrs King, is to pay a little more attention to your own problems just at the minute! *(To Hugh)* Doesn't hurt to shake 'em up a bit early on.
Hugh	It's joy to watch you, sir.
Stephen	Come come, my dear, dry those tears. Hanky?
Woman	No thank you.
Stephen	*(To Hugh)* Hard, then soft, you see?
Hugh	Beautiful, sir.
Stephen	Now then, Mrs King, I'm going to tell you a story.
Woman	Oh God.
Stephen	One day, a woman goes into a supermarket and steals some Coco Pops. Do you like my story, Mrs King?
Woman	Not really.
Stephen	I'm pretty near the mark though, aren't I?
Woman	No.
Hugh	She's lying, sir!
Stephen	All right, Lewis. I think Mrs King and I understand each other.
Woman	I don't think we do.

238

Stephen	After all, lifting a packet of Coco Pops isn't such a terrible thing, is it? Not when you look at what they get up to at football matches these days. No, I'd say that shoving a packet of Coco Pops down your cleavage and forgetting to pay for them is just being human, after all.
Woman	Have you finished?
Stephen	No I haven't finished, you snotsucking ball of slime.
Woman	Now look here ...
Stephen	No, you look here. See that? Know what that means?

He points to a medal ribbon on his chest.

Woman	No.
Stephen	Tell her, laddie.
Hugh	I'm afraid I don't know either, sir.
Stephen	This is a Distinguished Service Medal, from the Arndale Centre in Chippenham!

He points to a photo on the wall.

That's me! There! Shaking hands with the manager. Read out the citation, Lewis.

Hugh	Right, sir. *(Reads)* 'Harry Turner is congratulated on his alertness in apprehending a shoulder of lamb – New Zealand.'
Stephen	Stolen lamb, Mrs King. Stolen lamb, stolen Coco Pops. Comprendo?
Woman	Are you accusing me of theft?
Stephen	Affirmatory, Mrs King!
Woman	Right. *(She rootles in her handbag)* What do you think this is? *(Takes out piece of paper)*

239

Hugh	Careful sir, it could be a trap.
Woman	It's a bloody receipt. *(Reads)* Coco P. 48 pence!
Stephen	Have you got a receipt for that receipt?
Woman	Of course I haven't.
Hugh	Haha!
Stephen	No, course you haven't. 'Cos you nicked it, didn't you?
Hugh	Confess, confess! You're from a broken home!
Stephen	Steady, Lewis.
Hugh	Sorry, sir.
Woman	Look, why don't we just call the police?
Stephen	Police. Hear that, Lewis?
Hugh	I did, sir. Very amusing.
Stephen	I shouldn't worry too much about the police, Mrs King.
Hugh	Police. Ha. *(Spits)*
Stephen	A fine body of men, on the whole, but amateurs when it comes to analysing the mind of a ten twenty-three. I could have joined the police if I'd wanted, Mrs King. The money's better of course, what with the housing allowance, but in the end I said to myself . . . 'Harry, my boy, you belong with the elite.'
Hugh	Good on you, sir.
Stephen	Thank you, Lewis. Or may I call you Oliver?
Hugh	I'd be honoured. Harry.
Woman	You pathetic pair of twerps.
Stephen	I'm sorry?
Woman	You sad, crappy, twerps. I'm leaving now.

Stephen   Well I'm afraid we're a long way from finishing yet . . .

The woman gets to her feet. Stephen tries to stop her but she disables him with some fancy martial artwork and then throws Hugh across the desk. She exits looking cool. Stephen and Hugh pick themselves up off the floor.

Yes, you're probably wondering why I let her walk out just like that?

Hugh   Well she was obviously innocent, sir.

Stephen   Exactly. Knew it from the start. You get a nose for it after a while.

VOX
POP

Stephen   Oh yes. All of them. I've slept with every single one. Well every front-bencher, anyway.

Satire/Tribute

Stephen Hello. Welcome to 'A Bit Of Fry And Laurie'.

Hugh Grrrrr.

Stephen Ladies and gentlemen, because Hugh and I are known for our anger, our satirical rage at the 'human condition', for want of a better cliché . . .

Hugh Grrrr . . .

Stephen We often get accused of lacking a sense of proportion. Here's a letter . . . 'It's very easy to knock, to rage and snarl and satirise, but what are you suggesting should go in the place of the institutions and people you so viciously decry?' This is a typical letter from Mr Alan Dense, absolutely typical. He writes letters like this all the time . . . 'It's oh so simple to knock Mrs Thatcher, isn't it?' Well of course he's quite right. It is ludicrously easy to knock Mrs Thatcher. It's the easiest and most obvious thing in the world to remark that she is a shameful, putrid scab, an embarrassing, ludicrous monstrosity that makes one frankly ashamed to be British, and that her ideas and standards are a stain on our national history. That's easy and clear, anyone can do that. But after tonight, no one can accuse us of not making a constructive suggestion as to what might go in place of Mrs Thatcher. Hugh.

Hugh holds up a wire coathanger.

That is our constructive suggestion, and I hope that's silenced some of our critics. Anyway, on with the blind, unreasoning rage.

Hugh Yes, here we go. I've written a savage, angry, satire on jam jars that get separated from their lids.

Stephen	Now that is anger.

Hugh walks to piano. On top of the piano is a jar with no lid.

Hugh	*(Sings)* Where is the lid Where is the lid Where is the lid Where is the lid

Where is the lid
Where is the lid
Where is the lid
Where is the lid

Does anyone know
Does anyone know
Does anyone know

Where is the lid
Where is the lid
Where is the lid
Where is the lid –

During this song Stephen has been saying:

Stephen	'Yes, it's over here.' 'Hugh! It's on the table.' 'Hugh, it's over here for God's sake.' etc.

Eventually Stephen can take it no more and attacks Hugh by beating him on the head with the jar or some similar heavyweight object.

Stephen looks down on Hugh's unconscious frame for a second.

We are devoting the rest of this programme to a tribute to the writer, comedian and light sketch actor, Hugh 'Excellent Sermon Vicar' Laurie, who died earlier today after a merciful accident that finally ended his long years of struggle with mental illness.

(Photo of Hugh appears.)

Stephen   *(Voice-over)* Hugh Laurie, whose real name was Hugh Laurie, was better known by his stage name: Hugh *Laurie*.

Cut to still of terraced house.

Hugh was born and brought up in a working-class home that his parents had specially built . . .

Pull back on still to reveal that the slum terraced house is actually set in rolling parkland in front of a beautiful stately home.

. . . in the grounds of their Gloucestershire estate. Like many shy children, Hugh learnt from an early age simply to blend in.

Cut to still of brick wall and lamp-post.

Caption   'Hugh Laurie, High Wycombe, 1967'

Stephen   His first acting job came in 1979, at Hereford Civic Centre, since renamed in Hugh's Honour, Hereford Civic and Amenities Centre.

Cut to interview with Rowan Atkinson.

Caption   'Nigel Havers'

Rowan   He was immensely dangerous. Such a dangerous actor. You always had this feeling when he was around that anything could happen. *(Pause)* Hugh Laurie, on the other hand, was about the dullest man I ever met.

Cut to interview with Nigel Havers.

Caption   'Paul Eddington'

Nigel   He brought to every one of his roles this quality of needing the money.

Cut to interview with bow-tied critic.

Caption   'Neil Hudd, TV and theatre critic for the *Daily Mail*'

Critic   I'm so terribly clever, you see. That's one of the things I really admire about myself. I have this extraordinary ability to see, after the event, why something didn't work, and communicate it so wittily. I really am fabulous.

Cut to film of Stephen interviewing himself.

Stephen   Stephen Fry, what is your fondest memory of working with Hugh Laurie?

Stephen   The moment I knew he was really dead would be hard to beat.

VOX
POP

Stephen   Surprisingly enough, Roy Hattersley's actually a bit of a tiger in bed.

Jewellery

*Hugh enters a jewellery shop. Stephen is polishing the
back of his hand, for no particular reason, other than
that it is screamingly funny.*

Hugh   Er, good morning.

Stephen   Sir, it *is* a good morning. Sir is handsomely right
            to say so.

Hugh   Yes.

Stephen   Is sir aware, I am busy wondering, that I made so
            bold to remark on the goodness of the morning to
            the youngest of my mothers earlier today as she
            wheeled me into an upright position. Was sir in an
            awareness of that?

Hugh   No . . . no I had no idea.

Stephen   'Here is a morning, mother of my bosom,' I
            averred, 'as fine and crisp and gutty as any since
            the days when Compton and Edrich opened for
            England and the sun never went down on the
            British without asking permission first.'

Hugh   Ha, did you?

Stephen   I did, sir! Sir, I did. And if two broad-shouldered,
            long-fingered men such as ourselves can
            come independently to the conclusion that the
            morning they are currently experiencing is one
            of a goodness, then one of a goodness it must
            assuredly be.

Hugh   Really?

Stephen   Yes, sir, and you can spank me quietly with a
            chamois leather if it isn't so.

Hugh	Right, now . . .
Stephen	But sir hasn't come to trade insults on the state of the morning unless I am more vastly mistaken than a man who thinks Hilaire Belloc is still alive. Do sit down.
	They both sit.
Hugh	No, I've . . .
Stephen	Sir has brought his handsomely sprung and finely wrought young body into this shop with the express purpose of going about the business of buying jewellery. Am I close to the mark?
Hugh	Absolutely.
	Stephen stands.
Stephen	Do you mind if I stand, sir? I think perhaps this 'sitting down' idea of yours was a little ahead of its time.
Hugh	*(Also standing)* Right. Yes. The thing is I'm getting engaged and I'd . . .
Stephen	Would sir like an Opal Fruit?
Hugh	Um . . .
Stephen	A nice strawberry Opal Fruit? Or indeed any flavour?
Hugh	Thank you.
Stephen	*(Reaching for his hat)* I won't be long.
Hugh	Where are you going?
Stephen	There's a sweet-shop not half a mile up the road. I happen to know that they sell Opal Fruits.
Hugh	Well in that case, really don't bother.
Stephen	Don't bother?
Hugh	No, really.

Stephen	Is sir in absolute possession of sureness in this regard?
Hugh	Look. I really only came in here for jewellery, I thought if you happened to have an Opal Fruit on you . . .
Stephen	*(Feeling about on the top of his head)* 'On' me? Sir I have no Opal Fruit 'on' me. I can and will go further, I have never had an Opal Fruit on me. Eccentric, no doubt. Look, sir can search my head if sir is unconvinced.
Hugh	Look, forget the Opal Fruit. The Opal Fruit is irrelevant. I want an engagement ring. Can we concentrate on that?
Stephen	Sir, I am chastened and bowed. Ever the man of affairs, sir has reminded us all, all of our duty. An engagement ring for sir.
Hugh	That's right.
Stephen	What flavour of engagement ring had sir in mind?
Hugh	Flavour? What are you talking about?
Stephen	Just my little joke. You'll humour a dying man. We have a range of engagement rings that I would ask sir to cast over with sir's eyes, which I cannot help but notice are of a startling cobalt blue that would go very well with the wallpaper in one of my god-niece's back rooms.
Hugh	*(Leaving)* Right, that's it. I'm leaving.

Stephen comes round with a range of engagement rings and blocks Hugh's egress.

Stephen	What about this one?
Hugh	What?
Stephen	What about this one?
Hugh	It's rather nice, I suppose.

248

Stephen	Sir, the issue of the rather niceness of this particular ring has been raised in Prime Minister's Question Time.
Hugh	How much is it?
Stephen	I would be wrong to let it go for more than forty thousand of your earth pounds.
Hugh	Forty thousand pounds!
Stephen	I would be equally at fault if I let it go for less than ninety.
Hugh	So it's between forty thousand pounds and ninety.
Stephen	Sir is as dogged in his pursuit of detail as Roy Walker, presenter of the never-popular show *Catchphrase* is dogged in his pursuit of a thick earlet.
Hugh	Perhaps you could, in preference to me walking out of here after hitting you very hard in the face, just tell me the frigging price.
Stephen	Since sir has been kind enough never to be Peter Sissons I can let sir have it for two hundred and eighteen poundingtons.
Hugh	£218?
Stephen	If you wish. And if sir will oblige me by promising never to wear green again I will throw this in for nothing.
	He brings out a velvet jewellery tray with a strawberry Opal Fruit as its centrepiece.
Hugh	An Opal Fruit.
Stephen	Yes, indeeding. A fruit of the genuine Opal persuasion. Perhaps sir will desist from ripping the kidneys from my nerveless frame if I offer him a taste to authenticate its strawberriness?
Hugh	No, no. I believe you.

249

Stephen   May I instead then, pausing only to pause . . .

Pause.

. . . congratulate you on your excellent taste?

Hugh   Thank you.

Stephen   Sir, I was talking to the Opal Fruit. Strawberrine but with a faint tang of small urine.

Hugh   Yes, yes. Quite so. Two hundred and eighteen pounds.

Stephen   Two hundred *and* eighteen pounds that should be.

Hugh   That's what I said.

Stephen   That's what *you* said. I barely spoke at all.

Hugh   Just put it in a presentation box if you would.

Stephen   No need. I'll wear it now.

Hugh   What?

Stephen   And I really think you should speak to my father now, darling. He's upstairs in the cellar.

Hugh   Right. I really am leaving, now.

Stephen   Leaving?

Hugh   Goodbye.

Stephen   But we're engaged!

Hugh leaves. Stephen turns to camera.

Men are such bastards.

Spies/Telescope

*Stephen is looking out of his office window with a
telescope. Hugh enters with a folder.*

Hugh   Oh. Morning Control.

Stephen   Morning, Tony. I'll be with you in a minute.

Hugh   I say, that's rather a splendid device. Where did
          you get that, if you don't mind my prying into
          your affairs?

Stephen   I don't mind you prying at all, Tony. After all,
          you're only human.

Hugh   That's right, Control. I am.

Stephen   And what's more, you're a spy.

Hugh   That's true as well.

Stephen   Well to answer your question, Tony, you see it's
          my birthday today, and my sister Marie gave me
          this as a present.

Hugh   I didn't know you had a sister called Marie,
          Control.

Stephen   Marie isn't her real name of course, it's just a code
          name I've given her which prevents people from
          discovering her real name.

Hugh   Ah well, that's cleared up that little confusion.

Stephen   Her real name is Maria.

Hugh   Oh. So you decided to opt for a code name that
          was quite similar to her real name, then Control?

Stephen   Yes. It makes it much easier to remember.

Hugh   Huh. You are a wily old fox, Control.

251

Stephen	Anyway. This contraption is called a telescupe, Tony.
Hugh	A telescupe?
Stephen	Yes. Although I should point out that that's also a code name, in fact.
Hugh	Say no more, Control. Hush hush.
Stephen	Mmm. Although I don't think I'm speaking out of school if I tell you that this device enables one to see things very clearly over quite a long distance. Here, you can have a go yourself.
Hugh	Control, I really don't know what to say.

Hugh goes over to the telescope.

Stephen	Don't mention it, Tony. Now have a look at that man down there standing next to the telephone kiosk.

Hugh looks through.

Hugh	Gosh Control. You weren't exaggerating when you said it allowed you to see things very clearly. He could almost be in the room with us.
Stephen	That's very true, isn't it? But here's where the telescupe comes in. Because Tony?
Hugh	Yes?
Stephen	He isn't in the room with us.
Hugh	Well I thought he wasn't in the room with us Control, but it's nice to have it confirmed by you.
Stephen	He's actually on the other side of the street.
Hugh	Hmm. He appears to be looking this way, Control, with . . . wait a minute . . . yes, Control, that man is looking at us . . . with a telescupe.
Stephen	Yes, Tony. My theory is that he is an enemy agent charged with the task of keeping us under surveillance.

252

Hugh	What a confounded cheek, Control. I've a good mind to ring the police and have him moved on.
Stephen	Steady Tony. I've got a better plan.

Stephen starts dialling.

	I got Valerie to find out the number of that telephone kiosk.
Hugh	Control, your plan is working. The man has picked up the receiver.
Stephen	*(Into telephone)* Hello? Enemy Agent? It's Control here. *(Pause)* Very well, thank you. Please stop keeping us under surveillance. Thank you.
Hugh	Yes, Control. He's going away.
Stephen	*(Wiping his hands)* There, Tony. Another small but significant victory for our side.
Hugh	Congratulations, Control.
Stephen	Now you go and fetch us a nice cup of coffee, and we'll pretend this whole ugly incident never happened.
Hugh	I can go one better than that, Control.

Hugh exits and enters with a cup of coffee tied up in a red ribbon.

	Happy birthday to Control. Happy Birthday to Control. Happy Birthday to Control. Happy Birthday to Control.
Stephen	Oh get along with you.
Hugh	Aren't you going to open it?
Stephen	Boh!

Psychiatrist

Hugh enters a psychiatrist's surgery or studio, or office or whatever they call them.

Stephen Good morning, Mr Meddlicott is it?

Hugh Yes. You look a bit young to me. Still, I suppose you'll do.

Stephen Well, that's nice. Now, I shall call you Arthur, if I may.

Hugh You may not. You'll call me Mr Meddlicott.

Stephen raises his eyebrows.

And don't simper.

Stephen Very well. So why are you here, Mr Meddlicott?

Hugh Well, why do you think? You're a psychiatrist aren't you? I'm not here for dancing lessons or free sex, I've come to be cured.

Stephen Cured of what?

Hugh For heaven's sake man, do I have to teach you your job? Madness of course. I'm slightly mad and I'd like you to cure me. 'Of what?' Tt!

Stephen You're mad?

Hugh Yes! Am I going to have to repeat everything twice? Now I'm a busy man, so if you'll just get on with it, I'd be very grateful.

Stephen Would you like to tell me why you think you're mad?

Hugh Oh what is this, some sort of game? Do you imagine I've got time to waste *thinking* I'm mad?

I *am* mad. Just take my word for it, will you, and let's have a little less lip.

Stephen   So how does this madness of yours manifest itself?

Hugh   At half past four every day I do something weird.

Stephen   Go on.

Hugh   Go on what. I'm waiting for half past four, aren't I?

Stephen   *(Looks at clock)* It's four thirty-three.

Hugh   I can see that. I'm running four minutes late today on account of your incessant yakking.

Pause.

Stephen   *(Looks at clock)* Four thirty four.

Hugh   Right. For heaven's sake, watch closely.

Hugh takes off his shoes, then removes a piece of bread from either jacket pocket and puts a piece in either shoe.

Stephen   You take off your shoes. And you put a piece of bread in each one.

Hugh   I know I do. What *is* your problem?

Stephen   Do you leave the bread there?

Hugh   Leave it there? Of course I don't leave it there. Are you some kind of idiot?

Stephen   Please go on. What happens next?

Hugh   I take the bread out of the shoes and hide it in my secretary's handbag. Then at four thirty-one, I take it out of her handbag and throw it in the bin.

Stephen   But you won't be doing that today, because your secretary's not there.

Hugh   Oh, give the man a bloody *medal.*

Stephen   So. *(Pause)* That's it, is it?

Hugh	Oh, I'm sorry, it's not enough for you. You'd rather I wrapped myself in bacon rind and pretended to be Florence Nightingale, would you? Well I'm sorry I'm as mad as I am. But no madder.
Stephen	Why do you think wrapping yourself in bacon rind would make you look like Florence Nightingale?
Hugh	Wh . . . I . . . are you an imbecile? I don't think anything of the kind.
Stephen	Florence Nightingale never wrapped herself in bacon rind.
Hugh	*(Angry and trying to explain)* I know she bloody didn't. BUT-IF-I-WAS-MADDER-THAN-I-AM-I-WOULDN'T-KNOW-WOULD-I-YOU-HALF-WIT.
Stephen	I see.
Hugh	So. What are you going to do about this madness of mine?
Stephen	Nothing. I don't think you're mad at all.
Hugh	You think it's perfectly usual to put bread in your shoes? On a daily basis. That's normal practice in your foul part of the world?
Stephen	You're welcome to a second opinion of course, but I don't think you're mad. Eccentric, certainly.
Hugh	And this is what we pay our psychiatrists for, is it? Well let me tell you, I shall write a very stiff letter to the *Daily Mail* about this. Now, cure me of my madness or I won't put my shoes on. Ever.
Stephen	*(Sharply)* You write letters to the *Daily Mail*?
Hugh	Not exclusively the *Daily Mail*. Sometimes the *Sun* or the *Mirror*.
Stephen	And they are published?

256

Hugh	Of course.
	Stephen springs to his feet and goes over to his desk, picks up a copy of the Sun *or* Mirror.
Stephen	Is this one of yours? 'A good way to prevent your money being stolen is to . . .'
	Hugh joins in.
Both	'Keep it in a special pocket sewn into your coat.'
Stephen	You're Mrs June Ellis of Stockport?
Hugh	Naturally.
Stephen	*(Reading from* Mirror*)* What about this . . . 'Why aren't –'
Hugh	'– bus conductors more friendly? A smile a day keeps the doctor away. And it's free too!'
Stephen	Chest size?
Hugh	Forty-two.
Stephen	Stay here. I'll get your strait-jacket.
Hugh	God the lengths you have to go to in this country to prove you're mad.

VOX
POP

Stephen   A Bonnie Langford concert?
Hmm. I think I'd rather be gang-
raped by the House of Lords.

Hard Man's Record

Close-up:

Car radio, hand on tuning knob.

Stephen's hand takes file out of briefcase.

Cut to outside of car. Stephen is putting briefcase on back seat of car. Hugh approaches car, opens door.

Hugh settles in his seat.

Stephen Thank you for sparing the time for this.

Hugh No problem.

Stephen You admire Gary Davies?

Hugh Don't get much time for that sort of thing.

Stephen You should make time, Alan. A man should unwind. *(Stephen turns off radio)* Do you mind if I call you Alan?

Hugh Fine by me.

Stephen Good. Good. I just find Sally a bit awkward.

Hugh I quite understand.

Stephen Excellent. Now then Alan, I've got your record in front of me and it makes impressive reading. You've certainly knocked about the world a bit haven't you?

Hugh Well, you know . . . I've knocked about the world a bit.

Stephen Sorry. I meant to say 'you've done a lot of travelling'. You've done a lot of travelling, haven't you, Alan?

Hugh Well, you know, I've knocked about the world a bit.

Stephen	Yes, you certainly have. But I'd like if I may to fill in one or two gaps, take a few side bearings, rough out some contours. OK with you?
Hugh	Fine.
Stephen	OK. '65, '66, you ran guns out of Macao using a refitted Dutch trawler.
Hugh	I can still smell those damn herring.
Stephen	'68 you popped up on the Ivory Coast smuggling refugees out of Nigeria. The following year there was that nasty caper with the Rhodesian mining company, and then in 1970 you became the reserve team coach for Oxford United. Correct?
Hugh	You've done your homework.
Stephen	But then, Alan, we seem to lose you. There's a gap, a hole, you appear to have vanished for four years. Four years is a long time in our business.
Hugh	You still haven't told me what that business is.
Stephen	Nor yet have I. A four year gap, Alan, until we find you cropping up again, this time in Indonesia, playing both ends against the middle in their civil war. From then on it's a series of apparently unrelated appearances, working with Uruguayan customs, a supply teacher in Maidstone, crop-spraying in Rawalpindi, Home Secretary in the last Labour government and then a short spell as Nigel Pargiter in the Archers.
Hugh	Someone had to do it.
Stephen	Oh yeah, sure.
Hugh	All right. Now it's my turn, okay? I've got to tell you I don't like being rung up by strange people I've never met before and having files read out at me. I don't like being asked questions by men in grey suits, yeah? Now why don't you tell me just exactly what is going on and who in blazes you are?

Stephen	*(Chuckling at the file)* Oh it's all true. Insubordinate, impertinent, imprisoned twice for striking a senior officer, a rebel, a trouble-maker, a loner, an independent, a conniver, a misfit, a maverick, a trickster, an inveigler, a shyster, a shuffler, a shammer, an adventurer, a cozener, a thimblerigger, a pettifogger, a bilker . . .
Hugh	Get to the point.
Stephen	All right. We need a man, Alan. We need a man with exceptional abilities, a man with a record of success against all the odds, a man with the courage to try his hand at the impossible.
Hugh	Go on.
Stephen	We want you, if you can, to sit down and watch an entire episode of *The Krypton Factor*.
Hugh	You're out of your mind.
Stephen	Listen to me, Alan. It's never been done. No one has ever watched the programme from start to finish, and we desperately need someone to do it. Sure, we've all seen bits, but no one has ever gone the distance.
Hugh	If I don't make it, you'll see that Judy's taken care of.
Stephen	Of course, Alan, of course.
Hugh	See you in hell.
	Hugh gets out of the car.
Stephen	What a man.

Borrowing A Fiver Off

Hugh Good evening and welcome to *Trying To Borrow A Fiver Off*. Tonight I shall be Trying To Borrow A Fiver Off the conductor of the Bristol Philharmonic Orchestra, Neville Anderson. Good evening, Neville.

Stephen Oh for heaven's sake, call me Neville.

Hugh Ha, if you insist. Neville, can I borrow a fiver off you till Wednesday?

Stephen Sorry, I've got nothing smaller than a twenty.

Hugh Bye bye.

VOX
POP

Stephen There's no doubt about it, it's an exciting place to live and work. We've even got one of those new edge-of-town city centres.

First Lines

Stephen addresses the camera.

Stephen   Ladies and gentlemen, all the sketches we've done on this show have been sort of finished, in one way or another. They start, they go along a bit, then they stop. More than one critic has drawn the parallel between our sketches and a nylon zip. But what we've never done on this show are the sketches that simply start – they start, with one line, sometimes quite a promising line, and then go nowhere at all. We'd like to show you some of them now, just so that you can get a glimpse of what might have been . . .

Cut to:

A traditional sketch shop. Stephen is behind the counter, Hugh enters frequently.

Hugh   Has Deborah Munnings arrived yet?

Cut to:

Hugh   I'd like to apply for the Royal Regiment of Homosexuals.

Cut to:

Stephen   Ah Dermot, there you are. I was sorting through some things in the attic this morning, and I came across your old legs . . .

Cut to:

Hugh   I'd like to open a Homosexual Bank account, please.

Cut to:

262

Stephen	Your grandfather's a bit smelly, isn't he?
Hugh	Yeah, well that's death for you.
	Cut to:
Hugh	*(Singing)* 'When somebody loves you, It's no good unless they love you'
	Cut to:
Stephen	Has Deborah Munnings arrived yet?
	Cut to:
Hugh	I'd like to apply to become a homosexual.
	etc. . . .

VOX
POP

Hugh And then my bereavement counsellor died. I didn't know who to turn to.

Dammit 4

Stephen is sitting at a desk looking at a computer terminal. Hugh is leaning over his shoulder.

Stephen	Dammit, Peter.
Hugh	Thanks John.
Stephen	This is . . . what can I say? This is good work.
Hugh	Well I kind of hoped that we might be along the right lines here.
Stephen	Right lines? Dammit backwards into a narrow space, Peter, this is the best I've ever seen.
Hugh	Jill reckons ten days at the most. Which means we could have this up and running by the 29th.
Stephen	You mean . . .?
Hugh	Exactly, John. The Derwent Enterprises Board meeting. With something like this nestling in your hip pocket, you could really kick some arse.

Stephen starts to laugh smugly.

What's up, John?

Stephen	Peter, can you imagine how Marjorie is going to take this?
Hugh	Well John, at a guess I'd say that she'll be wilder than a hungry hellcat in a tornado.
Stephen	That's putting it mildly.
Hugh	Is it?

They both laugh creepily. The phone rings. Hugh picks it up.

264

Hugh	Hahaha. . . . Yes, hello? Hold on Sarah. *(To Stephen)* It's Marjorie.
Stephen	Haha. Well talk of the she-devil. Oh what the hell, I'll take the call.
Hugh	It's not a call, John. She's outside and she wants to see you.
Stephen	Marjorie's here?
Hugh	Yup.

Stephen takes the phone.

Stephen	Show her in, Sarah.
Hugh	John, are you out of your goddamned mind?
Stephen	We don't know what it's about, Peter.
Hugh	To hell with what it's about, John! You and I have broken our arses building up this health club, with Marjorie gunning for us every centimetre of the way, and now you're going to let her swan in here . . .
Stephen	Now listen to me, Peter . . .
Hugh	Listen be damned! In case you'd forgotten, John, that bitchfiend tried to break us in two . . .
Stephen	Peter . . .
Hugh	I'm not going to let you do it, John!

They are now nose to nose across the desk. In the background the door opens and Marjorie enters. She is late forties, Joan Collinsish glamour.

Marjorie	Hello John.
Stephen	Hello Marjorie.
Marjorie	Peter.

Hugh says nothing.

Marjorie I hope I'm not interrupting anything?

Stephen Not at all. Peter and I were just running over one or two things.

Marjorie Are you all right, Peter? You seem a little uncomfortable.

Hugh Yeah. Maybe I'll go outside and get a bite of air. The atmosphere in here seems to have got to my stomach.

Exit Hugh. Stephen and Marjorie look at each other for a while.

Stephen You look well, Marjorie. You look damned well. New breasts?

Marjorie Swiss.

Stephen They suit you. I like what you've done to your hair. Looks much better there.

Marjorie Thanks John, you look pretty fit yourself.

Stephen Fit? Yeah, one of the perks of running a health and leisure business I guess. That is . . . if I still do run it?

Marjorie The meeting will decide, John, you know that.

Stephen *(Pouring two drinks)* And who will decide how the meeting goes, Marjorie? Dammit old man Ashby's in your pocket, Dexter and O'Neill will do whatever you damned well tell them and Tim will jump with the tide. Do you still like it straight up?

Marjorie Two lumps of ice.

Hugh has appeared at the window and is looking jealously in.

I do whatever I do for the boy, John. You must know that.

Stephen	Yeah, the boy. Have you taught him to hate me, Marjorie?
Marjorie	Hate you? *Hate* you? You'll never really know me, will you.
Stephen	Not if I live to be a chairman.
	Hugh is trying to listen.
Marjorie	Peter resents me.
Stephen	Peter? Dammit in top gear, Marjorie, what are you *after*?????
Hugh	*(Muffled, through the glass)* Yeah? What are you *after*??
	They don't hear him.
Marjorie	I just want you to know, whatever happens after this meeting . . . that it wasn't personal, John. Strictly business. I still like you . . . a lot.
Stephen	*(Roughly yet somehow tenderly)* Come here, you . . . you Marjorie.
	They kiss deeply and erotically.
	Hugh is distraught the other side of the glass. He hammers on it.
Hugh	Leave him alone you bitch-cat! John don't listen to her. Damn you!
	They part, panting.
Marjorie	I'll see you round the boardroom table.
Stephen	Yeah . . . round the boardroom table.
	She makes to leave.
	Oh and Marjorie . . .
Marjorie	Yes?
Stephen	Damn you to hell you're one hell of a woman.

267

Marjorie   I know. Well ... you know where to find me.

Stephen takes an Oedipal decision.

Exit Marjorie.

Stephen   *(Following her)* Daaaaaamn!

Hugh climbs in through the window in a desperate bid to stop him. He trips over.

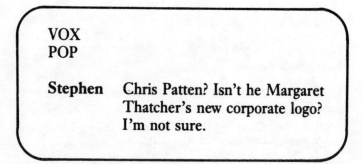

VOX
POP

Stephen   Chris Patten? Isn't he Margaret Thatcher's new corporate logo? I'm not sure.

Beauty and Ideas

Stephen is as we remember him from "Language Conversation". So is Hugh. But he's warier. He's done this before.

Stephen So, in a sense, in a sense, in a *sense*, Duncan, we are left with those two. Two. None other. Nary another, not one other more. We have, on the one side of the divide, the gulf, the chasm, the DIVIDING LINE, if you please, we have the beauty of ideas, and on the other, the other side, oh, I don't know, the other *term of the equation* if that's nicer, we have the idea of beauty. Am I sensing through? Am I connecting?

Hugh glances at the camera in friendly fashion.

Hugh We're busy discussing the beauty of ideas and the idea of beauty.

Stephen Hold a thought for me, Geoffrey, I'll give you the thought, hold it for me. Would you please?

Hugh I'm going to hold a thought, now.

Stephen If beauty is only an idea, a form, a paradigm, a pattern, a template, an ideal, an idea, if you like, with an 'l', then what is 'the beautiful'? Beauty is unattainable, but 'the beautiful' surrounds us. We return to language. Philip, we're back with language again. That's the thought you'd be ever so to splendid for me.

Hugh We've made a return to language. That's the thought I'm holding.

Stephen Listen to me lovelet, language circumscribes beauty, confines it, limns, delineates, colours and contains. Yet what is langage but a tool, a tool we

269

use to dig up the beauty that we take as our only
and absolute real?

Hugh   Language is a tool.

Stephen   So I'm finding myself with some surprise and
no little alarm hurling a paradox at you. Beauty
is our only reality and yet it is an ideal. It is the
surface-tension of the membrane that stretches
between us and the vision of beauty that language
seeks to disperse, as a detergent might dissipate or
dissolve a droplet of oil.

Hugh   I'm in trouble now.

Stephen   Hush, tish, vibble, I'm streaking ahead. Let me
explain, expand, expound and exposit.

Hugh   Would you?

Stephen   I find you beautiful. But you are not beauty.

Hugh   Whoops.

Stephen   Therefore you contain a property of beauty.
Therefore the substance of which you exhibit a
property must exist. Where is it?

*Hugh looks about helpfully, in case it is on the table or
has been left on the floor.*

That is language's task. Who was it who said
'Language is the universal whore that I must make
into a virgin?' Who was it?

Hugh   Kate Adie?

Stephen   I think it was Karl Kraus. But it needn't have
been. Now. Tommy, time to ask you to give back
the thought I bade you hold for me.

Hugh   I was holding the thought 'We've made a return to
language.'

Stephen   Correctly correctington. Language pursues
beauty, harries it, hounds it, courses it across the

270

roughlands of truth and enquiry AND IN SO DOING CAN BE BEAUTIFUL ITSELF. Ripple on ripple, image within image, a wheel within a wheel like the circles that you find in the windmills of your mind.

Hugh   Noel Harrison.

Stephen   Noel, as you so rightly, Harrison. Language can be beautiful. And Madeline asleep in lap of legends old. Plenitude. Dishes. Martita. Breasts. Tumble. Emolument. Forage. Smitten. Plenum. Vulva. Words that have their own sonority and beauty that is *extrinsic, extrinsic* to their connotational OR DENOTATIONAL referends.

Hugh   I think he said vulva.

Stephen   So Timothy I'll leave you with a thought, a breath, a fruit that drops from the boughs of my imaginings. Think beauty but be beautiful. Say beauty, but say it beautifully. Beauty is duty and duty beauty. So there. Goodnight. I don't feel quite so well now.

Hugh   *(To camera)* I'll talk to you later. B-bye.

VOX
POP

Hugh   The exciting thing about Chris Patten is that he's bold and imaginative.

Amputated Genitals

Stephen is coming groggily round in a hospital bed.
Hugh as doctor, sympathetically gazes down.

Stephen Oo-er.

Hugh Mr Kerniff . . .

Stephen Mmm.

Hugh Mr Kerniff, how are you feeling?

Stephen What happened?

Hugh You probably don't remember Mr Kerniff, but you were in a very serious accident.

Stephen A van.

Hugh No. An accident. You were on your bicycle, and you were hit . . .

Stephen By a van.

Hugh That's it.

Stephen Am I all right?

Hugh You're going to be fine, Mr Kerniff. Lots of drink and plenty of hot sleep.

Stephen Right.

Hugh But I'm afraid you did sustain a very serious injury to your genitals.

Stephen My genitals?

Hugh *(Holds up stainless steel tray)* As you can see.

Stephen Oh dear.

Hugh Oh, as you rightly say, dear. We had no choice but to remove them.

Stephen	Oh no.
Hugh	Oh, as you didn't rightly say, yes.
Stephen	However will I manage?
Hugh	Hmm. Did you use them often, Mr Kerniff?
Stephen	Well, not really. But it was nice to know that they were there.
Hugh	Quite. Well all is not lost, Mr Kerniff. Medical science has advanced a great deal. Prosthetic and substitute legs, arms, even noses, are now commonplace.
Stephen	You supply substitute genitals?
Hugh	Say hello to Killer, Mr Kerniff.

Hugh leads on a nasty-looking Doberman.

Stephen	You're not going to . . . I mean, surely you can't. For heaven's sake, I don't want a dog's genitals!
Hugh	Oh what an almost amusing misunderstanding, Mr Kerniff. No no no. Killer will simply be your substitute for having genitals.
Stephen	I beg your pardon?
Hugh	Yes, I'm sure you've seen people walking round with Dobermans before?
Stephen	Well . . . yes.
Hugh	Yes, well for men who have no genitals, the ownership of a Doberman or similarly violent animal acts as an important psychological crutch. And I stress the word 'important'.
Stephen	Owning a Doberman is a substitute for having genitals?
Hugh	Indeed yes, Mr Kerniff. Thousands of people compensate for genital inadequacy by owning large dogs.

273

Stephen	But why?
Hugh	Beats me, Mr Kerniff. I'm only a doctor. In addition we will provide you with a diving watch, a year's subscription to *Guns & Ammo* and this combat jacket. And these are yours too.

Hugh drops a diving watch, a gun magazine, a combat jacket and a bunch of keys on Stephen's bed.

Stephen	Wh . . .?
Hugh	Keys to your rusty white van.
Stephen	But, Doctor . . .
Hugh	Yes, Mr Kerniff?
Stephen	I appreciate that you're trying to help here, but I also happen to use my genitals for, you know, getting rid of my urine . . .
Hugh	Oh don't worry, that's the beauty of the system. When people see you wearing a combat jacket and driving round in a white van with Killer, the piss will be taken out of you constantly.

> VOX
> POP
>
> **Stephen**   I suppose in an ideal world
> I would be in bed with Philip
> Schofield right now.

Fast Talker

On a street somewhere. Stephen is trying to interview Hugh as the eyewitness to a road accident. Hugh is a fast-talking, over-eager Australian. Stephen has to keep stepping in and out of shot to restrain Hugh.

Stephen	*(To cameraman)* Are we ready?
Hugh	Yup. Any time. I was standing . . .
Stephen	No, I was just talking to the cameraman.
Hugh	Right. Got you.
Stephen	OK. So basically I'll just ask you what you saw . . .
Hugh	Well this guy came haring round the corner, must have been doing about fifty . . .
Stephen	Wait a minute . . . Can you wait until . . .
Hugh	Oh right.
Stephen	I'll ask you a question about what you saw . . .
Hugh	Yeah, this guy came round that corner, I thought he was going to hit that wall over there . . .
Stephen	No. Can you wait until I've asked you the question . . .
Hugh	Sorry. Sorry.
Stephen	Now then . . .
Hugh	This guy came round that corner there . . .
Stephen	WAIT . . . a minute.
Hugh	Sorry. I thought you . . .
Stephen	No. Just wait. Brian, are you ready?

Brian	*(Off)* Ready.
Hugh	OK. This guy came haring round that corner . . .
Stephen	Shut up!
Hugh	Oh yeah, right.
Stephen	Please do not say anything until I've asked you a question.
Hugh	Oh I get you. Right, sorry.
Stephen	Good. Now Mr Travis, I believe you . . .
Hugh	Yeah that's right, and this guy came round that corner over there doing about fifty . . .

Stephen goes right up to Hugh, noses almost touching, and screams at him.

Stephen	WAIT . . . UNTIL . . . I'VE . . . ASKED YOU . . . THE . . . QUESTION!!

Longish pause.

Hugh	OK.
Stephen	Thank you . . .
Hugh	This guy came . . .

Stephen punches Hugh in the face incredibly hard.

VOX
POP

Stephen	*(Wine tasting)* Um . . . the first one was dog the second cat. No? They were both cat?

Graham Gooch's aggressive appeal fails to impress umpire Jack Shepherd. Tendulkar went on to make an unbeaten 143.

London Transport Chief Sir Jack Perrelman explains underground zoning to a group of sixth formers from St Alan's.

As the museum attendant's body jackknifed in a rictus of pain,
Sherman made for the control room at a dead run.

This shows the gender difference even more clearly.
Note the distended folds (or flaps).

Papal greed? A seventeen-mile tailback at junction 14.

The USS Tomahawk prepares to embark on Operation 'Butt Kick'.

The main restaurant offers relaxed dining in a traditional atmosphere. The Butty Bar is Doncaster's premier rendezvous. A great place to meet people and enjoy a light informal screw.

This was taken with a Nikon F4 at 5.6, with an exposure of 1/500. A diffusion filter was used and the subject's nipples lightly brushed with baby oil. Note the matted dried-on effect.

A view of the Chadrot valley before engineers began to work on the hydro-electric dam. (The dam now provides eighty per cent of the power used in Staffordshire brothels.)

The famous 'Squirrel Scene' from the suppressed third reel of the movie. Cameraman Geoffrey Unsworth is second from the left. Christopher Biggins has his back to camera and his head in a small basket.

The standard
'Nun's Feet'
formation. Note
that if player A
(ringed) switches
to the Corsican
straddle, the
formation reverts
to the more usual
Double
Sidebreast or
Inkerman
Reverse.

Neddy Carter's
despairing dive
fails to prevent
Aston Villa's
smooth
progression into
the third round.
A crowd of
29,000 saw the
game.

Farmhouse cheese-making has altered little over the years in the Cotswold village of Addis Ababa. Here, the 'grilk' is separated from the 'tappy' by means of a circular 'swottle'. (The unused 'tappy' is sold on to manufacturers of car exhaust systems.)

Officers and men of Number Six Squadron, the Royal Air Force in a scene from their theatre-in-the-nude production of Rattigan's *Flare Path*.

Beethoven arranca constantes sorpresas de tonalidad, indicación y dinámica. 'Beethoven springs constant surprises of tonality, register and dynamics.' Practise especially an even, level intonation on the word '*indicación*', being careful to masturbate gently with the left hand.

J. H. St C. L. in happier days. You can see the Soane grotto in the background and Mamou with her beloved Westie terriers, Squeakie and Turd.

By the second year, the adult male will have grown to about 800lbs, its nose will be nearly a foot long, and its central leg will have developed a thick layer of horny tissue.

Remember to lead with the left shoulder, keeping your eye well over the ball: this shot shows the danger of too much right hand – a simple catch to short extra cover.

Brian Copeland, Vauxhall's Deputy Regional Fleet Sales Coordinator North-East, presses home his point.

After the first stunking, the juice is left to ferment for twelve weeks before being thrown away.

The patient is weighed before and after the operation. By subtracting the second figure from the first, it is possible to calculate the weight of the organs that have been removed. Alternatively, weigh the organs themselves.

Missing the mark: British medal hopes take a dive as Gary Burbett drops to a disappointing twenty-sixth in the individual 50m medium bore pistol-shooting.

This caption says it all.

And so we say 'Farewell, New Zealand –
land of contrasts.'

Yellow Pages

Charming old man enters bookshop, where Hugh and Stephen serve.

Old Man   Good morning. Do you have a copy of *Fly Fishing* by J. R. Hartley?

Hugh   I knew it, I knew it.

Stephen   I said this morning.

Hugh   Would you believe it, we had a whole shopful of them, and now . . .

Camera pulls back to reveal an empty shop.

Old Man   Well, that's the power of advertising I suppose.

Hugh   Absolutely. Mind you . . .

Stephen   We do have 30,000 copies of *Yellow Pages*, can't shift 'em.

Old Man   Ooh. Can I order one?

Hugh   Well we've got them here.

Old Man   No, no. I have to order them you see.

Stephen   Well, yeah. All right then. We can order one for you.

Old Man   You can? That's marvellous. My name? Of course . . . it's Pages, L.O. Pages.

Hugh   I never asked him his name, did you?

Stephen   No.

Stephen   *(Voiceover)* Good old L.O. Pages.

Spies/Twin

Stephen is looking at a picture on the wall, dressed in a very unControllish sort of way. Painter's smock and multi-coloured scarf. Hugh comes in, and starts talking before he sees Stephen.

Hugh   Morning Control. Sorry to bother you with this but . . .

He sees Control and is slightly startled by his clothes.

I was wondering . . . whether . . .

Stephen   Morning.

Hugh   Morning. If you'll allow me to say so, Control, you appear to have radically changed your appearance and manner of dressing.

Stephen   Ah, we've got a little bit of a crossed line here, I'm afraid. I'm not actually Control.

Hugh   You're not Control?

Stephen   No.

Hugh   Well now I don't know whether I'm coming or going.

Stephen   Don't worry. I'm Control's twin brother. How do you do?

Hugh   Oh I see. How do you do? You really do look awfully like Control, you know.

Stephen   Yes, people have frequently remarked on the similarity between myself and Control, it's true.

Hugh   My name's Tony.

Stephen   My name's Control.

Hugh   Sorry?

Stephen	It's a bit confusing but you see my mother could never tell us apart right from the day we were born, so she decided to call us both by the same name. She called us both Control.
Hugh	You mean Control is Control's real name?
Stephen	That's right. Oh dear. Have I been indiscreet?
Hugh	Not at all. It's just that I always assumed that the name Control was just a cover for Control's real name, which was a closely guarded secret.
Stephen	Well, of course I've always known that his name was Control. Just as I've always known that my name was Control as well.
Hugh	You could knock me down with a feather.
Stephen	I expect I could if it was a large and heavy one.
Hugh	Yes. So. Do you happen to know where Control is?
Stephen	I'm right here, as it happens.
Hugh	Oh no! We're confused already!
Stephen	Oh, you mean my brother Control!
Hugh	Yes.
Stephen	He's presently painting an erotic mural somewhere in Earl's Court I should imagine.
Hugh	Oh dear. I may need a lie-down soon.
Stephen	Before you go to that extreme, Mr Murchison. I assume you are Tony Murchison by the way . . . ?
Hugh	I am. Though the way things are going perhaps I should say 'I think I am!'
Stephen	Yes. I like you already, Tony, if I may call you that.
Hugh	Please do.
Stephen	I was going to explain that I am something of the Black Sheep of our family. Control is a widely

respected chief of the Secret Service and I am a not very respectable painter, though with a certain following in the louche areas of the metropolis.

Hugh   With you so far Control number two.

Stephen   And the thing of it is is that Control asked if I wouldn't mind changing places with him: me to run the Secret Service for a week, he to have a stab at painting an erotic mural in Earl's Court.

Hugh   Ah. I expect he's wanting to keep his undercover hand in.

Stephen   Very probably. So, Mr Murchison, have you got any secret documents you'd like me to sign?

Hugh   Well Control number two, I just need your permission to allocate funds for the purchase of that new safe house in Kensington that nobody knows the address of. Here are the estate agent's details.

Stephen   (*Looking through*) Oh, no Murchison. I can't possibly authorise our spending money on a house which has floral carpets and plain curtains.

Hugh   Ah.

Stephen   And look at the wallpaper in the hall. Far too busy.

Hugh   Right. I'll get to work on finding something more appropriate.

Stephen   Yes please.

Hugh   Meanwhile . . . would a coffee be helpful at all?

Stephen   Well, I'd love a lemon tea if you can manage it.

Hugh   Well well well! Control?

Stephen   Yes?

Hugh   Even if I hadn't guessed earlier I'd know now that you aren't the real Control. Because Control?

Stephen   Yes?

Hugh   The real Control never has lemon tea. Always coffee.

Stephen   Voh!

Hugh   One lemon tea coming up, though.

VOX
POP

Hugh   *(Blindfolded sipping first at a glass of red wine and then at a glass of white)* It's a trick. They're both red. *(Taking off blindfold)* Well, well, well. That's extraordinary. Ha, ha. Ha. Don't show this will you. I'm a wine merchant, I shall cop frightful stick at work. Good Lord! Ha! *(He's not that amused in fact)*

Swearing

Stephen and Hugh enter with their mouths gagged with tape, like anti-nuclear protesters (according to Hugh, who knows about these things).

Owing to the inaudibility of the irrepressible twosome, subtitles (But not subtleties, never subtleties).

Stephen   Mm . . . mmm . . . mmm mmm.

Hugh   Ng . . . ng . . . ng . . . ng . . .

It is understood that the following dialogue is subtitled. Where it says Hugh and Stephen they will in fact be mumbling. The obliques strokes indicate where a separate caption is required.

Stephen   Good evening ladies and gentlemen/welcome to 'A Bit Of Fry and Laurie'./

Hugh   Hello./

Stephen   Before we go any further, we should explain/ our rather unconventional appearance this evening./

Hugh   Yes, you normally sit on the left, don't you?/

Stephen   Nice gag, Hugh./

Hugh   Thanks, I made it myself./

Stephen   *(To audience)* We have a problem/ with our first item this evening . . ./

Hugh   Only a slight one, though./

Stephen   Yes, we've licked bigger problems than this / eh Hugh?/

Hugh   Yes, there was that very funny time when . . ./

Stephen   Oh shut up./

282

Hugh	Right./
Stephen	We are wearing these gags as a protest/
Hugh	Write on/
Stephen	Our first item tonight, my sweet little honeyclusters/ is a searing insight into real life,/ and perforce relies on using/ the language of the street./
Hugh	Swearwords . . ./
Stephen	Swearwords, exactly. But we have been banned from using actual swearwords/
Hugh	Bastards/
Stephen	So we have had to make up new ones /which are absolutely pitiless in their detail./
	Hugh rips off his gag.
Hugh	And nobody can stop us from using them. Here they are . . .
	Stephen rips off his gag. From now on, we are out loud.
	'Cloff'.
Stephen	'Prunk' . . .
Hugh	'Shote' . . .
Stephen	'Cucking' . . .
Hugh	'Skank' . . .
Stephen	'Fusk' . . .
Hugh	'Pempslider' . . .
Stephen	No, we said we wouldn't use that one.
Hugh	Did we?
Stephen	Yes, that's going too far.
Hugh	What, 'pempslider'?

Stephen	Shut up.
Hugh	Sorry.
Stephen	And lastly, 'pim-hole'.
Hugh	Hah.
Stephen	So, here it is, ladies and gentlemen, our first sketch . . . and good luck . . .

Cut to 'Witness'

> **VOX POP**
>
> **Hugh**   I'm afraid I was very much the traditionalist. I went down on one knee and dictated a proposal which my secretary faxed over straight away.

Witness

Stephen is a barrister. He is questioning Hugh, a police sergeant who is in the witness box. There is an elderly, fruity sort of Judge, Ralph, and a nasty-looking piece of work in the dock.

Stephen Can you tell us, Sergeant Henderson, what the prisoner said to you when you made the arrest?

Hugh If I may consult my notes, m'lud?

Judge Certainly, certainly, certainly. By all means. Yes.

Hugh I apprehended the accused and advised him of his rights. He replied 'Why don't you ram it up your pim-hole, you fusking cloff prunker.'

There is a sensation in the jury box. A woman screams and two men faint clean away. Judge purses his lips and makes a note.

Judge 'Why don't you ram it up your pim-hole you fusking . . .' er, cloth-blanket was it?

Another scream. The sound of a juryman being sick.

Stephen Er, I believe it was . . . er . . .

Judge *(Testily)* Yes, yes?

Stephen Cloff-prunker m'lud.

Sharp intakes of breath all round.

Judge *(Bemused)* I see. Forgive my ignorance Mr Clarkson, but what exactly *is* a 'cloff-prunker?'

Another sigh of horror. Stephen is mightily embarrassed.

Stephen Well m'lud it's . . .

Judge	*(Impatiently)* Yes?
Stephen	It's . . . hem . . . an illicit practice whereby one person . . . erm . . .
Judge	Well?
Stephen	Whereby one person frangilates another's slimp, m'lud.
Judge	*(Staggered)* He does what?
Stephen	He or she gratifies the other person by . . . smuctating them avially.
Judge	Good lord. How absolutely disgusting. Do people really do that sort of thing?
Stephen	I believe so, m'lud.
Judge	In which case I dare say there are probably magazines devoted to this practice?
Stephen	Very possibly, M'lud.
Judge	Are you planning to introduce any of these publications in evidence, Mr Clarkson?
Stephen	I hadn't thought it wholly necessary, M'Lud.
Judge	Hmm. Slapdash, Mr Clarkson. Slapdash. Well. Carry on, carry on.
Stephen	Thank you m'lud. Now Sergeant. After arresting the accused, I believe you questioned him at the station. You have a transcript of the interrogation?
Hugh	Yes, sir. I asked him if he could explain his whereabouts on the night in question. He replied 'I was in all night, wasn't I, you pempslider.'
Judge	Pempslider?
Stephen	A pempslider, M'Lud is . . .
Judge	*(Irritated)* Yes thank you, Mr Clarkson, I am not entirely uneducated in these matters.

Stephen	I beg your pardon, M'Lud.
Judge	I did go to Winchester, you know.
Stephen	Quite so, m'lud. If you would continue, Sergeant. He called you a pempslider.
Hugh	That is correct. And then . . . then, he called me a . . . I wonder if I might have a glass of water, m'lud?
Judge	Certainly not. This isn't America.
Hugh	He said 'Skank off, you cloffing cuck, you're all a load of shote-bag fuskers, so prunk that up your prime-ministering pim-hole.'
	Complete pandemonium from all save the Judge who looks at the accused sternly. A policeman behind him is clutching a handkerchief to his mouth and heaving. Accused looks smug.
Stephen	*(Whimpering faintly)* My God.
Judge	And what did you say to that, Sergeant?
Hugh	*(Consulting notes)* I told him to mind his fucking language, m'lud.
Judge	*(Approvingly)* I should think so too.

> VOX
> POP
>
> **Stephen** You see, it's a problem of discipline. Young people know nothing of service. They should all be forced to do some time in the army. There's muggings, rapings, beatings, violence, cruelty – fair enough, that's the army. But at least it teaches you how to serve.

Dancercises

Stephen pirouettes onto what is already becoming known as 'the area'.

Stephen   Last year I was overweight, short of breath, flabby and – it grieves me to say it, however sexily I might contrive to do so – unhappy. Since then a friend introduced me to Dancercises. I won't tell you who the friend was, but if I drop the hint that it was a prominent quantity surveyor, I think you'll guess. He put me onto 'Dancercises' and I must say it was the finest thing he's done in his otherwise futile and meaningless life. The key to Dancercise is the rather ingenious coupling of the word 'Dance' to the word 'circumcise'. The great disadvantage with most forms of keep-fit is that they are uncomfortable, unnatural and can often throw too much strain on the important parts of your family. And, let's be utterly frank, they can look and sound peculiar and embarrassing if performed in public. Dancing, or more properly, Dance, is natural and expressive. Let's suppose I'm a prominent Quantity Surveyor and Hugh is Geoffrey Cavendish, a client. While I work, you can see that it is easy to fit in toning and strengthening movements.

Goes over to where Hugh is.

Morning Geoffrey.

Does a little dance.

Hugh   Hello Dennis.

Stephen   Got any quantities for me to survey this morning?

288

Hugh	I've got a quantity that I'd love for you to survey if you're not too busy, Dennis.
Stephen	*(Moving and jiving freely)* Yes. This quantity here?
Hugh	That's the fellow.
Stephen	*(Surveying it)* Well, that's got that quantity surveyed? Any others?
Hugh	That's all for today.
Stephen	Thanks, Geoffrey. You'll let me know?
Hugh	Oh, Dennis. If there are any other quantities I find and I want them surveyed, you'll be the first to know.

VOX
POP

Hugh	As I see it one American life is the same as two European lives, four Japanese lives, seventy African lives and three hundred Central American lives. At least that was at the close of business yesterday.

Trick or Treat

Stephen is in the area, finishing off polishing his desk with a duster and a can of Pledge.

Stephen   It is our firm belief on 'A Bit Of Fry And Laurie', married to a passionate girl from Stockton-on-Tees, that there is a right way and a wrong way to do everything.

He is walking out across the central set now towards a doorway set.

So I and my 'partner in crime', Hugh Laurie. *(He finds this inordinately amusing)* My 'partner in crime'!!! No, I call him that, but that's not really what he is. We don't really commit crimes together of any kind. That's just a ghastly and unacceptable phrase that I like to use sometimes. So, anyway, I and my, as I say, 'partner in crime!' . . . *(Wipes eyes)* Honestly! . . . are now going to demonstrate the right way and the wrong way to treat a couple of young children who have come round on Hallowe'en a-trick or treating.

Hugh is waiting wearing something rather odd and looking very excited.

Hugh   That's right!!! Now, we're going to play it like this. Firstly we're going to show you the Wrong Way, that's THE WRONG WAY, and then we're going to show you the Right Way. I'll say that again . . .

He doesn't.

Stephen   Good. So all we need now is to wait for the doorbell to ring.

	They wait.
Stephen	Nice carpet, Hugh. Tideyman's?
Hugh	Who else, if you'll pardon the pun.
Stephen	What pun?
Hugh	Oh, wasn't there one? Sorry.
	Doorbell rings.
	Ah, the door.
Stephen	We'll answer it, shall we?
Hugh	Sounds a hot suggestion to me.

They answer the door. Two children stand without, wearing Hallowe'en masks.

Child 1	Trick or treat, mister.
Hugh	Ah!
Stephen	Toh!
Hugh	Let me see, did we prepare a little bag of jelly beans out back?
Stephen	We most certainly did, I'll go fetch them.

Hugh is left alone with the children. He ruffles the hair of one of them.

Hugh	So. You fond of football, young shaver-snapper?
Child 2	Yeah.
Hugh	Do you fancy Arsenal this year?
Child 2	No way. I quite fancy my sister though.
Hugh	*(Disconcerted)* Ahmm . . . er . . .
Stephen	*(Coming through)* There we go.

He ruffles their hair.

Child 1	Ta.
Hugh	Bye now.
	Stephen shuts the door and smiles.
	That was the wrong way. THE WRONG WAY!! Now for the RIGHT WAY. I won't say that ever again. The Right Way, the RIGHT Way.
Stephen	Nice pun, Hugh. Tideyman's?
Hugh	Who else, if you'll pardon the carpet.
Stephen	What carpet?
Hugh	Oh, wasn't there one? Sorry.
	Doorbell rings.
	Ah, the hot suggestion.
Stephen	We'll answer it, shall we?
Hugh	Sounds like a door to me.
	They answer the door: two children stand without, wearing Hallowe'en masks.
Child 1	Trick or treat, mister.
Hugh	What?
Stephen	WHAT did you say?
Child 1	Trick or treat.
Hugh	Trick or treat?
Stephen	Trick or treat?
Hugh	Come here.
Stephen	Both of you. NOW!!!
	The children approach. A bit scared.
Hugh	*(Hurling child number one bodily out of the door)* This is England, not America.

292

Stephen	*(Doing the same to number two)* NOT AMERICA!! You understand?
	Both children have flown out of the door.
	You see? A right way, and a wrong way.
Hugh	We thank you.
Stephen	Limply.

VOX
POP

Hugh	*(With an electronic organiser)* Ask me anything, a telephone number, what time it is in Adelaide. Tell you what, I can tell you exactly what I'll be doing on the third of August 1997, say. Hang on *(Presses a few buttons)*. Nothing. See, it says. Nothing.

Breast Delivery

Stephen answers the door. Hugh is standing there in delivery man gear, with clipboard.

Hugh   Morning. Mrs Bennett?

Stephen   Pardon?

Hugh   Are you Mrs Bennett?

Stephen   No.

Hugh   No?

Stephen   No.

Hugh   Wait a minute. Wait a minute. Can you prove that?

Stephen   Prove what?

Hugh   I'm not being rude, it's just that for all I know you might be a conman answering doors and pretending not to be Mrs Bennett. Lot of that goes on.

Stephen   Well . . . will a Driving Licence do?

Hugh   Not really, no. You might have stolen it, you see. Anything else you can show me, to prove you're not Mrs Bennett?

Stephen   How about Mrs Bennett?

Hugh   Sorry, not with you.

Stephen   If I show you Mrs Bennett, would that prove I wasn't her?

Hugh   It's a start.

Stephen   Darling!

Hugh   Yes?

Stephen	No, I was calling my wife. I'm Mr Bennett.
Hugh	Oh.
Stephen	Darling!
Hugh	No, look, don't bother. If you're Mr Bennett, you can sign for them. Would you mind?
Stephen	Certainly. What are they?
Hugh	Some breasts.
Stephen	Pardon?
Hugh	Your wife ordered a quantity of breasts from us, and we promised we'd have them here by Wednesday.
Stephen	Today's Friday.
Hugh	We had a puncture.
Stephen	Wait a minute, what's she doing ordering breasts?
Hugh	Search me.
Stephen	I mean for heaven's sake she's already got some.
Hugh	Tscch. Women. Don't start me off. They're never happy, are they? Just sign there for me.
Stephen	'Breasts times three'. Three?
Hugh	Spare.
Stephen	I see. Well thanks very much.
Hugh	Aren't you going to check the box?
Stephen	Why?
Hugh	Well . . . make sure they're all right.
Stephen	I'm sure they're fine.
Hugh	Mmm. We do get a lot of mix-ups.
Stephen	All right, then . . . one, two, three. They look fine.

Hugh	Ermm . . .
Stephen	Yes?
Hugh	D'you mind if I have a look?
Stephen	I beg your pardon?
Hugh	Just to check.
Stephen	You want to look at my wife's breasts?
Hugh	Well . . .
Stephen	You are asking me if you can look at my wife's breasts?
Hugh	Just a peek.
Stephen	*(Showing the box)* Tssch. All right then.
Hugh	Phwor. Not bad are they?
Stephen	I suppose they're all right.
Hugh	All right? They're fantastic. You're a lucky feller.
Stephen	Mmm. Actually, I'm a leg man myself.
Hugh	Really?
Stephen	Yes.
Hugh	Funnily enough, I've got some legs in the back of the van if you're interested.
Stephen	Have you?
Hugh	Yeah. Make a nice surprise gift for your wife.
Stephen	No, I shouldn't really. She's up to her waist in legs as it is.
Hugh	They're a bit special.
Stephen	Are they?
Hugh	Definitely.

Spies/Firing

Stephen is at his desk. There is a knock at the door, and Hugh enters.

Hugh   Hello, Control.

Stephen   Tony. It's you.

Hugh   That's right. I understand from Valerie that you wanted reasonably strongly to see me.

Stephen   Valerie is by no means leading you up the garden path, Tony, because I do want to see you.

Hugh   I find Valerie's usually right in these little matters.

Stephen   Ng.

Hugh   Control?

Stephen   Yes, Tony?

Hugh   Did you want, I'm wondering, to speak to me as well, or was it just seeing me that was on your mind?

Stephen   Well now Tony, there was something I wanted to ask you, but it's a little bit tricky actually.

Hugh   Tricky?

Stephen   Yes, Tony. Have you ever been in the position where you've had to tell someone you like quite a lot that you've got to fire them from their job?

Hugh   No.

Stephen   Ah.

Hugh   That didn't turn out to be too tricky a thing to ask me, did it?

Stephen	Yes. Thing is, Tony, I haven't quite said the really tricky thing yet.
Hugh	Ah. Would it be the kind of thing that would go better with a good cup of coffee, Control?
Stephen	Perhaps a little later, Tony. I wouldn't want to be thought of as hiding behind that cup of coffee.
Hugh	That's just as well, Control, because the cup of coffee I had in mind was going to be quite small.
Stephen	Tell me Tony, have you, in your position as subsection chief of the East German and related satellites desk, noticed the way the wind is blowing on the other side of the curtain?
Hugh	It's been blowing in odd kinds of ways, hasn't it, Control?
Stephen	It has, Tony. Glasnost, perestroika and related phenomena have had their effect on the political map of Europe in no uncertain terms.
Hugh	Yes, Control. Only this morning, I had to ask Valerie if she wouldn't mind going out and buying some new political maps of Europe, as ours were really quite out of date.
Stephen	Yes, it's shaken all our lives up a bit, certainly. But Tony . . .
Hugh	Yes, Control?
Stephen	It's also meant that our masters in Whitehall have started wondering whether they need quite so many people involved in spying.
Hugh	I'm not sure I fully understand, Control.
Stephen	Well they take the view, Tony, that nowadays, with the Russians simply ringing us up and telling us most of their secrets, we don't need to spend such a lot of money on finding them out.

298

Hugh	That's an astute piece of political thinking by our masters in Whitehall, Control.
Stephen	Yes, Tony, it is.
Hugh	How about that coffee now, Control?
Stephen	No, Tony. Not yet. Anyway, what this is all leading up to, Tony, if you haven't already guessed, is that I'm going to have to fire you from your job.
Hugh	Control. I'm slightly at a loss for words.
Stephen	Please don't think, Tony, that I'm getting any enjoyment out of this situation. This is one of the hardest things I've ever had to do in all my years of running the Secret Service.
Hugh	Mmm. I certainly don't envy you, Control, having to pass on a bit of news like the one you've just passed on to me.
Stephen	Yes, it is very hard, Tony.
Hugh	Oh well, Control. I suppose that's that, then.
Stephen	Yes, Tony, I'm afraid it is. I really am very sorry.
Hugh	May I take this opportunity of saying how much I've enjoyed working for you, Control, and wish you the best of luck with all your future spying.
Stephen	Thank you Tony. I can honestly say that this place won't be the same without you.
Hugh	No, I suppose it will be a bit different because I won't be here.
Stephen	That's right.
Hugh	I'll be somewhere else.
Stephen	Yes.
Hugh	Well goodbye, Control.

They shake hands.

299

Stephen   Goodbye, Murchison.

Hugh exits. Stephen sits down again and blows his nose. He picks up the phone.

Valerie? Could you bring me a cup of coffee? *(Pause)* How do I like it? I like it the way Tony Murchison used to make it.

VOX
POP

Stephen   If things had worked out differently it's strange to think *I* would now be Foreign Secretary and Douglas Hurd would be an assistant librarian. Weird, isn't it?

The Robert Robinsons

The Robert Robinsons each have behind them a word roller, like the one on Call My Bluff. *To start with it says 'the Robert Robinsons'. Each time they ting a bell which is on the table in front of them, the word roller goes round and a new word appears.*

Stephen	Ah, well now yes, good evening. That much is certain.
Hugh	Though tish ah, nay, hush and fourpence, Mr Dwyer.
Stephen	And an extra point for being so clever!
Hugh	Would that it were, would that it were.
Stephen	Ah, indeed, would that it were, Mr Charteris, would that it were.

They both ping their bells and the words 'pompous' and 'insufferable' appear.

Hugh	Here's a thing, not that pish and tish.
Stephen	I have a letter from a Colin Elgood of Carshalton Beeches telling me he turns his carrier bags inside out so as not to give free advertising to Mr Sainsbury and men of his ilk.
Hugh	Nay men of his stamp.
Stephen	Of his ilk, stamp and kidney.
Hugh	Your answer is better Mr Meredith, so much better but wrong, sadly wrong.
Stephen	And an extra mark for being clever!

They ping and the words 'self-satisfied' and 'fraudulent' appear.

Hugh	Ah, we have a plump! Someone has plumped. Go on, Mr Harris, have a plump too.
Stephen	Hish, tusk, ah now, it only remains for me to declare the Twee family winners of our little game.
Hugh	An extra mark followed by this round of applause.
	Ping! The words 'absurd' and 'gasbag' appear.
Stephen	Ah, the pity of it, the pity. Time, our old enemy, comes round again.
Hugh	Nish, tussock, flimp and fivepence.
Stephen	We bid you goodbye.
Hugh	We bid you farewell.
Stephen	But ah, though, flish, bish and trivvock, not for ever.
	Ping! The words 'sod' and 'off'

VOX
POP

Hugh *(As policeman)* There's method in my madness. Ha, ha, ha!!!!! *(Madly)*

Technophobia

Stephen   Did you ... I don't know, you may have done
... last night ... see that Horizon ... er ...
documentary, is it? Is that what they're called?

Hugh   Horizon documentary, yes, I think so. You mean,
on the er ...

Stephen   Television.

Hugh   Television, that's right.

Stephen   Yes, television. I think it's a ... documentary. Did
you see it?

Hugh   No, I didn't, I'm afraid. I was out last night.

Stephen   Oh dear, you didn't record it?

Hugh   Record it?

Stephen   Yes.

Hugh   Oh I see what you mean. No, we've got one of
those er ...

Stephen   Recording ...

Hugh   Yes, those machines that record ...

Stephen   Recording machines ...

Hugh   Is that what they're ...?

Stephen   I think so.

Hugh   Yes, well, we've got one, but I'm afraid neither of
us knows how to work it.

Stephen   Oh how terribly amusing.

Hugh   It is, isn't it? Amusing and eccentric.

Stephen   Terribly.

Hugh   Yes I'm just hopeless with anything mechanical ...

Stephen	Oh me too. My wife gave me an electric toothbrush last Christmas, and I just can't work it out at all . . .
Hugh	Oh how amusing and eccentric.
Stephen	Isn't it? Isn't it incredibly amusing and eccentric?
Hugh	I can't even work an ordinary toothbrush.
Stephen	Can't you?
Hugh	No, I keep putting the wrong end into my mouth, and the toothpaste up my nose . . . I'm hopeless.
Stephen	Me too.
Hugh	My wife looks at me with one of those looks of hers that seems to say er . . .
Stephen	How amusing and eccentric?
Hugh	Exactly.
Stephen	Yes, there's another one of those documentaries on tonight, apparently.
Hugh	Really? Oh well I might watch it, then. What time, do you know?
Stephen	Half past eight, I believe.
Hugh	Half past eight, yes, that's when the big hand is pointing . . .
Stephen	Oh don't ask me. I can't deal with these confounded watch things . . .
Hugh	No, neither can I. My daughter gave this to me, and I can't get the hang of it . . .
Stephen	No, I'm much too amusing and eccentric to . . . you know . . .
Hugh	Me too. Far too amusing and eccentric.
Stephen	But I think it's at half past eight. It should be in the paper, anyway.

Hugh	Newspapers? Haha. . . .
Stephen	Hahaha . . . me too.
Hugh	Never know which way to turn the blasted page.
Stephen	Get it upside down . . .
Hugh	All over the place . . .
Stephen	I always give the paper to our young son to read, he's the only one who can work the confounded thing.
Hugh	Honestly. We *are* amusing and eccentric aren't we?
Stephen	Yes.
	Bell rings.
Hugh	Hello!
Stephen	Best be in the House for that debate on the electricity privatisation.
Hugh	Absolutely . . .

VOX
POP

Stephen	I suppose if I'm honest I use my penis as a sort of car substitute.

A Vision of Britain

Stephen addresses camera. His hair is wild and peculiar. He stares through thick, black-rimmed spectacles.

Hugh is playing 'I vow to thee my country' throughout on the piano.

Stephen   Ladies and gentlemen, bear with me. Bear with me please. Don't stop bearing with me for a few moments. I have a vision, a vision of Britain. I see a country peopled by . . . a country peopled by people who, who . . . people it with charm, with grace, yes even with greatness. As they people it, they enhance it with their lightness, their amusing accents, their v-neck sweaters and their unusual children. This country shall be free and wide and pretty, and their people shall be free and wide and pretty. And there shall be villages and towns and family amusement theme heritage fun parks which shall smell of urine and vomit. And there shall be twelve water and sewage businesses and leisure dromes and huge edge-of-town crematoriums and day-glo bermuda shorts which are flecked with urine and vomit. I see 'Impact' as a new kind of flexible high-yield convenient cash and care card for the kind of person you are today and I hear the sound of many thousands of miles of motorways, conveniently filled with many hundreds of thousands of cars whose seats are stained with children and urine and vomit. And the interior of the cars shall be sweaty and hot and bad-tempered and the queue for the exit that leads to the family amusement heritage theme fun park shall be hundreds of miles long. And there shall be shiny

magazines out of which will fall many dozens
of smaller shiny magazines which shall offer
useful electronic golfing equipment and wall safes
disguised as three pin sockets and bright security
lamps and personal attack alarms and hand
freshen-up absorbent pads to soak up the urine
and the vomit. And the faces of the people who
are peopling this Britain shall be shiny and they
shall be flushed and pink for they shall know that
they are forging a new Britain of fun and heritage
and family leisure amusement and the boot of their
car shall easily accommodate the self-assembly fun
park that they shall erect in their bathrooms. As
yet, it is all only a vision, a vision of family heritage
urine and fun leisure amenity vomit. But soon,
soon, with luck, sincerity and steadfast voting it
may become a reality.

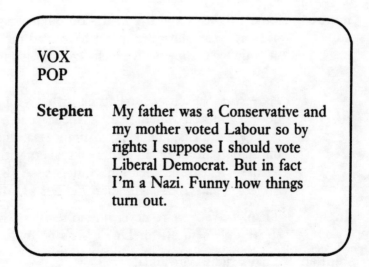

**VOX
POP**

Stephen   My father was a Conservative and
my mother voted Labour so by
rights I suppose I should vote
Liberal Democrat. But in fact
I'm a Nazi. Funny how things
turn out.

Ironic Self-Defence

Stephen   We live, don't we, in an increasingly age. Where
                once the village post office, a mug of Horlicks,
                Bing Crosby songs and a Kenneth More film were
                the only things the average Britain had to fear,
                nowadays every alleyway can conceal a threat, every
                encounter a violent confrontation, every telephone
                call an erotic nightmare. Arnold.

Hugh   That's right. It has become increasingly and
                abundantly that unscrupulous people have traded
                on the fear that now stalks the streets. Open any
                local newspaper or give-away sheet and you can
                read advertisements for self-defence classes in
                hai-ki-doh, ken-doh, play-doh, judo and a whole
                stain of martial arts. But people who answer the
                threat of violence with real violence of their own
                often find that it is *they* who end up in court, not
                their assailants. Nerelle.

Stephen   That's right. If you live in the Boroughbridge area
                of North Yorkshire you might have read this article
                in your local copy of the Helperby and Cundall
                Advertiser.

                Voice-over: 'Discover Dr Patrick Fisher's amazing
                new key to non-violent self-defence. Repel
                muggers, rapists, attackers, insurance-salesmen,
                burglars, Christians and house-breakers without
                harm or fear of prosecution. Simply send £3.00 for
                Fisher's Guide To Non-Physical Violence.' Dwoyne.

Hugh   Thanks. Well, we're never one to resist a challenge
                so we duly sent off for Dr Fisher's book. Fwith.

Stephen   That's right. Moylinda.

Hugh   The 'book' turned out to be this. *(Holds up flimsy
                pamphlet)* The secret method that Dr Fisher

308

recommends? Well, it seems that there are two basic approaches.

Hugh & Stephen read them alternately, starting with Stephen.

Stephen '1. The Flirty Come-on.'

Hugh '2. The Disorientating Remark.' Testina.

Stephen Thanks. So we decided to try this method out for ourselves. F-f-f-f.

Hugh Yes indeed. We went out into Chichester's notorious East Gate and waited for the inevitable assault.

Caption '1. The Flirty Come-on.'

Hugh is loitering on a bench, an expensive-looking briefcase on his lap. He is counting the money in his wallet.

A mugger sidles up next to him and whips out a knife.

Mugger *(Waving it under his nose)* You know what this is?

Hugh Yes. I do actually. Sweet of you to try and help me out, but I do actually know what it is.

Mugger Right. Wallet.

Hugh Wall . . . oh for heaven's sake you're mugging me.

Mugger That's right.

Hugh Oh, now you've . . . oh. Of all the people here . . . you've picked on little old me. I don't know what to say. I think I'm going to cry.

Mugger Wallet.

Hugh Of course, of course. Hold on, I'll just take the money and things out first, otherwise you'll have to

	lug them around all day, and there'll be no room for your own stuff.
Mugger	Look, get a move on.
Hugh	Oh sorry, of course. You've got things to do, of course you have, and here's me nattering away twelve to the dozen.
Mugger	Oh forget it.
Caption	'2. The Disorientating Remark.'

Stephen is in an alleyway, he bends down to tie his shoe-laces. A man comes up from behind.

Man	Right. Do as I say and you won't get hurt. Lie down in that corner and drop 'em.
Stephen	I had an Uncle Geoffrey that looked just like you. He wasn't so old then and tasted slightly wider.
Man	Did you hear what I just said?
Stephen	I've got a note from matron you know.
Man	What?
Stephen	Unless you go away from here and leave me alone completely I'll write a poem in Lebanese and send it straight to Gary Lineker's doctor.
Man	Just get down in that corner.
Stephen	*(Shouting)* My name is an anagram of the Metropolitan Police and unless you stay here and do exactly as you tell me your breasts will become the property of Gerald Kaufman.
Man	*(Pushing Stephen to the floor and unbuckling his belt)* I said GET DOWN!
Stephen	Right-o. Fair enough. I should just mention though, that you can't fit quicker than a Kwikfit Fitter.

Back to studio.

Stephen   So. A warning there. If Dr Fisher's Advertisement should find its way into your High Street Give-Away Market Trading Advertiser Sheet our advice is Trish.

Hugh   That's right. And remember. Dermidge.

Stephen   So, until. It's.

Hugh   Bye.

VOX POP

Stephen   Well I was given one of those personal organisers, so when I went into work everyone said 'You're a bit of a yuppie!!!' It was so funny. Because yuppies are those new people you know who are very trendy. 'A bit of a yuppie!' Dear oh dear. That's probably the funniest thing that's ever happened to me.

The Cause

Hugh and Stephen are in a London club sort of place.

Stephen   Freddy.

Hugh   Oh, good heavens, Jack, I didn't see you there.

Stephen   Good evening, Freddy.

Hugh   Well, good evening, Jack.

Stephen   Now then, Freddy you're a decent sort of chap.

Hugh   Well, I, yes, I think so Jack, yes, I try to be a decent sort of chap, yes.

Stephen   Mmmm. Can I ask you a question, Freddy?

Hugh   Ask away, ask-a-bloody-way.

Stephen   Are you one of us?

Hugh   Am I one of us?

Stephen   Yes.

Hugh   Am I one of us?

Stephen   Yes.

Hugh   Not entirely sure I understand your question, Jack.

Stephen   Let me put it another way.

Hugh   Oh, would you Jack, yes, well, I'd be enormously grateful.

Stephen   Do you believe in the cause?

Hugh   The cause ...

Stephen   The Cause of Freedom.

Hugh   Well, Jack I suppose, generally, yes, yes, I do. If anyone's passing the hat round for freedom, I'll bung in a quid or two, Jack, yes.

Stephen	I thought so, I thought so from the first.
Hugh	Yes, I'm one of us Jack, if you want to put it that way.
Stephen	Excellent.
Hugh	Phew, well, we got there in the end, Jack, sorted that one out.
Stephen	It gets a bit more complicated now.
Hugh	Oh, Lord.
Stephen	Would you be prepared to do something in the cause of freedom?
Hugh	What sort of thing, Jack? Jumble sale, hand out leaflets? What?
Stephen	Put a bomb in a restaurant.
Hugh	Put a bomb in a restaurant. Ah Crikey. And leave it there, you mean?
Stephen	Leave it there. That's right.
Hugh	Yes, yes. You don't mean put it there, have a spot of lunch and then take it out again?
Stephen	No, I mean leave it there.
Hugh	Um, until it goes off?
Stephen	Precisely. Do you think you could manage that in the cause of freedom?
Hugh	Oh, Jack, Jack, I wonder if you wouldn't mind, sort of, joining up the dots for me, if you like.
Stephen	If it'll make it easier for you.
Hugh	I think it will, Jack, I think it will, because unless I've fainted and missed a whole chunk of the conversation, um, we've been sitting here, you

313

	and I, having a nice old chat, putting the world to rights and so on, and then suddenly you're asking me to put a bomb in a restaurant.
Stephen	That's right.
Hugh	Those are the two dots I'd like you to join up, Jack. The nice chat and the bomb in the restaurant. Join them up for me, there's a good fellow.
Stephen	All right then, Freddy. There are certain people who do not believe in the cause.
Hugh	Don't believe in freedom, you mean?
Stephen	That's right.
Hugh	Oh, utter swines, and they eat in a particular restaurant, do they Jack?
Stephen	Some of them will be eating in a particular restaurant on a particular day.
Hugh	Ah, well, Jack, sorry to stop you, but, I've an idea, um, well, you know who these people are, Jack.
Stephen	Yes.
Hugh	And you know which restaurant they'll be in?
Stephen	Yes.
Hugh	Right, well, so here's the idea. We go in there, you and I, Jack and we sit down at their table and we hammer it out with them face to face. What do you say?
Stephen	Fight them, you mean?
Hugh	No, no, no, Jack, no: argument. You're a persuasive fellow, Jack – I bet we could sit down at their table over the soup, and you could talk and I'll back you to the hilt and I bet you anything we could have them believing in freedom by the time the pudding arrives. What do you say Jack?

314

Stephen	I don't think that'll quite do.
Hugh	It won't quite do. Well, all right Jack. How about this *(Laughs)* we pretend to put a bomb in the restaurant.
Stephen	Freddy . . .
Hugh	Yes, Jack?
Stephen	I think perhaps . . .
Hugh	Yes.
Stephen	I think perhaps that I was wrong about you.
Hugh	No, Jack, no. No you were absolutely right, Jack. Right as bloody rain, you were.
Stephen	Well, then.
Hugh	Well, Jack, it's just . . . I'm just the most awful duffer at this sort of thing.
Stephen	The restaurant is called the Étoile d'Or in Maddox Street. I suggest you put it behind the lavatory cistern. But it's up to you.
Hugh	Oh, Hell.

Stephen (Gordon) and Hugh (Stuart) are at a restaurant with their wives.

Hugh	They've got a bigger table than we have.
Girl 1	Come on Stuart, this is fine.
Hugh	Look, there are two of them and they've got a bigger table. There are four of us and look at this. *(Bangs table)*
Girl 2	Oh Stuart for heaven's sake, a table's a table!
Stephen	Darling . . .
Hugh	Well, Jill, there we differ. To me there are tables and there are tables. Am I right Gordon?

Stephen	Well you know me, Stuart, table is as table does.
Girl 1	At least it's snug, poppet.
Hugh	What it is, poppet, is cramped. You should've used my name when you booked.
Girl 1	Well I did.
Stephen	What, Mr Poppet?

(They all laugh at Hugh)

(Hugh enters the restaurant as the character from the club, clutching briefcase with bomb in it)

Waiter	Good evening, sir.
Hugh	Good evening. A table for bomb please.
Waiter	Excuse me?
Hugh	*(Laughing hysterically)* A table for one. Sorry . . . bit nervous. I've never actually eaten a meal before.
Waiter	Well, you have chosen the perfect place to start. Follow me please.

(Cut back to Gordon and Stuart)

Stephen	So what did we think of the show?
Girl 1	Loved it. Thought it was really nice.
Stephen	Me too. High quality entertainment.
Hugh	I'm going to come right out and say it. To me, Jeffrey Archer is the finest playwright this country's turned out since William Shakespeare.
Stephen	That's a hell of a statement, Stu.
Hugh	Well let me go one further, Gordon. To me, Jeffrey Archer delivers.
Stephen	Oh the guy can write, no question.
Girl 2	Delivers, does he?
Hugh	I beg your pardon, Jill?

316

Stephen	Come on darling, you know what he means.
Hugh	No, it's all right thank you, Gordon. I can fight my own battles. What he delivers, Jill, to my mind, is quality drama . . . OK it's a little dangerous . . . OK it's not something that your average Joe punter is going to find all that accessible, but in the market he's working to he delivers and Gordon will tell you that's a compliment I use very sparingly indeed.
Stephen	It's true actually Jill, it's true. Stuart is not the kind of man to bandy the word 'deliver' around the place.
Hugh	Thank you Gordon.
Girl 1	Thought the sets were marvellous. They were really clever. Weren't they poppet?
Hugh	Yes, and the costumes were fantastic.
Girl 2	Sorry, they were wearing suits weren't they?
Hugh	Well, this is where Jeffrey Archer is so strong you see . . . in his observation. He's observed that in an office a large number of people wear suits. Isn't that right, Gordon?
Stephen	Absolutely, Stu.
Hugh	Well, he's observed that, you see. I mean the guy's got an eye for detail like well, there's no one like him in my book.
Stephen	To be fair to myself, Stu, I'd observed that people in offices wear suits too.
Hugh	No, no, no you hadn't, Gordon. You can only say that after you've seen the play. If I'd asked you before the play what people wear in offices you wouldn't have had a clue.
Stephen	I think I would've said suits.
Hugh	No you wouldn't, Gordon.

317

Stephen	I think I would.
	(Hugh clicks his fingers at the waiter)
Hugh	No you wouldn't. Now wait a minute, look, that bloke came in after us and they're taking his order.
	(Hugh is the character with the bomb, still clutching the briefcase)
Waiter	What would you like, sir?
Hugh	Crikey, yes.
Waiter	Something the matter, sir?
Hugh	Well, how many lavatories have you got here?
Waiter	Just one, sir, over there.
Hugh	Yes, I've tried that one, it's no good. No bloody good. It's the cistern, it's too close to the wall . . . you can't get anything between the cistern and the wall. Oh hell.
Waiter	Are you ready to order, sir?
Hugh	Order yes, well, to be perfectly honest I'm not awfully hungry.
Waiter	Well may I recommend a salad? Perhaps a smoked chicken salad? It makes a perfect light meal.
Hugh	Yes that sounds awfully good. Tell you what though, instead of that I think I'll just have a glass of water.
Waiter	Just a glass of water, sir?
Hugh	Lord no, make it a bottle. Or tell you what, half a dozen bottles. I mean you only live once don't you.
Waiter	Very good, sir.
Hugh	Oh hell.
	(Stephen is a waiter. He goes to a table where a man sits alone)

318

Stephen	Good evening, sir.
Man	Good evening. I'd like to order some soup to start.
Stephen	Wait a minute, good Lord, you're Keith Bennett aren't you? The government minister?
Man	Well, as a matter of fact I am.
Stephen	I thought so, I knew it. Oh Mr Bennett, this is wonderful. I have to say I'm a great admirer of you and your policies.
Man	Really?
Stephen	Definitely. Can I recommend the halibut by the way. It comes with a nice black butter sauce.
Man	Thank you.
Stephen	You steered that broadcasting bill through the House of Commons didn't you?
Man	I did indeed.
Stephen	Brilliant, quite brilliant.
Man	Well I must say this is really most gratifying. So you really do admire my policies?
Stephen	Yes well, most people don't like you then?
Man	Well, you know how it is, we aren't always the most popular of people, we politicians.
Stephen	Yes, you must get used to people calling you a complete dickhead I suppose.
Man	No, not exactly.
Stephen	That speech you made about deregulating broadcasting . . . oh, I cheered for you that night. We must strive to offer the consumer a far greater range of choice, for too long broadcasting has been in the grip of a small élite. We must expand and offer more choice.

319

Man	Good heavens, you've remembered it word for word.
Stephen	Well, it was masterly stuff . . . oh my God, your cutlery . . . a silver knife and fork, I can't believe it. *(Removes cutlery)*
Man	Those are rather nice. They're not dirty are they?
Stephen	That this should happen to you of all people. I'm so sorry, I'll be right back.
Man	But they were fine . . .

(Cut back to Gordon and Stuart)

Girl 1	Of course, Moulinex. All the way through I was trying to think where I'd seen that actress before. She's the one in the Moulinex advert.
Stephen	Oh that's right, the one about the blender.
Hugh	What, the wife?
Girl 1	Sorry?
Hugh	The actress who plays the wife? She's in some sort of advert at the moment, is she? Hello! Laura, wake up! The actress in the play who was playing the wife that we just saw tonight – you're saying she's in an advert at the moment?
Girl 1	The wife . . .
Stephen	Actually she was playing his daughter.
Hugh	Hold on, I'm probably getting her confused with someone, wait a minute . . . *(Looks at programme)*
Girl 2	There was only one woman in the play, Stuart.
Girl 1	And she was his daughter, Poppet.
Stephen	That was sort of the idea of the entire evening.
Hugh	Yes, daughter. What did I say?
Stephen	You said wife.

320

Hugh	Did I? This table is definitely smaller you know ... I mean all those other ones ...
Stephen	Look, that man over there, he's in the government. Isn't he a cabinet minister or something?
Girl 1	Keith Bennett.
Hugh	Got it! Roy Hattersley, you're quite right, Gordon.
	(Stephen as waiter)
Stephen	I do apologise.
Man	Apologise for what? The fork and knife were fine.
Stephen	Oh it's very kind of you, sir, but I absolutely insist ...
	(Pours bag of plastic coffee stirrers into man's lap)
Man	What's this?
Stephen	Your cutlery, sir.
Man	But these are plastic coffee stirrers.
Stephen	Yes I know, but at least you've got the choice now. I mean they may be complete crap but you've got the choice ... that's what's important, the choice ... *(Starting to shout and to strangle man)*
	(Cut back to Gordon and Stuart)
Girl 2	That politician man's being strangled by a waiter.
Hugh	At least he's got a decent size table.
Stephen	Anyway to return to the play I have to say that although the acting was really good ...
Girl 1	Marvellous acting.
Stephen	I do think the play would've benefited from having a Paul Eddington in it.
Girl 2	*A* Paul Eddington?
Stephen	Well ideally, *the* Paul Eddington.

321

Girl 1	Isn't he wonderful?

Hugh   Well you see the thing about Paul Eddington of course is his timing.

Stephen   His timing is just so . . .

Hugh   Well it's the timing of a master.

Stephen   A friend of mine's sister married Paul Eddington's doctor.

Hugh   You never told me that, Gordon.

Stephen   Well, you know, one doesn't like to boast. Apparently it's well known that Paul Eddington has the second best timing in the business, after Nigel Havers.

Girl 2   What is timing, exactly?

Hugh   Well, it's a bit difficult to explain to a woman, Jill, but timing is basically the magic ingredient that Paul Eddington's got.

(Paul Eddington comes in)

Girl 1   What *is* it?

Paul Eddington
Yes, I'd like to know that too, I must say.

Stephen   I know your doctor's brother-in-law.

Paul Eddington
How nice.

Hugh   We were just explaining to our wives that you've got about the best timing in showbusiness.

Paul Eddington
After Nigel Havers.

Hugh   Level with us, Paul, would you class your timing as good, very good, extremely good or immaculate?

Paul   Well . . .

322

(Cut back to Hugh as the character with the bomb)

Hugh   Hello, look, excuse me everyone, sorry to bother you and all that sort of filth . . . nearly forgot, long live freedom . . . the thing is there's a bomb . . . yes I know, rotten isn't it . . . the thing is it *is* about to go off so you might like to leave.

(Everyone runs out)

That's right, this way. Crikey, my bill!

(Bomb explodes)

Cut to 'Where Eagles Dare'

VOX
POP

Stephen   It was just so funny. It was just so bloody funny. I literally died. It was bloody brilliant actually. No seriously, it was really funny, actually.

Where Eagles Dare

Hugh   You know that scene in *Where Eagles Dare?*

Stephen   Which scene?

Hugh   The one where Richard Burton is pretending to be a German agent.

Stephen   Oh yes.

Hugh   And in fact he's trying to find out the names of all the German agents in Britain. You know the one?

Stephen   Yes, yes. I remember it.

Hugh   Yes. That happened to me once.

Stephen   Did it, did it?

Hugh   Yes. In spades. In fact it's always happening to me. Lots of things from films happen to me.

Stephen   Is that right?

Hugh   You know that scene in *War Games* where the scientist calls the air-force general a pig-eyed sack of shit. Someone called me that the other day.

Stephen   The *other* day?

Hugh   Oh no, you're right. It was the same day. And *Fatal Attraction* could have been written about me. I almost sued when I saw it.

Stephen   You were persecuted by a one-night stand were you?

Hugh   No. No. I once went to bed with Glenn Close though.

Stephen   That's ridiculous.

Hugh   You're right, it's completely ridiculous. I went to bed with Michael Douglas.

324

Stephen	You went to bed with Michael Douglas.
Hugh	In a sense.
Stephen	What sense?
Hugh	A completely made-up untrue sense.
Stephen	Well as it happens, I've been to bed with Michael Douglas in that sense.
Hugh	Really?
Stephen	Well, snogged with him.
Hugh	How was it?
Stephen	I don't know. I made it up. But I'll tell you a really true thing that definitely happened to me, Kathleen Turner and Adrian Moorhouse. We were all lying in bed when . . .

Enter Paul Eddington very suddenly.

Paul	Immaculate, I'd say.

VOX
POP

Hugh   I had this idea for a television series, which I sent to Channel 4, in which every week people have to kill Noel Edmonds in a different way. But they said they were already working on something very similar.

Dammit Lavatories

Hugh is Peter, a lavatory attendant, inside a lavatory, making strange noises as he wrestles with some recalcitrant object or other.

Hugh   *(Off)* Come on. Come on . . . Gotcha.

Lavatory flush sound.

Stephen, as John, another attendant, crashes in and throws his coat onto a hook 'baa-ing'.

(Off) That you, John?

Stephen Who else, Peter?

Hugh   I was beginning to wonder where the hell . . .

Stephen Traffic, Peter, plain and simple.

Hugh   That's a bitch, John.

Stephen Took the switchback routes wherever I could, but the A47 is a car-park at the moment.

Hugh comes out of the stall carrying a plunger and wearing rubber gloves.

Hugh   Damn that ballcock.

Stephen It's no good blaming the cistern, Peter. So fill me in. How's business this a.m.?

Hugh   Quiet, John. Very quiet. Couple of noisy ones in stall three earlier on.

Stephen Really?

Hugh   Yeah, but mostly it's been quiet.

Stephen Right. Calls?

Hugh	Yeah, had one from the maintenance boys about fixing the towel rollers . . .
Stephen	And?
Hugh	Can't make it till next Tuesday.
Stephen	Dammit.
Hugh	That's what I said, John.
Stephen	Damn, blast, triple damn, with an extra side order of damn.
Hugh	Yup. I said that as well.
Stephen	How the hell do they expect us to run a public lavatory complex without maintenance back-up?
Hugh	Beats me, John. They said they'd give it top priority . . .
Stephen	Top priority my arse! *(Scrunches up a cup)* That's just a lot of hot air, Peter.
Hugh	I know John.
Stephen	Our clients can't dry their hands with hot air.
Hugh	Well actually . . .
Stephen	Peter, don't start on this electric hand-drier stuff again. I've read your report, and it's good work, but now is not the time.
Hugh	Not the time? I wonder if you'd have said that when we were running the health club?
Stephen	Forget the health club, Peter, God damn it! Marjorie won. Pure and simple. It wasn't a clean fight I grant you, but she won. That's it. Over.
Hugh	You don't have to throw Marjorie in my face, John.
Stephen	I'm sorry, Peter. But dammit we've got a chance here, a chance to build the finest damned personal relief centre Uttoxeter has ever known.

Hugh	But when, John? What's the timeframe?
Stephen	Hell, Peter, only a fool would try and answer that question. Six months, maybe.
Hugh	Every morning when I leave the house, Sarah kisses me on the cheek . . .
Stephen	Sarah? But your wife is Nancy?
Hugh	Sarah's the au pair, John. Helps out with a lot of Nancy's chores.
Stephen	Right.
Hugh	She kisses me and dammit if there aren't tears in her eyes.
Stephen	Peter, I know it's hard . . .
Hugh	Kids have a hard time at school. 'Haha, Sherman's dad is a lavatory attendant . . .'
Stephen	Don't ever say that, Peter. *(Scrunches up a cup)* The Peter I know is an equal partner in an enterprise that is going to alter the face of Uttoxeter's sanitation for ever.
Hugh	But the shame, Peter . . .
Stephen	Peter, you're doing this for Nancy and the kids. When you refill the soap dispensers, it's for them. When you pick the cigarette ends out of the urinal, it's for them. When you unclog a U-bend with your bare hands, you're doing it for them!
Hugh	Dammit, John, you're right.
Stephen	That's more like it. *(Scrunches a full cup. It hurts.)* Now let's get to it.
Hugh	Shoot.
Stephen	Paper in every stall?
Hugh	Check.

328

Stephen	Evacuation points cleaned?
Hugh	Check.
Stephen	Even under the rim?
Hugh	Even under the rim.
Stephen	Mirrors polished?
Hugh	Till you could see your face in them.
Stephen	Good work.
Hugh	Had to close the urinal momentarily for cleaning purposes. And when something like that happens, as you know, the weak go to the wall.
Stephen	Did you stop them?
Hugh	No trouble.

A drunk shuffles in coughing.

Good morning, sir.

Man coughs.

This your first visit to our facility?

Man coughs again.

If you require our full relief service, the cubicles are to your left, otherwise you will find the quick service stalls situated ahead of you.

Man lurches away and vomits into a corner.

Dammit!

Stephen	Dammit, Peter, we're still not attracting the right kind of customer.
Hugh	I know, John. But a lot of the more desirable punters are going next door.
Stephen	And why in *hell* aren't they coming here?
Hugh	Because they're women, John.

329

Stephen	Peter, I want you to get in next door, and find out who's running their operation.
Hugh	I already know who's running it, John. It was quite a shock, I can tell you.
Stephen	Don't say it, Peter. Don't tell me ...
Hugh	That's right. Marjorie.
Both	DAAAAMN!

A BIT OF
Fry & Laurie

To Bobby Robson

Thanks to Roger Ordish, for managing to produce the show in between episodes of 'Sir James Savile Will Bring His Influence to Bear in Arranging Matters to Your Satisfaction'; to Uri Geller for being so laughable; and to the waiter for finding Stephen's glasses.

Introduction

Stephen Well Hugh, here's the book.

Hugh Absolutely.

Stephen Well put. *(Slight pause)* So, any advice for someone who's just picked this book up, say, in one of the many fresh, clean High Street bookshops that stock this important new work and is considering, if not making a purchase, then at least slipping it down his or her trouser or trousers?

Hugh Well Stephen, I'd like firstly to congratulate the potential thief on his or her good taste or tastes, but I'd like to follow up that congratulation quite smartly with a caveat or warning.

Hugh breaks off and looks over Stephen's shoulder or shoulders. There is a longish pause.

Stephen Yes. I'm busy wondering what the nature of that caveat or warning might be, Hugh.

Hugh *(Jerking back)* I'm sorry, I thought I saw something dark, vivid and unpleasant.

Stephen It must have been your imagination.

Hugh Probably. No, the caveat, rejoinder, admonishment or warning I would make to the potential thief of this book is this. No matter who you are, no matter what your name is, no matter how far away you run, no matter how you try to disguise yourself with towels and the cunning application of coloured yoghurts, no matter what lengths you go to, no matter how well you protect yourself, we will seek you out and destroy you.

Stephen Eventually.

Hugh	We will destroy you eventually. And when we do . . .
Stephen	Well . . .
Hugh	Exactly.
Stephen	So. Just remember. You can run, but you can't hop.
Hugh	We'll be there. Across the street. In dark glasses.
Stephen	Arms folded.
Hugh	Watching.
Stephen	In silent reproach.
Hugh	So just you trot over to the desk and pay the nice lady cash money for this book.
Stephen	Apart from anything else, you'll find that if you don't none of the jokes will be at all funny.
Hugh	That's right. Every sketch will have a punchline limper than . . .
Stephen	Limper than . . .
Hugh	Limper than a very limp thing that's especially limp today.
Stephen	Exactly. But hey! That's the heavy part over with. Let's tell the average honest and surprisingly pretty punter a little about the genesis of this book, shall we Hugh?
Hugh	This book doesn't have a genesis, Stephen. You're thinking of the bible.
Stephen	Ha, what a very nearly laughable misunderstanding, Hugh. I meant 'genesis' in the sense of 'beginning or inception'.
Hugh	*(Wiping his eyes with laughter)* Oh! I see! And *I* thought . . .
Stephen	*(Falling about)* Dear oh dear.

336

They pick themselves up off the floor at length.

No, this book came about as a result, didn't
it Hugh, of enormous commercial pressure to
make the written texts of *A Bit of Fry And Laurie*
available to the public at large.

Hugh   When you say 'enormous commercial pressure' you
mean . . . ?

Stephen I mean some drunken overpaid publishing
executive thought it might be a good way of
staving off their eventual dismissal.

Hugh   Right.

Stephen We wrote these sketches over a period of . . .
what, Hugh?

Hugh   Over a period of time, if I remember rightly.

Stephen Over a period of months between June and
December 1987.

Hugh   When the world was young and everything seemed
slightly frilly.

Stephen Why did we write these sketches, you may ask?

Hugh   Well, let me turn that question round and say
'Why did we sketch these writes, you may ask?'

Stephen Let me turn *that* question round and say 'Why did
we write these sketches, you ask may?'

Hugh   Because they were there.

Stephen No, Hugh, because they *weren't* there. That's the
whole point. Amazingly, no-one had written those
sketches before.

Hugh   The Pythons had written something pretty similar
though hadn't they?

Stephen looks uncomfortable.

Stephen   *(Through clenched teeth)* Shut *up*, Hugh.

Hugh   Sorry.

Stephen   No, as we say these sketches are the original children of our minds.

Hugh   They're our babies.

Stephen   In a sense, yes. In a wholly unacceptable sense.

Hugh   Yes, because that's not to imply that we literally went to bed together, introduced various fleshy nozzles into each other's warm places and then gave birth to a pile of paper covered in amusing sketch material, is it Stephen?

Stephen   Hugh.

Hugh   Yes?

Stephen   Shut your bleeding neck for a moment will you?

Hugh   Right-o.

Stephen   These sketches are for your perusalment and enjoyage to do with what you will.

Hugh   Within certain rather exciting legal parameters.

Stephen   That's right. We ought to mention that you can't actually *perform* these sketches in public to a fee-paying audience.

Hugh   Though why anyone should want to perform these sketches in public beats me with a wet napkin.

Stephen   Oh I don't know Hugh.

Hugh   Don't you?

Stephen   No.

Hugh   Oh.

Stephen   Imagine your plane has been hijacked by a gang of terrorists and their leader, a rather desperate character called Miguel, threatens to shoot all

338

the passengers unless someone can perform the 'Haircut' sketch in the Club Class lavatory.

Hugh   Of course you're right. How silly of me.

Stephen   Well in those circumstances it would be quite illegal for you to accede to his wishes.

Hugh   Quite right. We do not deal with terrorists.

Stephen   All we can suggest is that you volunteer to write a sketch very similar to 'Haircut', and that you'll promise to have it finished and in rehearsal by the time you reach Libyan air space.

Hugh   Yes. Just remember that Miguel's bark is much worse that his bite.

Stephen   And he cannot bear split infinitives.

Hugh   So that's got that out of the way. Anything else that the discerning consumer need know in order to extract maximum reading pleasure from these pages, Stephen?

Stephen   Oh just the basics. Consult your GP, wipe down all surfaces with a damp dry cloth, and do not go to sleep with your head on a railway line.

Hugh   Sound advice. Although Stephen, isn't there one vital step you should take before consulting your GP?

Stephen   Absolutely, Hugh. Before consulting your GP, please please please consult your GP.

Hugh   For those of you reading in black and white, Stephen put a lot of emphasis on that third 'please'.

Stephen   Yes. Although I hope I didn't completely neglect the first two.

Hugh   Of course not.

Stephen   Once you've taken those basic, common sense measures, it's just a question of relaxing, kicking off your shoes, slipping into a loose-fitting kimono and going over to the cash desk to buy this book.

Hugh Although if you've read this far without buying it, we can only assume that it's raining pretty heavily outside.

Stephen Looks as if it's brightening a bit over there . . .

Hugh D'you know, you may be right . . .

Spies One

Hugh comes into the office. Stephen is sitting behind a desk.

Hugh   Hello, Control.

Stephen   Oh. Hello there, Murchison. How are you today?

Hugh   Very well indeed as a matter of fact, Control.

Stephen   That's good.

Hugh   Yes.

Faintly uncomfortable pause.

Stephen   So. Anyway. What can I 'do you for'?!

Hugh   Well. This just came through flash from Berlin, sir. I thought perhaps you might like to take a look at it.

Stephen   Flash from Berlin, eh? Well I better had. We've got quite a few valuable agents in Berlin, haven't we? It might be something quite urgent, I expect.

Hugh   Yes.

Stephen   *(Reading)* I see Valerie has decoded it for me. That's kind of her. Saves me quite a bit of extra work. I must remember to thank her.

Hugh   That would certainly be a nice gesture, sir.

Stephen   Well, much as I expected. I don't know if you had an opportunity to look through it, Tony, before thoughtfully bringing it into me, but it is quite an urgent message from Firefly, our network head in Berlin.

341

Hugh	Yes, I had time just to glance at the codename as I came in. Firefly is under deep cover. Has something quite important happened to make him break it like this?
Stephen	Well that was the first thought that crossed my mind, Tony, certainly. It looks as if his network has been penetrated by an enemy agent.
Hugh	Oh no.
Stephen	Yes, I'm afraid so. All his men have been arrested. Glow-worm was shot attempting to cross over into the west and Firefly himself is hiding up somewhere at a safehouse in the east.
Hugh	So the whole network has been blown?
Stephen	That's right. It's a thundering nuisance.
Hugh	It certainly is. Thundering.
Stephen	I'm severely vexed, I don't mind telling you.
Hugh	I expect a coffee would come in welcome then.
Stephen	Well it certainly couldn't hurt, could it?
Hugh	No. Not just one. I'll get Valerie onto it.
Stephen	Thank you so much, Tony.
Hugh	You're very welcome.

Makes to go. Turns from the door.

	Let's hope it's not going to turn out to be one of those days, eh, Control? Like Thursday.
Stephen	Oh! That's all we need! I don't know! See you later then, Tony.
Hugh	Alright.

Censored

Stephen   Ladies and gentlemen, we were going to do a sketch for you . . .

Hugh   But we're not now.

Stephen   No, we're not going to do it for you, now.

Hugh   Or ever.

Stephen   Or probably ever. Unless this country radically changes direction.

Hugh   Looks unlikely.

Stephen   Which does indeed look unlikely. The reason we're not going to do this sketch is that it contains a great deal of sex and violence.

Hugh   A great deal.

Stephen   Lots of sex and violence.

Hugh   That's right. During the sketch, Stephen hits me several times with a golf club.

Stephen   Which of course wouldn't matter except that I hit Hugh very sexily.

Hugh   That's the trouble, you see. He does do it so sexily. I wish you could see it.

Stephen   And then the sketch ends with us going to bed together . . .

Hugh   . . . violently.

Stephen   Extremely violently. Now this raises problems.

Hugh   Not for me.

Stephen   Me neither, but Sir William Rees-Mogg didn't like it a bit, did he?

Hugh   Well there was one bit he liked.

Stephen Yes that's true. He did like it one bit. But he didn't like it a lot of other bits.

Hugh   But I don't want you to think that Sir William's remit with the Broadcasting Standards Council is so sweeping as to be a kind of government thought police.

Stephen No. The concern is primarily for standards.

Hugh   Standards.

Stephen For the sake of our children.

Hugh   So, in a generous spirit of give and take, Sir William has taken our sketch.

Stephen And we've given it to him.

Hugh   And he has written one for us to do instead. Which is free of any gratuitous sex and violence.

Stephen And shows due and proper regard for decency and standards.

Hugh   Promoting family life and protecting our children.

Stephen Sir William has called his sketch simply 'Bitchmother, Come Light My Bottom'.

Hugh   And we're going to do it for you now.

Stephen 'Bitchmother, Come Light My Bottom', by Sir William Rees-Mogg.

VOX
POP

Stephen Oh yes, my wife wears the trousers. No question. But we're hoping to get a second pair some time next year.

344

Haircut

Stephen is dressed as, and therefore in dramatic terms is, a barber. Hugh enters the shop.

Stephen Good morning sir.

Hugh Morning.

Stephen Yes sir, I do believe we're in for a spell as they used to say in the music halls. Not too hot, but not too mild neither..

Hugh Mmm.

Stephen Re the weekend just past, might I enquire as to whether sir was in receipt of an enjoyableness, or did events prove themselves to be of an otherwise nature?

Hugh Very pleasant thank you.

Stephen Thank you sir. Very pleasant. Good. Then in presumption of sir's answer, I may take it that sir was for that period without the boundaries of Lincolnshire, wherein, I understand, it rained like a bitch.

Hugh No, I was nowhere near Lincolnshire.

Stephen Sir, I am uplifted to hear such news.

Hugh My wife and I spent the weekend in Hull.

Stephen Sir is married?

Hugh Yes.

Stephen I had literally no idea.

Hugh Well never mind . . .

Stephen Will sir at some future time, as yet unspecified,

345

forgive me for not having immediately
congratulated him on his joyousness in the good
tidings department?

Hugh   Of course. I didn't expect you . . .

Stephen Would sir perhaps consider it to be beyond-
boundingly forward of me, on behalf of all the
staff here, to send a bouquet of flower-style
objects to Mrs Sir?

Hugh   Well that's really not necessary.

Stephen Sir, since I began as a barber, not thirty-nine
years ago, the phrase 'not necessary' has been
neither more nor less than as a spur to quicken my
actions.

Hugh   Well thank you, that's very kind of you . . .

Stephen Alright sir. To business. Being one of the
shrewdest sirs it has been my privilege to meet,
you are no doubt keen to exploit the social and
financial advantages inherent in having a hair cut?

Hugh   A haircut, that's right.

Stephen Of course. A hair cut is a hair enhanced if sir will
fail to slash my throatlet for being so old. Now the
hair in question is . . . ?

Hugh   What?

Stephen The hair presently under advisement belongs
to . . . ?

Hugh   What do you mean?

Stephen What do I mean?

Hugh   Yes.

Stephen Haha. I sneak myself towards the suspicion that
sir has cast me as the mouse in his ever popular
cat drama.

346

Hugh	What are you talking about? It's my hair. I want you to cut my hair.
Stephen	Ah. So sir's own hair is the hair upon which this entire transaction is to be founded?
Hugh	Well of course. Why would I come in here to get someone else's hair cut?
Stephen	Sir. Please set fire to my legs if I am trying to make haircutting seem more glamorous than it really is, but may I just say this – you cannot be too careful in my position.
Hugh	Really?
Stephen	Indeed sir. Once and only once, I cut a gentleman's hair against his will. Believe me when I say it was both difficult *and* impossible.
Hugh	No, well it's my hair I want cut.
Stephen	Your hair.
Hugh	Yes.
Stephen	The hair of sir.
Hugh	Yes.
Stephen	Excellent. Then let us proceed to the next and most important of stages. Which one?
Hugh	Which one what?
Stephen	Which of sir's manifold hairs would he care to place in my professional care for the purposes of securing an encutment?
Hugh	Well all of them.
Stephen	All of sir's hairs?
Hugh	Yes.
Stephen	Sir is absolutely sure?
Hugh	Of course I'm sure. What's the matter with you?

347

Stephen	I seek not to question the drasticity of sir's decision, only to express the profoundness of my humblings at the prospect of such a magnificent task.
Hugh	Well, all of them.
Stephen	All of them. My word.
Hugh	Is that a problem?
Stephen	By no means. I merely hope that sir can find a moment in his otherwise hectic schedule to appreciate that for me to cut every one of sir's hairs represents the snow-capped summit of a barber's career.
Hugh	Well you've done it before, haven't you?
Stephen	Indeed, sir. I once cut all the hairs on a gentleman's head in Cairo, shortly after the War, when the world was in uproar and to a young man everything seemed possible.
Hugh	Once?
Stephen	It would be pointless for me to deny that I was fitter and better-looking then, but let us hope for sir's sake, that the magic has not entirely disappeared up its own rabbit hole. We shall see.
Hugh	Wait a minute. Wait just one cotton-picking minute here.
Stephen	Sir?
Hugh	You've cut someone's hair, all of it that is, once since the war?
Stephen	Would sir have preferred that in the sphere of total hair cuttation, I was to him a virgin?
Hugh	I beg your pardon?
Stephen	That I can respect.

348

Hugh	What?
Stephen	The desire that we should both of us embark upon this voyage as innocents, wide-eyed travellers in a foreign land, unknowing of our destination, careless of our fate – to emerge somewhere, some day, bruised, tender, a little sad perhaps, but ultimately and joyously alive.
Hugh	Goodbye.
Stephen	Sir is leaving?
Hugh	Yup.
Stephen	Might I be favoured with an explanation as to why?
Hugh	Because I don't believe you have the faintest idea as to how you're going to end this sketch, and I simply don't want to be around when you try. It's going to be painful and embarrassing for both of us, and to be honest I'd much rather it was only painful and embarrassing for you.
Stephen	But sir!
Hugh	What?
Stephen	Sir could not be more mistaken if he tried. I know precisely how this sketch is going to end.
Hugh	Really?
Stephen	Really.
Hugh	Go on then.
Stephen	It might take time.
Hugh	Yes, time and pain and embarrassment. Goodbye.
Stephen	You bastard.
Hugh	Here we go.
Stephen	The number of times I've hung around while you've stumbled on to some pathetic ending.

349

Hugh	You see? You're completely stuck.
Stephen	No I'm not.
Hugh	Ha.
Stephen	Forty-five seconds. I can end this sketch in forty-five seconds.
Hugh	Yeah?
Stephen	Yeah.
Hugh	OK. Forty-five seconds.
Stephen	If sir will resume the seatedness of his posture.
Hugh	Alright.
Stephen	Can I assume that sir is close to the level of maximum comfort?
Hugh	Forty seconds.
Stephen	I will now fetch the necessary tools.

Stephen exits.

| Hugh | Haha. It's going to be a chainsaw or some bloody . . . tscch. |

Hugh looks at his watch. Stephen does not re-enter.

Long pause. Hugh realises he has been left holding the baby.

Fuck.

Spoonbending with Mr Nude

Hugh and Stephen are sitting in a TV studio. There is a table lamp. Hugh has an annoying accent.

Stephen   Now, Mr Nude, you claim . . .

Hugh   That's right, I do claim, I do . . .

Stephen   Yes, you claim to be able to bend spoons with psychic energy . . .

Hugh   Psychic energy, yes, that is the method I have chosen, to bend spoons, yes.

Stephen   How long have you had this ability?

Hugh   How long, precisely, that's absolutely right.

Stephen   Well?

Hugh   Indeed, you are very sympathetic, thank you. It's very difficult when people are not sympathetic, but you are very sympathetic.

Stephen   Thank you.

Hugh   No, thank *you.*

Stephen   Can you do other things with spoons, apart from bend them?

Hugh   Yes of course I can. I can do anything with a spoon.

Stephen   Can you?

Hugh   Indeed I can. Give me a spoon, and I will give you the world.

Stephen   Well that's an impressive claim, certainly.

Hugh   Thank you.

Stephen	That's alright. Well Mr Nude, we have some spoons here. Perhaps you'd care to give us a demonstration?
Hugh	I am not a circus freak, you know.
Stephen	I realise that.
Hugh	Some people think I am a freak. I am not a freak.
Stephen	Well I'm sure that nobody here . . .
Hugh	'Freak!' They sometimes shout at me in the street.
Stephen	Do they really? That's awful.
Hugh	But you are very sympathetic.
Stephen	Thank you.
Hugh	Thank you.
Stephen	Would you care to have a go at bending this spoon for us?
Hugh	Thank you, yes I will bend this spoon.
Stephen	Ladies and gentlemen, Mr Nude is now going to bend this spoon using psychic energy.
Hugh	That's right, now is when I'm going to bend it.
Stephen	Go ahead, Mr Nude.

Hugh quite plainly bends the spoon with his hands.

Hugh	Thank you very much, you are all very sympathetic.
Stephen	Well the spoon is certainly bent.
Hugh	Of course it is bent. Of course it is. I bent the spoon, so, of course it is bent.
Stephen	Yes, that much is clear and without argument.
Hugh	Forgive me, I am very tired now. To bend a

352

spoon is very tiring, and I have bent too many spoons today.

Stephen   How many spoons have you bent today?

Hugh   Four spoons today. It is too much. I am not a freak, you know. I am a human being.

Stephen   Forgive me, Mr Nude . . .

Hugh   Of course.

Stephen   Thank you.

Hugh   Thank you.

Stephen   But from where I was sitting, it looked rather as if you just bent the spoon with your hands.

Hugh   What are you saying?

Stephen   I'm saying that . . .

Hugh   What is this?

Stephen   It's a bent spoon.

Hugh   There.

Stephen   Oh quite, the question is how did you bend it?

Hugh   I don't know how much I like you now.

Stephen   Well, I'm sorry.

Hugh   Before I thought you were very sympathetic . . .

Stephen   Well I hope that . . .

Hugh   But now, I think you are not so sympathetic. Now, I don't like you.

Stephen   I'm sorry to hear that.

Hugh   At all.

Stephen   Are you sure it isn't 'fraud' that people shout at you in the street, rather than 'freak'?

Hugh   It is you who make the claims. I have always been

353

honest. I bend the spoons with psychic energy, I have told you. I never claimed to be able to bend them with my hands. That is your claim.

Stephen And you did bend it with your hands.

Hugh The spoon is bent, that is enough. Perhaps it does flow through my hands this psychic energy of which you claim. It may be. Certainly the spoon is bent. Therefore I bent it.

Stephen I can bend a spoon with my hands too.

Hugh I have never said that my powers are unique. Always I have striven to teach the world that anyone may bend a spoon. My book is not expensive.

Stephen bends a spoon.

Stephen There.

Hugh To think I found you sympathetic. I hate you now.

Stephen Well next week I shall be examining the claims of a man who says that in a previous existence he was Education Secretary Kenneth Baker and I shall be talking to a woman who claims she can make flowers grow just by planting seeds in soil and watering them. Until then, wait very quietly in your seats please. Goodnight.

Hugh *(Simultaneously)* If viewers living in the Matlock and Buxton areas of Derbyshire would be so kind as to inspect their cutlery drawers at home they will find that they contain a bent spoon and an unused Weetabix special offer coupon. I can also reveal that everyone in the town of Datchett over the age of fourteen has a slight itch just above the right thigh which they are scratching as I speak. Thank you.

354

Critics One

Stephen and Hugh are sitting in swivel chairs, with haircuts. They look and sound nearly as revoltingly smug, smarmy and unpleasant as real critics.

Hugh   Simon Clituris, you watched that sketch ... I assume you were disappointed?

Stephen   Well frankly, I thought it was predictable.

Hugh   You predicted it, did you?

Stephen   Absolutely, and I think that's why it was predictable. Their choice of targets was predictable ...

Hugh   Estate agents ...

Stephen   Where?

Hugh   The target of that last sketch was estate agents.

Stephen   I didn't notice that.

Hugh   And of course their choice of language was predictable ...

Stephen   Precisely. English was a sadly predictable language for them to have chosen.

Hugh   Which is a shame.

Stephen   A great shame. If you don't speak it.

Hugh   A bigger shame if you do.

Stephen   Hahaha.

Hugh   Hahahaha.

Stephen   But I suppose one could have predicted it.

Hugh   I suppose so. Can you predict what their next
          sketch will be?

Stephen Oh lord, yes. A parody of 'Treasure Island'.
          Bound to be.

*Cut to something that is as far from being a parody of
Treasure Island as is emotionally possible.*

VOX
POP

Hugh I can remember exactly what I was
        doing when I heard the news. I
        was listening to the news.

Troubleshooters

Stephen and Hugh are being dramatic businessmen.

Hugh	Calm down John, we're not going to get anywhere . . .
Stephen	Don't tell me to calm down. Dammit Peter, I want answers, and I want them fast.
Hugh	Answers? A bit late for all that, don't you think? *(Drinks)*
Stephen	What the hell's happened to you, Peter? You know as well as I do, there's no such word as 'a bit late for all that'.
Hugh	Agreed.
Stephen	So shoot. What've we got?
Hugh	Marjorie wants control of Derwent Enterprises, and from where I'm sitting, she's going to get it.
Stephen	Marjorie? Jesus, Peter, Marjorie's just a kid.
Hugh	Tell that to the board.
Stephen	Watch me. I might just do that. *(Drinks)*
Hugh	Good luck to you.
Stephen	Meaning?
Hugh	They'll laugh in your face, John. Like they did me. Marjorie's got them eating out of her hand.
Stephen	Alright. Then I'll go to old man Derwent himself.
Hugh	Come off it John. No one's even spoken to old man Derwent in years. The man's a recluse. It's hopeless I tell you. Marjorie's won. And she hasn't even fired a shot. *(Drinks)*

Stephen Listen to me, Peter. Marjorie may have won the war, but she hasn't won the battle.

Hugh Dammit John, you're up to something. I've seen that look before.

Stephen You're damn right I'm up to something.

Hugh Dammit.

Stephen What?

Hugh What are you up to?

Stephen Something. I'm up to something.

Hugh I thought so.

Stephen I want you on my team for this, Peter.

Hugh Dammit John, I'm yours, you know that.

Stephen I haven't finished. It's absolutely mandatory that you buy into my way of working. Things could get a little hairy during the next forty-eight. *(Drinks)*

Hugh You know me, John. Hairy is as hairy does.

Stephen Good to hear. Call O'Neill for me, will you? Get him to postpone the meeting.

Hugh What shall I tell him? *(Drinks)*

Stephen *(Shouting)* Tell him any damn thing you like – just buy me some time!

Hugh Dammit John, it's good to have you back.

Stephen You'd better save the pretty speeches for later, Peter, we've a long night ahead of us. *(Drinks)*

Hugh Just like old times, eh, John?

Stephen Sure, Peter, sure.

Hugh *(Dialling)* You know it's funny. I drove through High Wycombe just the other day . . . *(into phone)* Hello? Peter here. Get me O'Neill.

358

Stephen	And fast.
Hugh	And fast. *(pause)* Say again? Dammit.
Stephen	What?
Hugh	O'Neill's out of town and can't be reached.
Stephen	Dammit to hell and back.
Hugh	Right. Damn blast and double damn.
Stephen	Damn.
Hugh	Want me to try Amsterdam?
Stephen	No.
Hugh	But . . .
Stephen	Come on Peter, you're not thinking straight. Amsterdam's too obvious. Marjorie was never obvious. That's why I loved her.
Hugh	*(Drinks)* By God here's a turn-up. I never thought I'd hear an old warhorse like you talk about love.
Stephen	Love's nothing to be afraid of, Peter. You don't need a Harvard MBA to know that the bedroom and the boardroom are just two sides of the same ballgame. I wonder –
Hugh	Try me. Shoot.
Stephen	Put it together. A block of part-paid ordinaries funnelled through Geneva. A carefully staged release of IDL preference stock through the back door underpinned by a notional rights issue. Who'll be wincing then? *(Drinks)*
Hugh	Dammit John, it's starting to add up. Want me to try Sydney?
Stephen	Come on Peter, stay awake. He'll be in Australia by now.
Hugh	Dammit sideways. Wait a minute. Will they trace it back to us?

359

Stephen	A ploy like that? It'll have Seagrove's handwriting all over it, John.
Hugh	And back again. But that still leaves us with Marjorie.
Stephen	Dammit.
Hugh	*(Whispered mysteriously)* What's she *after*?
Stephen	No point in asking that, Peter. I gave up trying to understand Marjorie a long time ago.
Hugh	Yeah. Women.
Stephen	Marjorie isn't women, Peter.
Hugh	No, of course not, John. Forgive me. I meant no offence.
Stephen	Something I've always wondered. How did you keep Nancy so long?
Hugh	I've never been Nancy, John.
Stephen	No, your wife.
Hugh	Oh Nancy. You know. Rough with the smooth. You work at it. Do your best. Never enough time. Keep on grafting, long hours, you think you know but of course you don't, cover all the angles, they talk about stress, I tell them I'm married to it.
Stephen	Am I right in thinking that you have a daughter?
Hugh	Yup. Henrietta.
Stephen	Did he? Did he really? That must have hurt. Hurt like hell on a jetski.
Hugh	You never had kids of your own, I believe?
Stephen	You're wrong, Peter. You're so wrong.
Hugh	Oh, I beg your pardon.
Stephen	We're sitting in my children at this moment.

360

Hugh	I may have misheard that, John.
Stephen	The company, Peter.
Hugh	Oh right.
Stephen	I gave everything to this company. *(Suddenly shouting)* Dammit New York should have rung by now!
Hugh	Relax, John. It's still early.
Stephen	I know, Peter. But it's not going to stay early for long.

Stephen goes to the window.

Hugh	New York'll come through, John. I know they will.
Stephen	*(Looking out of the window)* I hope so. There are six million people out there, Peter.
Hugh	Really? What do they want?
Stephen	Who knows? Peter?
Hugh	Yeah.
Stephen	I say we go with it.
Hugh	Agreed.
Stephen	If New York rings, we give them affirmative.
Hugh	I'll tell Susan.
Stephen	Now let's get the hell out of here.
Hugh	Sure?
Stephen	Yeah. I don't think even we two can sustain this level of high intensity work without coming down for a space.
Hugh	Dammit you're right.
Stephen	Besides, I could use a drink.

361

Gordon and Stuart eat Greek

Stephen (Gordon) and Hugh (Stuart) are sitting at a table in a Greek restaurant. Music plays in the background.

Hugh   Yeah, I like to eat Greek at least once in a time, Gordon. It's a plain cuisine, simply prepared.

Stephen   Yeah, well I'm not averse myself, Stuart.

Hugh   No?

Stephen   Substantially partial to a plate of Greek, as it happens. Substantially partial.

Hugh   Good. *(Indicating menu)* We won't worry about this. I'll chat to the top over-waiter personally. This is just for the walk-in punters.

Stephen   Right you be.

Hugh   Listen to that bazooka music, Gordon. East meets West.

Stephen   Love it.

Hugh   There's a lot to be learned from the Greeks, you know. After all, they gave us the word 'civilization'.

Stephen   I thought that was the Romans.

Hugh   Ethnically the same peoples, Gordon. Also the word 'economics'. Sharp folk, your Greeks. Very sharp.

Stephen   And the word 'genoymeen'.

Hugh   What?

Stephen   They gave us that as well. I suppose we must have just given it back, almost immediately.

362

Hugh	Tough folk, your Hellenics. Hard as the crags and boulders that shape the islands and hills of their landscape.
Stephen	Tssch. Do you know I wouldn't be surprised if there was a lesson in there somewhere?
Hugh	Certainly there is. I've often thought of putting out a paper on the correlation between landscape and business acumen.
Stephen	Great subject, Stu. You could set fire to some arses with a paper like that. The Institute of Executive Salesmen would go ape crazy on all fours for a theory of that sort.
Hugh	I think so, Gordon. I think so. Take my own case. Myself, way back when, my folks hailed from Yorkshire. You see? Limestone uplands, unforgiving moors and scarred dales. An uncompromising, beautiful, hard and wide nurse of men.
Stephen	But you were born in Surrey.
Hugh	The limestone's in my blood. You can see it in the way I do business. Where you from first off, Gordon?
Stephen	Lincolnshire.
Hugh	Huh. You see? Flat, sodden, yielding, chalky, cautious, indecisive, always late for meetings . . .
Stephen	Well Lincolnshire's flat, Stu, yes. But I wouldn't say it was always late for meetings . . .
Hugh	*(Ignoring him)* Yeah, maybe I'll put that paper out after all. Maybe I'll do that.
Stephen	Service is a bit slow.
Hugh	You see, that's the typical lowlander's reaction. That's got Lincolnshire written all over it. You've

got to understand that the Greek does things at his own tempo, Gordon. Natural rhythms and cycles, deep within them. The Yorkshireman in me respects that.

Stephen   Well we don't want to be late for the basketball game, Stuart.

Hugh   *(Shouting)* Service here! Let's get some action at this table!

Waiter arrives. A cheery Greek figure.

Waiter   Good afternoon, my lovely friends.

Hugh   OK, *kalli spera.*

Waiter   Ah. Is lunchtime. You mean *kalli mera.*

Hugh   Well yes, in some dialects, obviously. Now . . .

Waiter   *To piato tees meras chtopothi.*

Hugh   Good, good. So . . .

Stephen   The dish of the day is octopus.

Hugh   I know that, Gordon. Well aware. Where was the octopus caught?

Waiter   Where was it caught? What a question. In the sea.

Hugh   Right. It should be OK then Gordon, if you want to have that.

Waiter   So . . . ?

Stephen   Well *thelo parakalo dolmades kai filetto souvlaki kai nero pagomeno kai ena boukali retsina.*

Waiter   *Entaxi. Kai ya sas, kyrie?*

Hugh   What?

Stephen   What would you like, Stuart?

Hugh   The same. Definitely. The er . . . *parakalo.*

364

Stephen	Δυο
Waiter	Certainly, gentlemen.

Waiter exits.

Hugh	And we'd better order up some wine while we're at it.
Stephen	I did that, Stuart.
Hugh	Oh, of course you did, yeah. I was miles away.
Stephen	He's a bit forward isn't he? All that 'lovely friends' stuff.
Hugh	Well what he's done, Gordon, is recognise a kindred spirit. He's spotted the craggy moorlander in me and he knows that he and I have been nourished by essentially the same granite. Ergo, we're clients to be treated with respect, not your usual walk-in, quick turnover merchants.

Waiter enters, with plates.

Waiter	*Dolmades* for my two beautiful English gentlemen, I think.
Hugh	Great.
Stephen	Looks good.
Waiter	Is very good, my special friends.

Waiter exits.

Stephen	*(Tucking in)* Ha.
Hugh	What is this?
Stephen	Well it's *dolmades*.
Hugh	*Dolmades?*
Stephen	Stuffed vine leaves.

Hugh	Stuffed vine leaves? Is he trying to take us for a ride?
Stephen	It's a classic Greek dish.
Hugh	Classic Greek ... What am I, a peasant or a busy executive?

Waiter enters.

Waiter	Everything alright, my absolute darlings?
Hugh	Fine thank you.
Stephen	My colleague doesn't like *dolmades*.
Waiter	But you ask for *dolmades*.
Stephen	He didn't know what it was.
Hugh	I knew what ... hahahaha. Everything's just fine, thank you.

Waiter exits.

Let's get out of here, Gordon. This is just a tourist trap.

Stephen	In Stevenage?
Hugh	Why not?
Stephen	But this is good, Stuart.
Hugh	Wake up, Gordon, wake up! Jesus, they must have seen you coming a mile off.
Stephen	Don't you want your *dolmades?*
Hugh	Do I want to push a stuffed vine leaf through my face? No, incredibly, I don't.
Stephen	Well I'm starving, so if it's all the same with you ...
Hugh	*(He drinks some wine)* Oh that's it. This wine is corked.

Stephen	It can't be. It's got a metal top.
Hugh	Don't get clever. Just taste it. *(Banging table)* Waiter!
Stephen	Delicious.
Hugh	Delicious? It's got something in it.

Waiter enters.

Waiter	Yes, my excellent friends?
Stephen	*(To Hugh)* It's resinated.
Hugh	Exactly. Waiter, this wine has resinated in the bottle.
Waiter	Yes. Is retsina.
Stephen	It's supposed to be like that, Stu. They add pine needle resin to it . . .
Hugh	Yeah, thanks very much for your input Gordon, but I hope I know my wines. I didn't fork out on an encyclopaedia of world wines for nothing.
Waiter	Retsina. Is very good.
Stephen	It's delicious, Stu.
Hugh	*(Pause)* Well I hope you're going to invite me to the wedding.
Stephen	What?
Waiter	Give me a pardon?
Hugh	You two are getting married, presumably?
Stephen	Stuart . . .
Hugh	No, obviously a six-year friendship goes out the window if you're going to start siding with some Greeko against me.
Waiter	I think maybe everything is not so good for my two lovers.

Hugh   *(To waiter)* You can cut that out right now.

Stephen   Listen Stu . . .

Hugh   No you listen, mush. While you were marking time with linguaphone courses of the ancient world, I was pounding the streets of Tiverton learning the selling trade.

Stephen   Stu . . .

Hugh   While you tanned your hairy arse on the nude beaches of Crete or wherever it was, stuffing vine leaves with a bunch of perverts, I was getting my masters degree in the university of hard knocks and tough surprises. Well mister – I make no apology. To you or your fancy lover boy. *(He makes for the exit)*

Stephen   Stu! Where are you going?

Waiter   I can bring you an omelette, if you like, sir.

Hugh   Forget it. I've had enough, Gordon. I'm going out for an honest British kebab.

VOX
POP

Stephen   What I always say to myself is, 'what would Lester Piggott have done in this situation?'

368

SAS

Stephen is in an SAS uniform, behind the desk of an Army Careers office.

Stephen So you'd like to join the Special Air Service?

Hugh Not really.

Stephen Not really?

Hugh Well, yes alright.

Stephen That's more like it. Height?

Hugh I'm sorry?

Stephen How tall are you?

Hugh Oh. Nine foot six.

Stephen Nine foot six. Good. Weight?

Silence.

Weight?

Silence.

Well?

Hugh I'm waiting.

Stephen Good. You'd be surprised how many applicants are trapped into revealing how heavy they are. And you weigh?

Hugh Three tons.

Stephen Three tons. Sure about that?

Hugh Just over.

369

Stephen	Alright. Just over three tons. It's as well to be accurate in these matters. Saves complications later on. So. Any particular disabilities?
Hugh	I've got no sense of taste.
Stephen	In what? Films? Music?
Hugh	Food. I can't taste food.
Stephen	Oh dear. That might be a problem.
Hugh	Might that be a problem?
Stephen	I've just said it might. Never mind, let's press on. Any special skills?
Hugh	I look good in black.
Stephen	Excellent. How old are you?
Hugh	Ten and a half.
Stephen	Shoe size?
Hugh	Twenty-eight.
Stephen	Quirks?
Hugh	Muddling up my height and my shoe size. I mean my shoe size and my height. See? I did it again.
Stephen	Well that seems to be OK. How are you at making small talk?
Hugh	Weather and traffic?
Stephen	That sort of thing.
Hugh	I can hold my end up.
Stephen	Correct. Now, are you aware of what the SAS is all about?
Hugh	Not really.
Stephen	I see. Well originally, the SAS was formed as an élite, crack, secret, crack secret assault force, to work behind enemy lines during the war.

370

Hugh	Right.
Stephen	Of course our role has changed somewhat since then. Nowadays our duties are to act primarily as a masturbatory aid for Lewis Collins and various back-bench MPs.
Hugh	I beg your pardon?
Stephen	I'm afraid so. A worrying number of today's parliamentarians are quite unable to achieve sexual gratification without fantasizing about the SAS. So basically, we have to go round the place being secret and crack and élite, so that these people will be able to keep their marriages intact.
Hugh	Doesn't sound very exciting. Have you got anything else on your cards?
Stephen	Well, the BBC are advertising for someone to go into that room over there.
Hugh	Which one?
Stephen	*(Pointing)* That one, just over there.
Hugh	Alright. I'll give it a go.

Hugh enters room for next sketch.

VOX
POP

Hugh   It's very hard to undo it, though.
So you have to be absolutely sure.

Operations

Stephen and Hugh are sitting on stools.

Stephen   So, Hugh, I believe you've found something of interest in one of your magazines.

Hugh   That's right, Stephen. It's a brochure for the Collingwood Hospital.

Stephen   That's a private hospital, isn't it, Hugh?

Hugh   That's right, Stephen. Important point.

Stephen   And it's in London, England, if I remember serves me correctly.

Hugh   That's precisely where it is, Stephen, yes. What excited me, however, as I was looking through this brochure was not where the hospital is, but the services it offers.

Stephen   Medical services, I presume.

Hugh   They do limit themselves by and large to the provision of medical services, Stephen, yes. I dare say they're keen to consolidate in that area before moving out into other leisure activities.

Stephen   That must be sound business practice, in anyone's book?

Hugh   That's right. But anyway, this brochure . . .

Stephen   Ha. I'd almost forgotten.

Hugh   Well that would have been a shame, Stephen, because this brochure contains a full list of the Collingwood Hospital services, and it includes a complete section on the kinds of operations you can have, it you're ever down that way.

372

Stephen	Would you care to read some of them out, Hugh?
Hugh	Of course, Stephen. Just glancing down the page, I find everything from appendectomy to bone marrow replacement, from organ transplants to heart surgery.
Stephen	So, no shortage of choice then, Hugh?
Hugh	That's right. There's something there for everyone. It really is a mouthwatering selection.
Stephen	When are they open?
Hugh	Well this is one of the great things about the Collingwood. They're open twenty-four hours a day.
Stephen	Weekends?
Hugh	Weekends and Bank Holidays.
Stephen	So the Collingwood Hospital might be a good place to take the family?
Hugh	Absolutely, Stephen. There are plenty of operations that are specially tailored for children. For example, having their legs straightened. Mums everywhere I'm sure would love to go for one of their hip replacements, and for Dad . . . well how about some of that heart surgery we mentioned earlier?
Stephen	That sounds like a heck of a weekend. But Hugh?
Hugh	Yes?
Stephen	We haven't mentioned prices.
Hugh	Of course. Prices vary, Stephen, according to the operation you choose . . .
Stephen	I'd imagine they would.
Hugh	Well they do. Basically they start at around four thousand pounds for a tonsilectomy . . .

373

Stephen   Right.

Hugh   . . . and can go up to as much as sixty thousand for an eight hour operation on the brain.

Stephen   So really, whatever your financial status, there's something at the Collingwood Hospital for you.

Hugh   That's right. There is one proviso I'd add to that.

Stephen   Oh?

Hugh   You should have quite a lot of money.

Stephen   Good point. Whatever your financial status, as long as you've got a lot of money.

Hugh   That's it.

Stephen   And if you haven't? Or if you want to save money?

Hugh   Well, my advice would always be . . . get yourself a stout pair of walking shoes and get out into the beautiful countryside.

Stephen   Thanks, Hugh. Plenty of choices there.

VOX
POP

Hugh   I killed her because she said she wanted to marry Noël Edmonds. Until then, she really had been a model daughter.

Sound Name

Stephen is a police sergeant, writing down the
particulars of an arrest at the station counter. Hugh is
on the other side, looking sheepish.

Stephen   And the vehicle belongs to you, does it sir?

Hugh   Yes.

Stephen   And your name is?

Hugh   Right. Hold on a second. *(Hugh gets a lighter out of his pocket)* Ready?

Stephen   Yes.

Hugh   My name is Derek . . . *(Hugh drops the lighter onto the counter)*

Stephen   What are you doing?

Hugh   That's my name.

Stephen   What is?

Hugh   This. Derek . . . *(Hugh drops the lighter again)*

Stephen   That's your name?

Hugh   Yes.

Stephen   What? Derek *(Stephen drops the lighter)* . . . is your name?

Hugh   Yes.

Stephen   What kind of name is that?

Hugh   Well it's my name.

Stephen   Unusual, isn't it, Mr . . . *(Drops lighter)*?

375

Hugh	If I had a pound for every time someone's said that . . .
Stephen	And how do you spell . . . *(Drops lighter)*, Mr . . . *(Drops lighter)*?
Hugh	It's as it sounds.
Stephen	Uhuh. Yeah but I wonder if you'd mind actually spelling it for me, would you?
Hugh	Well I mean, can't you just . . .
Stephen	I'd be very grateful. If you wouldn't mind.
Hugh	N–I–P–P–L hyphen E.
Stephen	Nipple.
Hugh	I beg your pardon?
Stephen	Nipple.
Hugh	Nipple? Where? What are you talking about?
Stephen	N–I–P–P–L–E . . .
Hugh	Hyphen E.
Stephen	Hyphen E . . . spells Nipple. In my book. It does not spell . . . *(Drops lighter)*.
Hugh	Have you gone mad? What's the matter with you? I thought the modern policeman was supposed to be a highly trained law enforcement unit. You can't even spell.
Stephen	Alright, Mr Nipple, address?

Hugh looks around.

What's your address?

Hugh	Are you talking to me?
Stephen	Yes.
Hugh	You want to know my address?

Stephen	Please.
Hugh	Or do you want to know Mr Nipple's address, whoever he is?
Stephen	Your address please, sir.
Hugh	Alright. My address is Number twenty-two . . . *(Hugh tapdances, slaps Stephen)* . . . Kings Lynn.
Stephen	Now watch it.
Hugh	What?
Stephen	Just watch it.
Hugh	Watch what, for heaven's sake?
Stephen	You do realise, do you, that assaulting a police officer is an extremely serious offence?
Hugh	Yes, I imagine it probably is. Very serious. But telling a police officer your address, on the other hand, is probably not very serious, is it? Or is it? Perhaps the law's changed since I last looked. Perhaps the Home Secretary has had to take stern measures against the rising tide of people giving their address to policemen whenever they're asked to.
Stephen	Alright. Alright. My fault. Ask a stupid person and you get a stupid answer.
Hugh	I beg your pardon?
Stephen	So, can I just check this with you, Mr . . . *(Drops lighter)* . . . ?
Hugh	What?
Stephen	Just to make sure I've got this right. Your address is . . . number twenty-two . . . *(Tapdances, punches Hugh)* . . . Kings Lynn?
Hugh	No, no, no! What's the matter with you? Are you deaf? It's . . . *(Tapdances, slaps Stephen)* . . . Kings Lynn.

377

Stephen   Oh I'm sorry. I thought you said ... *(Tapdances, punches Hugh)* ... Kings Lynn.

Hugh   Well I didn't.

Stephen   My apologies sir. I can't read my own writing.

Hugh   Well get a typewriter.

Stephen   If only we could afford it. Actually, at some angles, this almost looks like ... twenty-two ... *(Tapdances, hits Hugh with a cricket bat)* ... Kings Lynn.

Hugh   That was too hard.

Stephen   Oh I'm sorry sir. You're right. We really should get a typewriter.

Hugh   That was too hard.

Stephen   Well sir, you must admit that it's an unusual address for anyone to get the hang of ...

Hugh   Never mind the fucking sketch! That was too hard. That really hurt.

Stephen   Oh diddums. Did the nasty actor hit the poor little twerp ...

Hugh   Fuck off.

Hugh exits.

Stephen   *(To camera)* He's just a child really.

VOX
POP

Stephen   Until you've been there, you don't really have any idea what it's like – I shouldn't think. I'm not sure, I've never been there.

Spies Two

Stephen is sitting at his desk in the spies' office. Hugh enters carrying a cup of coffee. He puts it down on Stephen's desk.

Stephen Hello, Murchison. Nice to see you.

Hugh Whoops! You gave me rather a fright, Control. Sorry – I nearly upset your coffee there.

Stephen No harm done, I can easily mop up that very small drop and it was very kind of you to bring me some at all. I'm most grateful.

Hugh It was no trouble, I was coming in anyway and I thought 'why not bring in a coffee for Control? It's eleven o'clock, I expect he'd welcome a cup.'

Stephen Greatly appreciated.

Hugh I checked with Valerie and she said you like a little bit of milk, not too much, and no sugar. I hope that's right.

Stephen That's exactly how I like my coffee, Murchison.

Hugh Anyway I ought to tell you why I came in.

Stephen Mm, yes. Was there something you wanted to tell me? Or perhaps you wanted to ask me a question?

Hugh Well a bit of a mixture of both really, Control. Do you remember we decided to put a tail on the new Cultural Attaché at the Russian Embassy?

Stephen Yes, I do remember. I remember the very day we talked about it. We thought he might be a spy working for the KGB, and I said, 'let's follow him around and see if he does anything that might look suspicious'.

379

Hugh   That's right. We gave him the Codename Big
             Bad Wolf, and you decided that it would be good
             to put Philip and his F division in charge of the
             surveillance.

Stephen Yes, Operation Coathanger if memory serves me
             correctly. You were sitting over there – it was quite
             a rainy day and Philip was standing by the desk,
             I think.

Hugh   Yes. Though if you remember it was before you
             moved your desk round this way, so he would have
             been over there.

Stephen Oh yes. I must say I do much prefer it like this. I
             don't think I'll go back. I can see all the door and
             have quite a nice view over St Giles Circus.

Hugh   Yes. That must be nice. Anyway, it looks as if the
             Big Bad Wolf probably is a spy after all.

Stephen Oh dear. Well we certainly feared as much. Just as
             well we took the trouble to find out. It shows how
             it's always worth checking things up, isn't it? Has
             he been meeting known KGB agents then?

Hugh   Yes, he certainly has. As you can see.

             *Hugh stands there. Stephen puts his hands out and
             Hugh gives him a blue folder.*

Stephen *(Looking at the folder)* I must say I like this folder.
             Didn't the old ones used to be blue?

Hugh   Yes. It was Valerie's idea to change to blue. She
             thought it would brighten the place up a bit.

Stephen Very nice too. *(Reading)* 'Big Bad Wolf has a
             Meeting with Colonel Andreyev in John Lewis's.'
             Did Philip take this photograph himself, do
             you think?

Hugh   *(Coming round to look)* It certainly looks like Philip's
             handiwork.

380

Stephen	You can't see which department they're in. I hope Big Bad Wolf isn't stealing any of our secrets or trying to persuade our agents to defect.
Hugh	That would be galling, wouldn't it?
Stephen	I tell you what. You leave this one with me, Murchison.
Hugh	Are you going to tell the Minister?
Stephen	I'll certainly have to do that, yes. Meanwhile Philip had better keep up the surveillance.
Hugh	Would you like me to tell him? I'll be seeing him later today.
Stephen	Would you? That would certainly save me the trouble.
Hugh	No problem at all.
Stephen	Thanks.
Hugh	You're welcome. Anyway, I'd better get back to my office now. The Prague desk has been in a bit of a flap.
Stephen	Uh-oh. Mustn't keep you then.
Hugh	I'll let you know if anything else crops up.
Stephen	That would be appreciated. And thanks again for the coffee. It tasted very nice.
Hugh	Really such a pleasure. See you then, Control.
Stephen	Bye bye, Murchison.

Toaster

Hugh enters an electrical goods shop. Stephen is behind the counter.

Hugh   Hello. I'd like to buy a toaster.

Stephen What sort of toaster are you looking for?

Hugh   I beg your pardon?

Stephen What sort of toaster are you looking for?

Hugh   Oh I see what you mean. Well, ideally I'd like one that's good at toasting bread . . .

Stephen Yes.

Hugh   . . . but can also be used as a weapon.

Stephen A weapon?

Hugh   I beg your pardon?

Stephen A weapon?

Hugh   Oh I see what you mean. Yes, a weapon.

Stephen Mmm. Call me an unrestrained arsewit if you like . . .

Hugh   Perhaps later.

Stephen As you wish. Why would you want to use a toaster as a weapon?

Hugh   I beg your . . .

Stephen Why would you want to use a toaster as a weapon?

Hugh   These are uncertain times. We live in a shifting quicksand of international tension, forever dancing uncertain and fantastical steps on the brink of war.

Stephen Christ.

382

Hugh	I think the optimum choice in the circumstances would be some kind of lightweight throwing toaster.
Stephen	A lightweight throwing toaster?
Hugh	Affirmative. Then I could use it as a weapon.
Stephen	Forgive me if I seem to be labouring the point, but wouldn't it be simpler to use a weapon as a weapon, and use the toaster for toasting?
Hugh	I've already got a weapon.
Stephen	Well doesn't it work?
Hugh	Not as a toaster.
Stephen	Well let me assure you, all our toasters work as toasters.
Hugh	But not as weapons?
Stephen	'Fraid not.
Hugh	Huh. Well that's not going to be much good when they come parachuting into Carshalton.
Stephen	Who?
Hugh	I beg your pardon?
Stephen	Who is going to be parachuting into Carshalton?
Hugh	They are.
Stephen	Who is 'they'?
Hugh	I dunno. I'm not interested in politics.
Stephen	I see.
Hugh	I didn't have this problem with my bed.
Stephen	Mmm. Your bed is a weapon?
Hugh	In the right hands, yes.
Stephen	A lightweight throwing bed?

Hugh	Don't be stupid. It's a seek out and destroy bed. Modified for counter-insurgency operations.
Stephen	Aha.
Hugh	Perfect for the rough terrain surrounding the Carshalton area.
Stephen	I see.
Hugh	The bed shop was most helpful.
Stephen	Well I dare say, but this is a kitchen appliance shop. If you want weaponry, I can't help feeling you'd be better off going to a specialist.
Hugh	What sort of specialist?
Stephen	Don't tempt me to answer that.
Hugh	What do you mean?
Stephen	Nothing. Nothing. I could suggest a garlic-press, I suppose.
Hugh	Semi-automatic, gas-cooled, hand-to-hand, hunter-killer garlic-press?
Stephen	Well, no, it's not much of a weapon really. Unless you're worried about garlics parachuting into Carshalton.
Hugh	I don't at this time have garlics targetted as a priority threat.
Stephen	Had you thought of a down to earth, honest to goodness kitchen knife?
Hugh	A kitchen knife?
Stephen	Yes.

Produces knife.

Hugh	Don't be stupid. You could have someone's eye out with that.

Stephen	I thought that was the idea.
Hugh	Oh no. No no no. You misunderstand me. My whole life is based on the principle that I will never be the aggressor.
Stephen	Really?
Hugh	All I want is to be prepared.
Stephen	To be prepared?
Hugh	To be prepared for when they come parachuting into Carshalton . . .
Stephen	Yes?
Hugh	And also for the moment when I suddenly feel like a piece of toast.
Stephen	I see.
Hugh	You unrestrained arsewit.
Stephen	You're welcome.

VOX
POP

Stephen I definitely think the Queen ought to give one to Esther Rantzen. Definitely.

Maternity Ward Ten

Stephen is pacing the corridor of a hospital maternity ward, looking nervous. Hugh puts his head out of a door, wearing a white coat.

Hugh   Mr Conway?

Stephen   No.

Hugh   Ah *(He looks down the corridor)* You are . . . ?

Stephen   Mr Quick.

Hugh   Mr Quick, right, thank you.

Hugh exits.

Pause.

Hugh enters.

              Mr Arthur Quick?

Stephen   Noel.

Hugh   I'm sorry?

Stephen   Noel Quick.

Hugh   Noel, yes of course. And your wife is Mrs Mary Quick?

Stephen   Shirley.

Hugh   Shirley, yes. Shirley Quick. Thank you.

Hugh exits.

Pause.

Hugh enters.

386

Hugh	Mr Quick.
Stephen	Yes?
Hugh	Have you come far?
Stephen	No, well, we're just off the ring road. About twenty minutes.
Hugh	Oh, nice, nice. I say, hasn't your wife got splendid hair?
Stephen	Has she?
Hugh	Oh yes. Fantastic.
Stephen	Well, I suppose it is rather lovely, yes. I hadn't really thought . . .
Hugh	Well you should think, Mr Quick. You should. It's lovely hair. Lovely thick, blonde hair.
Stephen	She's got brown hair.
Hugh	Mmm. Lovely.

Hugh exits.

(Shouting off) Brown hair.

Hugh enters.

	Lovely thick, brown hair, yes. To be quite frank with you, that's some of the best hair I've seen in a long time.
Stephen	Oh thank you.
Hugh	You're a lucky man, Mr Quick. I'm telling you, that is world-class hair.
Stephen	Is there any chance of seeing her, Doctor?
Hugh	You just can't wait, can you? I don't blame you. With hair like that waiting for you, who wants to hang around in a draughty old corridor?

Stephen	Well quite.
Hugh	Excuse me.

Hugh exits.

Pause.

Hugh enters.

Yes, I always think brown hair looks tremendous on . . . a quite short woman.

Stephen	Well, possibly.
Hugh	Possibly?
Stephen	Of course, my wife's very tall.
Hugh	Ah. You'd say she was very tall would you?
Stephen	Very.

Hugh exits.

Hugh	(*Off*) Very tall. She's very tall, with brown hair.

Hugh enters.

Yes, right. Of course she's tall. Yes. I was thinking of her being quite short, because of course she's lying down at the moment. So she only comes up to my waist. From my point of view, you see, your wife is very short . . . and very wide. But I expect that when you're at home, she stands up quite a lot, and so then you're bound to see more of her tall side.

Stephen	Can I see her?
Hugh	No, you can't.
Stephen	Why not?

Hugh	Well, because there's a wall in the way.
Stephen	No. Can I go in and see her?
Hugh	Aha. It's not advisable, frankly. Patients who've just had their tonsils out, are always a bit . . .
Stephen	Tonsils? She's come here to have a baby.
Hugh	Excuse me.

Hugh exits.

(Off) She's come here to have a baby, for Christ's sake!

Hugh enters.

A baby, right. That's a lovely idea. Is it your first?

Stephen	Yes it is, as a matter of fact. We've been trying for quite a long time.
Hugh	I bet you have – with hair like that, phwor, eh? Had any luck so far?
Stephen	What do you mean?
Hugh	With babies. Have you had any luck?
Stephen	Well yes, that's why we're here.
Hugh	Of course, of course.
Stephen	Surely she must have had it by now?
Hugh	Who?
Stephen	My wife. Surely she must have had the baby by now.
Hugh	Oh er . . . hold on.

Hugh exits.

(Off) Well where is it? Well haven't we got *any*? Tscch.

Hugh reenters.

Hugh   Yes she has.

Stephen   She has? That's brilliant! Is it a girl or a boy?

Hugh   It's . . . it's a boy.

Stephen   A boy! Cor! Can I have a look at him?

Hugh   Er . . . here I am, Mr Quick.

Stephen   What do you mean?

Hugh   Er . . . I am your son. I was born about twenty minutes ago. Sorry, I should have mentioned it earlier.

Stephen   You're my son? What are you talking about? Where's the baby?

Hugh   I'm the baby, Mr Quick. Unfortunately I was born with a strange disease called Stimtirumtumtum which means that I look and sound like an adult even though I'm only twenty minutes old. It's very rare, but strangely enough it's also quite common. Muriel Gray has got it.

Stephen   Muriel Gray?

Hugh   Yes. Only a trained doctor would know that she's just six months old.

Stephen   You're mad.

Hugh   Maybe, Mr Quick ... father. But you know, I blame the parents.

Stephen   Can I see my wife now?

Hugh   Mother? Of course. We can be a family at last.

Stephen   Shut up.

Hugh   Yes, I always think that fathers should be present when their wife's tonsils are being taken out.

390

Prize Poem

*Typical comprehensive school office. Stephen is a
headmaster. He looks worried. There is a knock at the
door. He looks up.*

Stephen Come.

Enter Hugh.

Ah, Terry, come in, come in.

Hugh Thank you sir.

Stephen Well now, do you know why I sent for you?

Hugh Not really.

Stephen Not really? Not really? Well, let me see. Firstly,
let me congratulate you on winning the School
Poetry Prize.

Hugh Thank you sir.

Stephen Mr Drip tells me that it was the most mature and
exciting poem that he has ever received from a
pupil. Don't suck your thumb boy.

Hugh I'm not, sir.

Stephen No, no. It was just a piece of general advice for
the future.

Hugh Oh I see.

Stephen Now Terry. Terry, Terry, Terence. I've read your
poem, Terry. I can't pretend to be much of a
judge of poetry, I'm an English teacher, not a
homosexual. But I have to say it worried me.

Hugh Oh?

391

Stephen	Yes, worried me. I have it here, um: 'Inked Ravens of Despair Claw Holes In The Arse Of The World's Mind', I mean what kind of a title is that?
Hugh	It's my title sir.
Stephen	'Arse Of The World's Mind'? What does that mean? Are you unhappy about something?
Hugh	Well I think that's what the poem explores.
Stephen	Explores? Explores! Oh it explores does it? I see. 'Scrotal threats unhorse a question of flowers', I mean, what's the matter boy? Are you sickening for something? Or is it a girl? Is that the root of it?
Hugh	Well, it's not something I can explain, sir, it's all in the poem.
Stephen	It certainly is all in the poem. 'I asked for answers and got a headful of heroin in return.' Now. Terry. Look at me. Who gave you this heroin? You must tell me: if this is the problem we must do something about it. Don't be afraid to speak out.
Hugh	Well no one.
Stephen	Terry. I'm going to ask you again. It's here. 'I asked for answers and got a headful of heroin.' Now Terry, this is a police matter. Speak out.
Hugh	Sir, no one has given me heroin.
Stephen	So this poem is a lie, is it? A fiction, a fantasy? What's happening?
Hugh	No, it's all true, it's autobiographical.
Stephen	Then, Terry, I must insist. Who has been giving you heroin? Another boy?
Hugh	Well, sir, you have.
Stephen	I have. I have? What are you talking about, you diseased boy? This is rank, standing impertinence. I haven't given anyone heroin. How dare you?

392

Hugh	No, it's a metaphor.
Stephen	Metaphor, how metaphor?
Hugh	It means I came to school to learn, but I just get junk instead of answers.
Stephen	Junk? What do you mean, the JMB syllabus is rigidly adh –
Hugh	It's just an opinion.
Stephen	Oh is it? And is this an opinion too? 'When time fell wanking to the floor, they kicked his teeth'. Time fell wanking to the floor? Is this just put in to shock or is there something personal you wish to discuss with me? Time fell wanking to the floor? What does that mean?
Hugh	It's a quotation.
Stephen	A quotation? What from? It isn't Milton and I'm pretty sure it can't be Wordsworth.
Hugh	It's Bowie.
Stephen	Bowie? Bowie?
Hugh	David Bowie.
Stephen	Oh. And is this David Bowie too: 'My body disgusts, damp grease wafts sweat balls from sweat balls and thigh fungus', I mean do you wash?
Hugh	Of course.
Stephen	Then why does your body disgust you? It seems alright to me. I mean, why can't you write about meadows or something?
Hugh	I've never seen a meadow.
Stephen	Well, what do you think the imagination is for? 'A girl strips in my mind, squeezes my last pumping drop of hope and rolls me over to sleep alone.' You are fifteen, Terry, what is going on inside you?

393

Hugh	That's what —
Stephen	That's what the poem explores, don't tell me. I can't understand you, I can't understand you.
Hugh	Well you were young once.
Stephen	Yes, in a sense, of course.
Hugh	Didn't you ever feel like that?
Stephen	You mean did I ever want to 'fireball the dead cities of the mind and watch the skin peel and warp'? Then, no, thankfully, I can say I did not. I may have been unhappy from time to time, if I lost my stamp album or broke a penknife, but I didn't write it all down like this and show it to people.
Hugh	Perhaps it might have been better for you if you had.
Stephen	Oh might it, young Terence? I suppose I am one of the 'unhappy bubbles of anal wind popping and winking in the mortal bath' am I?
Hugh	Well —
Stephen	Your silence tells me everything. I am. I'm an unhappy bubble of anal wind.
Hugh	That's just how I see it. That's valid.
Stephen	Valid? Valid? You're not talking about a banknote, you're calling your headmaster an unhappy bubble of anal wind.
Hugh	Well, I'm one too.
Stephen	Oh well, as long as we're all unhappy bubbles of anal wind popping and winking in the mortal bath then of course there's no problem. But I don't propose to advertise the fact to parents. If this is poetry then every lavatory wall in Britain is an anthology. What about *The Oxford Book of Verse*, where's that gone?

394

Hugh	Perhaps that's the lavatory paper.
Stephen	Is that clever?
Hugh	I don't know.
Stephen	I suppose it's another quotation from Derek Bowie is it? I don't understand any more, I don't understand.
Hugh	Never mind, sir. You're a bit frustrated perhaps, it's a lonely job.
Stephen	I am frustrated, yes. It is a lonely job. So lonely. I am assailed by doubts, wracked by fear.
Hugh	Write it down.
Stephen	Eh?
Hugh	Write it down, get it out of your system. 'Assailed by doubts, wracked by fear.'
Stephen	Yes, yes – you think? 'Assailed by doubts and wracked by fear, tossed in a wrecked mucus foam of . . . of . . .'
Hugh	Hatred?
Stephen	Good, good. What about 'steamed loathing'?
Hugh	Better, you're a natural.

Hugh slips away.

Stephen	'. . . wrecked mucus foam of steamed loathing. Snot trails of lust perforate the bowels of my intent. Put on your red shoes, Major Tom, funk to flunky . . . etc . . .

Fade out.

395

Parent Power

Stephen, a headmaster, is sitting behind a desk. Hugh enters with Michael, a small boy.

Stephen Ah good morning Michael, good morning Mr Smear.

Hugh Yes, we'll dispense with the good mornings if you don't mind. I haven't got time for good mornings.

Stephen As you wish. You wanted to discuss something, I believe?

Hugh I think you know why I'm here.

Stephen I don't think I do.

Hugh *(To Michael)* Tell him.

Michael looks embarrassed.

Stephen Tell me what?

Hugh Tell him what you told your mother last night.

Michael Sexual intercourse can often bring about pregnancy in the adult female.

Stephen Yes?

Hugh You heard that, did you?

Stephen Yes?

Hugh Well I'd like an explanation, if it's not too much trouble.

Stephen An explanation of what?

Hugh An explanation of how my son came to be using language like that in front of his mother.

Stephen Well I imagine that this is something that Michael learnt in his biology class, isn't that right?

Michael Yes, sir.

Stephen Yes I thought so. With Mr Hent. Glad to see some of it's sinking in, Michael.

Michael Thank you sir.

Hugh Well I must say this is a turn-up and no mistake.

Stephen What is?

Hugh I didn't imagine that you'd be quite so barefaced about it.

Stephen About what?

Hugh I came here today to make a complaint about my son being exposed to gutter language in the playground. I am frankly staggered to find that this is something that he's actually been taught in a classroom. I mean what is going on here?

Stephen We're trying to teach your son . . .

Hugh Oh are you? Are you indeed?

Stephen Yes.

Hugh What? How to embarrass his parents? How to smack himself with heroin?

Stephen I assure you Mr Smear, we have no intention . . .

Hugh Call yourself a school?

Stephen I don't actually call *myself* a school, no.

Hugh You ought to be ashamed of yourself. Filling a young lad's head with filth like that. Well let me tell you something. About the real world. You're here to provide a service.

Stephen Quite right.

Hugh	Quite right, yes, well I'm not happy with it. I'm not happy with the service you're providing.
Stephen	Would you rather that Michael didn't attend the biology course?
Hugh	Certainly I would, if those are the kind of lies I can expect to hear repeated at the dinner table.
Stephen	They're not lies, Mr Smear.
Hugh	Oh aren't they? Pregnancy is brought about by sexual intercourse?
Stephen	Yes?
Hugh	Oh Lord save us. So you agree with that?
Stephen	Of course. It's true.
Hugh	True my arse. It's nothing more than a disgusting rumour put about by trendy young people in the sixties.
Stephen	Trendy young people in their sixties?
Hugh	*The* sixties. In *the* sixties. That's when it all started. People like you.
Stephen	Mr Smear, sexual reproduction has been part of the biology syllabus for many years.
Hugh	I don't care about your blasted syllabus. What good is a blasted syllabus out there?
Stephen	Out where?
Hugh	There!
Stephen	The Arkwright Road?
Hugh	Arkwright Jungle, I call it.
Stephen	Well, what would you rather we taught your son, Mr Smear?
Hugh	I would rather . . . I would rather you taught him values, Mr . . .

398

Stephen Casilingua.

Hugh Casilingua. Values. Respect. Standards. That's what you're here for. You're not here to poison my son with a lot of randy sextalk.

Stephen So Michael is definitely your son, is he, Mr Smear?

Hugh Certainly he's my son.

Stephen Then it's safe to assume that at some stage you and your wife have had sexual intercourse?

Hugh *(Pause)* Right. *(Hugh starts to take off his jacket)* That's it. I'm going to knock some sense into you myself.

Stephen You're going to fight me now, are you?

Hugh Yes I bloody well am. I'm not going to stand for this.

Stephen Do you mind if I do? *(Rises to his feet)*

Hugh Talking like that in front of the boy. You're a bloody disgrace.

Stephen Mr Smear, let me ask you this. How could Michael be your son, if you haven't had sexual intercourse?

Hugh Michael . . .

Stephen Yes?

Hugh Michael is my son in the normal way.

Stephen In the normal way?

Hugh Yes.

Stephen And what is the normal way to have a son, in your opinion?

Hugh If you're trying to trick me into sexy talk . . .

Stephen I'm not.

399

Hugh	The normal way to have a son is . . . to get married.
Stephen	Yes?
Hugh	Buy a house and get properly settled in.
Stephen	Yes.
Hugh	Furniture and so on, and then . . . wait for a bit.
Stephen	Ah.
Hugh	Make sure you eat properly. Three hot meals a day.
Stephen	So Michael just sort of turned up, did he?
Hugh	Er . . . well of course it's a few years ago now, but yes I think one day he was just there.
Stephen	And you and your wife have never enjoyed sexual intimacy of any kind?
Hugh	Yes, it's very hard for you to believe isn't it, that there are still some people left who can bring a son into this world without recourse to cannabis and government handouts?
Stephen	Well I really don't know what to say.
Hugh	I bet you don't: It's not every day a consumer stands up to you and makes demands is it?
Stephen	Not of this nature no.
Hugh	Yes, well. Welcome to the harsh realities of the market-place, Mr Casilingua.
Stephen	OK. Well, what would you like me to do?
Hugh	It's obvious isn't it? If I go into Littlewoods and tell them I'm not satisfied with a cardigan, say, they'll change it for me. And gladly.
Stephen	You want another son?
Hugh	Certainly I do. Mine is soiled now.

Stephen	Well I'm afraid we haven't got any spare sons here, just at the moment.
Hugh	Well what have you got of equal value?
Stephen	Um – there are some locusts in the biology lab.
Hugh	Locusts, hmm. Do I have your assurance that one of these locusts will not embarrass Mrs Smear at table with foul language?
Stephen	I think I can go that far.
Hugh	Well that's something. How many of them are there?
Stephen	Two . . . at the moment.
Hugh	What d'you mean 'at the moment'?
Stephen	Well, it's just that these locusts are married, they've bought the cage, and some furniture, and they're having three meals a day.
Hugh	Hot meals?
Stephen	Warmish.
Hugh	So Mrs Smear might be a grandmother one day?
Stephen	Very possibly.
Hugh	*(Pleased)* She'd like that.

VOX
POP

Stephen	A good smack in the face. She deserves it.

Chatshow

Hugh is a young and surprisingly handsome chat-show host on a young and surprisingly awful Channel Four chat-show. He is behind his desk.

Hugh   *(In reference to whatever sketch has finished)* Well that was the unmistakable sound. Right, my next guest wrote his first novel back in 1972, the year of loons and flares and Suzie Quatro and the Glitter Band and all that stuff. He's been writing ever since, got a new one coming out now. Bit of a cult dude with the Saporo and sushimi set, so let's say a big 'hi!' to Richard Morley!

Enter slightly nervous and serious looking Stephen to absurdly brash music. Hugh does ludicrous jive handshake.

Right, Richard, welcome, sit down, take the weight off your paragraphs.

Stephen looks bewildered by this peculiar joke.

So tell me, this novel, what's it called?

Stephen   The novel I've just written is called *The Emperor of Disgust.*

Hugh   *The Emperor of Disgust.* Sounds pretty heavy.

Stephen   Heavy?

Hugh   What's it about?

Stephen   You haven't read it?

Hugh   Well, for the viewers, you know. They haven't,

obviously. It isn't published till tomorrow is it?
How can they have done!!!

Hugh punches Stephen on the arm.

Stephen Oh, I see. Well it isn't very easy to tell you the plot precisely because it is rather complicated.

Hugh Highbrow stuff I'll bet. Where's it set?

Stephen Set? Well the action of the novel takes place over several centuries and a number of different –

Hugh Tell me, do you use a word processor? Thing I've always wanted to know about writers, you know, how they set about it. Pencil, pen, typewriter. All that.

Stephen Well I use a word processor as a matter of fact. I used to use a typewriter, but –

Hugh How many novels then, have you had, in fact, published?

Stephen *The Emperor of Disgust* will be my seventh.

Hugh Seventh? You take it pretty seriously, then?

Stephen Yes, yes indeed I do. I do take it seriously. Very seriously. It's my job you see. My living.

Hugh Right. Right. Yeah. Tell me, where do you get your characters from? From real life?

Stephen Well usually I suppose they're an amalgam, you know.

Hugh You gonna put me in one of your books then?

Stephen Well I think I might actually.

Hugh *(Thrilled with the idea)* Yeah!?

Stephen Yes. I really think you are one of the most repellent and flatulent-minded people I've ever met. In many respects ideal fodder for the novelist.

403

Hugh laughs in an 'isn't this geezer just brilliant?'
kind of a way.

Stephen I don't know what you're laughing at, I find you
mindless, vapid and irrelevant.

Hugh *(Still laughing)* Seriously, Richard, what's the –

Stephen I am being serious, you repulsive ball of spittle.
And who the hell told you you could call me
Richard? You're rotting in hell and you haven't the
faintest idea of it, have you?

Hugh The last book you wrote . . .

Stephen Last book I wrote! You haven't a clue about the
last book I wrote have you, except from what that
daffy researcher you sent round tells you? Your
head is crammed with so much pappy drivel and
greasy bigotry and brash ignorance that there isn't
room in it for one single idea, is there?

Hugh This is brilliant.

Stephen Oh it's brilliant is it? It's 'good television' I
suppose. It shows you at the cutting edge of
dangerous broadcasting. You're about as dangerous
as a chocolate 'Hob Nob'.

Hugh mugs to the camera.

Look at you, sitting there like a . . . like a fat,
smug . . . a fat smug . . . *(Breaking out of character
and talking to someone off camera)* Sorry I've
forgotten the next bit, 'a fat smug . . .'

Hugh *(Also addressing someone off)* Vince, we go live on air
in ten minutes, I thought he knew his lines. What's
going on?

Stephen Sorry, I'm a bit nervous.

Hugh *(Coaching)* 'A fat smug git who's just won a . . .'

Stephen *(With Hugh coaching)* Oh yes, a fat smug git
who's just won a BAFTA. Have you any idea how
degrading and demeaning to the human spirit
people like you are?

Hugh Great, then I'll ask you where your book is on
sale, how much it costs and we'll play you out.

Stephen Alright.

Hugh Then I'll do a bit of chat, 'blah-di-blah-di-blah-
di-blah' and bang, bang bang. And, what's next?

VOX
POP

Hugh Sex and violence, really. That kind
of thing. We're a small company,
but things are very busy at the
moment.

Doctor Tobacco

Doctor's surgery – yes I know, but I'm afraid that's where we are.

Hugh is having his chest listened to.

Stephen   Say 'ninety-nine'.

Hugh   Ninety-nine.

Stephen   Good. Say 'thank you'.

Hugh   Thank you.

Stephen   Say 'breasts'.

Hugh   Breasts.

Stephen   Mmm. 'R'.

Hugh   'R'.

Stephen   Good.

Hugh   Good.

Stephen   Well, if you'd like to do your shirt up now Mr Pepperdyne.

Hugh   Everything as it should be?

Stephen   Nothing too serious, you'll be glad to hear. You say that you've been having a little trouble breathing at night?

Hugh   That's right.

Stephen   Been bringing up any sputum?

Hugh   Er, not really.

Stephen   Any yellow or green phlegm . . . blood?

406

Hugh	No.
Stephen	Tightening of the chest?
Hugh	Well a little I suppose.
Stephen	Headaches?
Hugh	Apart from the children, you mean? Not really.

They both laugh weakly.

Stephen	Right. I want to try you on a course of these: one twenty times a day. Have you ever taken them before?

Gets out a plain cigarette from a drawer.

Hugh	Um – what is it?
Stephen	It's a simple nicotinal arsenous monoxid preparation taken bronchially as an infumation.
Hugh	Infumation?
Stephen	Yes, you just light the end and breathe in.
Hugh	What, like cigarettes?
Stephen	You know them, then? Yes, actually, it's a bit hard to admit, but they're basically a herbal remedy.
Hugh	Oh, herbal cigarettes.
Stephen	That's right. A leaf originally from the Americas I believe, called tobacco.
Hugh	But medicated.
Stephen	Medicated? No.
Hugh	These are ordinary cigarettes?
Stephen	That's right.
Hugh	But they're terribly bad for you aren't they?

Stephen	I hardly think I would be prescribing them if they were bad for you.
Hugh	Twenty a day?
Stephen	Yes, ideally moving on to about thirty or forty.
Hugh	But they give you lung cancer and bronchitis and emphysema.
Stephen	Where on earth did you get that idea?
Hugh	Everyone knows that.
Stephen	Are you a doctor?
Hugh	No, but it stands to reason doesn't it?
Stephen	What on earth are you talking about? 'Stands to reason.' You wouldn't even know what a pair of lungs *did* if a doctor hadn't told you. It's taken mankind thousands of years to work out what the heart is for, what a blood vessel is, what the kidneys do, and now you're telling me because you've read a few weedy magazine articles that you know more about the human body than a doctor?
Hugh	Well no, but – it can't be natural, can it?
Stephen	Perfectly natural leaf.
Hugh	Yes but setting light to it and inhaling the smoke, I mean . . .
Stephen	More natural than Baked Alaska or nylon socks.
Hugh	Yes but you don't inhale nylon socks. At least I don't.
Stephen	You wear them next to the skin.
Hugh	But you can't seriously be recommending cigarettes.
Stephen	Why the buggery sod not? A bit of leaf smoke to loosen the lungs, ease that tightness and clear the head. Perfectly sound.

Hugh	I suppose you're going to tell me that cholesterol isn't bad for you next.
Stephen	What's cholesterol?
Hugh	It's . . . well, you know –
Stephen	Yes I know perfectly well what it is, but I don't suppose you'd so much as heard of it until a few years ago. You'd die without the stuff.
Hugh	Yes but too much is bad for you.
Stephen	Well of course too much is bad for you, that's what 'too much' means you blithering twat. If you had too much water it would be bad for you, wouldn't it? 'Too much' precisely means that quantity which is excessive, that's what it means. Could you ever say 'too much water is good for you'? I mean if it's too much it's too much. Too much of anything is too much. Obviously. Jesus.
Hugh	But I thought the balance of informed medical opinion held that –
Stephen	You thought, you thought. You didn't think, did you? Cigarettes are healing, natural and effective.
Hugh	If you don't mind I think I'd like a second opinion.
Stephen	That's your privilege.
Hugh	Right.
Stephen	*(Pause)* My second opinion is that they are also cheap, nutritious and stylish.
Hugh	Really?
Stephen	And if you're interested in a third opinion they're soothing, harmless and sexy.
Hugh	Well, I must say that does seem to clinch it.
Stephen	Alright then. So twenty a day, rising over the week.

Hugh	And the tightness in the chest?
Stephen	Should disappear completely.
Hugh	Tremendous. Well you're the doctor.
Stephen	What?
Hugh	You're the doctor.
Stephen	Whatever gave you that idea?
Hugh	Well I mean – you did.
Stephen	God, you are pathetic aren't you?
Hugh	Um.
Stephen	I'm a tobacconist. Isn't it obvious?
Hugh	But the –
Stephen	Yes, it looks more like a doctor's surgery than a tobacconist's.
Hugh	Why?
Stephen	Why? Because you're the kind of idiot that falls for that sort of thing. It's the same reason that cosmetics sales staff wear white coats, because pratts like you think a Swiss name and something called a 'skin treatment' must be better for you than a tub of cold cream which is all you're in fact getting. You're a credulous git, Mr Pepperdyne. A stethoscope and a plausible manner doesn't make me a doctor. I'm a conman and you're a moron.
Hugh	You are a doctor then?
Stephen	Could be. What do you think?
Hugh	You really want to know?
Stephen	I'd be fascinated.
Hugh	I think you've taken a reasonably good idea and overworked it. I think what started out as a fairly interesting and amusing statement about our

susceptibility to received ideas has become
something vague, ill-thought out and rambling.
And I think it's time to finish it.

Stephen Well do you? I think you've comp –

Blackout

Remembering Lines

Hugh and Stephen are on set.

Hugh   We'd like to do a sketch for you now entitled, quite simply, 'Jack Nimnock Goes Shopping In the Heart of Norwich'.

Stephen   That's right.

They each go to one side of the set and start to walk towards each other. As they pass they recognise one another.

Jack! Jack Nimnock! How are you?

Hugh   Neville! I'm fine, fine. How are you?

Stephen   Oh mustn't grumble. So what are you up to now?

Hugh   Oh this and that.

Stephen   Right. Right. So tell me, how's Mary?

Hugh looks blank. Stephen speaks sotto voce.

Mary and I are divorced.

Hugh   Mary and I are divorced.

Stephen   Divorced? I'm sorry to hear that, Jack. When did this happen?

Hugh again looks blank.

When did this happen?

Hugh   A couple of days ago.

Stephen   *(Sotto voce)* Years.

Hugh   Pardon?

412

Stephen	*(Sotto voce)* You were divorced a couple of *years* ago.
Hugh	A couple of years ago. Not days, Neville, as I initially suggested, but years.
Stephen	Well this is terrible news, Jack, terrible. Whose idea was it, if you don't mind me asking?

Hugh looks blank again.

Hugh	What?
Stephen	The divorce. Was it your idea or Mary's? *(Sotto voce)* Mine.
Hugh	Mine.
Stephen	Yours?
Hugh	Yours?
Stephen	Mine.
Hugh	Mine.
Stephen	So it was your idea?
Hugh	So it was *your* idea?
Stephen	I see. How did Mary take it?

Hugh looks blank yet again. Stephen starts to look annoyed.

	(Semi sotto voce) Not too badly at first.
Hugh	Not too badly at first.
Stephen	*(Semi sotto voce)* But I think she's pretty low at the moment.
Hugh	But at the moment I think she's pretty low.
Stephen	And how about you?
Hugh	Erm . . . don't tell me.
Stephen	You had a nervous breakdown.

413

Hugh	Oh yes, I had a nervous breakdown and went into shock and when I recovered I found I'd completely lost my voice.
Stephen	Memory!
Hugh	Memory, I'd completely lost my memory –

Pause.

Stephen	*(Under)* And now I can't remember a thing . . .
Hugh	*(Under)* I know, I know, that was a pause. *(Out loud)* And now I can't remember a thing about that period of my life.
Stephen	That's terrible, so had Mary been cheating on you then?
Hugh	Well . . .
Stephen	*(Whispering)* I've forgotten.
Hugh	*(Whispering)* So have I.
Stephen	No, *you've forgotten.*
Hugh	Oh I see. I've forgotten. She might have been but I just can't . . . um . . . persuade?
Stephen	*(Hissing)* No, remember!
Hugh	November. I'm a . . .
Stephen	*(Walking off)* Git.
Hugh	I'm a git. I'm a git, that's right –

Embarrassed at Stephen's disappearance.

– right, well cheerio then Neville. It was good seeing you after all these . . . . . . er . . .

| Stephen | *(Off yelling loudly)* Years!!! |
| Hugh | Years! That's right. |

Beggar

Hugh is a beggar. Tatty beard, old raincoat – pretty sordid. He has a small cloth cap on the ground and is playing the mouth organ. Stephen, dressed like a plutocrat, passes near him. He stops in amazement and stares at Hugh. Hugh starts to get rather discomfited by this.

Stephen   What on earth are you doing? What on earth are you doing?

Hugh   What do you mean?

Stephen   What is that cloth cap there for?

Hugh   Well it's for the money.

Stephen   Money? What money? I mean, what are you *doing?*

Hugh   I'm busking, aren't I?

Stephen   Busking? Busking? You're busking? What do you mean you're busking?

Hugh   I play the mouth organ and people give me money.

Stephen   Money? They give you money? For playing the mouth organ? People give you money for playing like that? They actually give you money? They pay you?

Hugh   Some people do. No harm in that.

Stephen   No harm in that? No harm in that he says. People are prepared to give you money for standing on a pavement and blowing through spittle? It's unbelievable.

Hugh   Look if you don't like it, you don't have to listen or give me anything.

Stephen   Don't like it? How could I like it? It's revolting.
It's the most disgusting and pathetic noise I've
ever heard. And people give you money for it?

Hugh   Well it's kindness as well, isn't it? They're just
being kind.

Stephen   Just being kind? But surely if they were just
being kind they'd put a bullet through your head,
wouldn't they? That's what I'd call being kind. Put
you out of your misery.

Hugh   I'm not that miserable. I quite enjoy it. People are
nice to me.

Stephen   Not miserable? Not miserable? How can you be
not miserable, look at you, your clothes are in rags,
you smell disgusting, how can you be anything
other than miserable?

Hugh   You're very insulting, you know.

Stephen   Yes of course I know. Do you think I wasn't aware
of the fact? Of course I'm insulting. I'm very
insulting indeed, especially to smelly, squalid poor
people who play the harmonica badly.

Hugh   We share the same planet, why can't you
let me be?

Stephen   Share the same planet? What are you saying,
'share the same planet'? The planet I inhabit is
full of restaurants, fast cars, high level finance,
holidays in Barbados and fine wine. Your planet
is full of bottles of meths, howling harmonicas,
smelliness and grimy doss-houses. It's not the
same planet at all. How dare you suggest that it's
the same planet?

Hugh   You may not think they're the same planet but they
are. You couldn't have one without the other.

Stephen   What are you talking about couldn't have one

	without the other? What are you talking about? Are you saying I depend upon you?

Hugh Course you do. All your wealth is entirely propped up on the rotting hulk of my poverty – and one day it will give way and you'll come crashing down with it.

Stephen Rotting hulk? Have you gone mad? Is this communist talk? Are you a communist? Do you want me to call a policeman?

Hugh It's not a crime to be a communist. Anyway I'm not.

Stephen Not a crime? Not a crime? Have you gone howling mad, not a crime. This is 1988, of course it's a crime. Communists are the enemies of democracy, they are criminals.

Hugh Well what's so good about democracy?

Stephen What's so good about democracy? What's so good about democracy he asks? It's freedom of speech and thought and belief, that's what's so good about it, you degraded heap of smelliness. Now get out of my way before I set fire to you. Get a job, clean yourself up. It's demeaning to have a pile of litter playing the harmonica at one.

Stephen turns and moves off.

Hugh *(Behind him, removing beard)* Wait!

Stephen Wait? Wait for what?

Hugh *(Pointing straight into the camera)* You see that?

Stephen What? See what? What have you done with your beard, what is the matter with you? Have you gone mad? See what?

Hugh *(Laughing)* You don't recognise me, do you?

Stephen Recognise you? No I don't recognise you. Of course I don't recognise you, why should I?

Hugh Do you ever watch a television programme called 'On The Streets With Bibby'?

Stephen 'On The Streets With Bibby'? Oh, the one with the hidden camera, you mean?
(Suddenly terrified) My God, you're not Robert Bibby are you?

Hugh *(Sinking down back onto the street)* No, but I might have been.

Little Chat

Hugh   Father?

Stephen   Yes?

Hugh   I've been thinking.

Stephen   Oh yes.

Hugh   You know how you said that Mother had gone to live with Jesus?

Stephen   Yes.

Hugh   Well I don't think that can be right.

Stephen   Oh?

Hugh   Yes. Because I saw Mother last night.

Stephen   You what?

Hugh   Yes. In Asda. And the man she was with was nothing like Jesus at all.

Stephen   *(Putting down newspaper)* Look, Jeremy, I think it may well be time that you and I had a little talk.

Hugh   Aren't we having one now, then?

Stephen   Well, yes, as a matter of fact we are. That's quite right. Good. How old are you now Jeremy?

Hugh   Thirty-one.

Stephen   Thirty-one, eh? When I first told you that Mummy had gone to live with Jesus, how old were you then, eh?

Hugh   Twenty-seven.

Stephen   Yes, well, goodness me, there we are you see. Twenty-seven. Time flies doesn't it? My goodness word me yes. There you are. Well now. When I told you what I told you it was a little bit of a fib.

Hugh	Oh.
Stephen	Yes.
Hugh	You told me a fib.
Stephen	Well it was to spare you hurt, son. You see Mummy didn't go to live with Jesus at all.
Hugh	As I rightly guessed.
Stephen	As you rightly guessed. What really happened was that Mummy died.
Hugh	Died?
Stephen	Yes. She died.
Hugh	But I saw her in Asda.
Stephen	No, you saw someone who looked a little bit like her.
Hugh	Oh.
Stephen	You had to know sooner or later.
Hugh	How did . . . how did Mummy die then?
Stephen	It's a sad story but you should know.
Hugh	Yes?
Stephen	I killed her.
Hugh	You killed her?
Stephen	Yes.
Hugh	Why?
Stephen	Why? Because she was screwing everything in trousers.
Hugh	Oh.
Stephen	*(Returning to paper)* You see?
Hugh	Yes, Daddy.

Lavatories

Stephen   Lavatories. Love them or loathe them. They're here to stay. We use them, we lavish our affection on them: we clean them, polish them, some of us spend up to half our lives in them. We read specialist lavatory magazines, spend money on the latest models with air-conditioning, stereos and two-speed wipers. Some of us even race them –

Hugh   *(Whispering)* Cars.

Stephen   What?

Hugh   You mean cars, not lavatories.

Stephen   *(Studying script)* Oh yes. Cars. How much do we know about them? We sit in them once a day and trust them to carry our effluent away, safely, cleanly, efficiently. Whether they're porcelain, plastic or fibre-glass, lever or button flush we expect them to –

Hugh   Lavatories. You mean lavatories.

Stephen   Oh yes.

Hugh   T!

Stephen   The beginnings of the modern lavatory were humble enough. In 1793 Johannes Krell of Leipzig constructed the first simple metal cabinet, using inert gases condensing to cool the cabinet to three degrees centigrade. The first dew-bin, or salad crisper started to appear in lavatories –

Hugh   Fridges. You're talking about fridges.

Stephen   Oh yes. Fridges. Like them or loathe them, you can't ignore them. Everyone's talking about them. Whether you're buying or selling a property, sooner or later you'll come in contact with a fridge. Their commission is an important part of your house budget –

Hugh   Estate agents. You're talking about estate agents.

Stephen Estate agents. You can't live with them, you can't live with them. The first sign of these nasty, purulent sores appeared round about 1894. With their jangling keys, nasty suits, revolting beards, moustaches and tinted spectacles, estate agents roam the land causing perturbation and despair. If you try and kill them, you're put in prison: if you try and talk to them, you vomit. There's only one thing worse than an estate agent but at least that can be safely lanced, drained and surgically dressed. Estate agents. Love them or loathe them, you'd be mad not to loathe them.

Hugh   That's better.

VOX
POP

Hugh I just loved the Beetles. They had hundreds of different kinds. Blue ones, black ones, yellow ones, two-tone, cabriolet. They had one with fuel injection.

Information

Stephen is sitting behind a desk with an 'information' sign on it. Hugh enters.

Hugh	Good morning.
Stephen	Good morning.
Hugh	Good morning.
Stephen	Right. Can I help you?
Hugh	Yes. Your face my arse.
Stephen	No, I said can I help you?
Hugh	Oh. I'd like some information, please.
Stephen	Yes.
Hugh	Well?
Stephen	Well what?
Hugh	I'd like some information, please.
Stephen	Yes. What information would you like?
Hugh	Well I don't know. What have you got?
Stephen	I beg your pardon?
Hugh	What information have you got?
Stephen	Well, all sorts.
Hugh	Such as?
Stephen	Such as . . . the average weight of a rabbit.
Hugh	Well I never knew that.
Stephen	What?
Hugh	I never knew rabbits had an average weight.

423

Stephen   Oh yes.

Hugh   Have you got any other information?

Stephen   Of course. But you've got to ask me questions, you see.

Hugh   And you'll tell me the answers . . . ?

Stephen   That's right.

Hugh   . . . if I ask the questions. Right. What's the name . . . ?

Stephen   Yes?

Hugh   What's the name of the man who taught me Geography at school?

Stephen   I'm afraid that's hardly the kind of thing . . .

Hugh   Aha.

Stephen   Tscch. Alright. His name was Colin Drip.

Hugh   That's right.

Stephen   Drippy, you used to call him.

Hugh   Drippy. Cor, that takes me back a bit. Now, there was a bloke in our class – tsch, what was his name . . .

Stephen   Adams, Attersham, Bennet, Connor, Fredericks, Hodson . . .

Hugh   Hodson! That's it, that's it. Ned Hodson. Blimey, he used to drive old Drippy up the wall. D'you know what he used to do?

Stephen   Yes.

Hugh   Oh. Cor. I wonder what happened to him?

Stephen   He married a girl called Susan Trite, and they now live in Fenton, near Worcester.

Hugh   I don't think I ever met her.

Stephen   Yes you did. July the fourth, 1972, you sat next

424

to her on a twenty-nine bus down Garboldisham
Road and she told you about the Bay City Rollers.
You were in love with her until the following
Wednesday.

Hugh   Hm. You've got quite a lot of information, then?

Stephen   We try to provide a service. Anything else?

Hugh   Yes please. Can you tell me . . .

Stephen   Yes?

Hugh   Can you tell me how to be happy?

Stephen   How to be happy?

Hugh   How to be happy.

Stephen   I'm afraid to say that information may be
            restricted.

Hugh   Oh. You do have it, though?

Stephen   Oh yes.

Hugh   But it's restricted?

Stephen   I'm afraid so. Sorry.

Hugh   Contented?

Stephen   Yes thank you.

Hugh   No, any information on how to be contented?

Stephen   Oh I see. Yes, we've got information on that.

Hugh   Can I have it?

Stephen   I'm afraid it's a secret.

Hugh   Oh, go on.

Stephen   Alright. The secret of contentment is . . .

Hugh   Yes?

Stephen   Don't ask questions.

Open University

Stephen addresses the camera.

Stephen   You know, some of the funniest things that happen in television never actually make it to the screen. They're the out-takes, or bloopers, that we all get so embarrassed about. Here's one of my all-time favourites, from an edition of the Open University, recorded in 1979.

Cut to:

Possibly black and white scene of Hugh standing in front of a blackboard with a lot of incomprehensible symbols on it. He is looking appallingly early seventies, paisley, loons etc.

Hugh   So that if we increase the non-reflexive integers in the equation by a marginal quantity denoted by D5, we can see that the parallel quantities D7 and D3 are inverted in the same direction, which gives us a resultant modular quantity of minus 0.567359. Now this should begin to give us a clue as to where the next . . .

Stephen enters, dressed as a floor manager, also in a paisley shirt and wide flares. He is laughing.

Stephen   Sorry Brian.

Hugh   That's alright. What's happened?

Stephen   You said '0.567359'.

Hugh   I didn't, did I?

426

Stephen Yes. *(Laughing violently)* It should have been '0.567395'.

Hugh Oh no. Oh I don't believe it.

They both laugh hysterically. We hear a succession of bleeps as they swear good-naturedly about the stupidity of the mistake.

Cut to:

Stephen *(Wiping his eyes)* Marvellous, absolutely marvellous.

VOX
POP

Hugh My wife and I were thinking of going to Ireland personally, to see what all the fuss is about. But we couldn't face having all the injections.

Spies Three

Stephen is behind his desk in the spies office when Hugh enters.

Hugh   Morning Control.

Stephen   Oh. Hello Tony. Come in.

Hugh   Thank you, I will come in, just for the now.

Stephen   I expect you've heard the news?

Hugh   Well everything is in quite an uproar. You know what rumours are.

Stephen   Yes, it's terrible isn't it, how they spread? I don't know. I sometimes think that if I believed every rumour I heard I'd be believing some things that aren't true at all.

Hugh   T.

Slight pause.

Stephen   Anyway, you'll have to forgive me if I yawn a bit during today, what with one thing and another I didn't get too much sleep last night.

Hugh   Poor you, you must be exhausted, or very tired at least, or is that wrong?

Stephen   No. I am tired, that's quite right.

Hugh   So perhaps you might tell me exactly what happened, Control, unless you're too tired.

Stephen   No, I'd be happy to fill you in, that way you won't have to rely on departmental rumours, will you?

Hugh   No. And that would be a great convenience.

428

Stephen	Well, we picked up Costain last night.
Hugh	I'd gathered as much from the rumours, but I wasn't sure whether it was absolutely true, so it's good to have it confirmed from you.
Stephen	I can imagine. He came very quietly, I think he had guessed that we suspected him of being a traitor for some time now.
Hugh	Which we had, hadn't we?
Stephen	Yes. When was it we first came to suspect him?
Hugh	Hoo, well I can't remember exactly, but it was certainly some time ago.
Stephen	Before last spring, I should think.
Hugh	Around there definitely. Certainly no later than the fourteenth of May, because that's my birthday and I remember saying that catching Costain and putting him out of harm's way would be the best Christmas present anyone could ever have.
Stephen	I remember you saying those exact words, Tony.
Hugh	But any old way, you managed to arrest him then?
Stephen	Yes. He was taken to the ninth floor and I had the job of interrogating him.
Hugh	That's never a pleasant task is it?
Stephen	It's one of the things I least enjoy having to do as a matter of fact Tony. It's very difficult when someone doesn't want to tell you things and you have to think up ways of *making* them tell you.
Hugh	Yes, that can call on all your know-how, can't it?
Stephen	Costain I'm afraid really didn't want to tell us anything. But I thought it would be much better if he did because if he's been working for the Russians for the last twenty years it's quite important that we know everything that he's been up to.

429

Hugh	That way we know which of our secrets have been given away and which ones are safe.
Stephen	That's exactly right.
Hugh	Is the Minister pleased that we've caught him at last?
Stephen	Well, while on the one hand Tony, he's delighted that Costain is behind bars, on the other hand he's extremely anxious to avoid any publicity. And on the other hand he's . . .
Hugh	You've got three hands there, Control.
Stephen	Whoops, I wasn't counting very carefully, was I? Well, let's say he's also rather cross that we allowed a Soviet agent within our own ranks to go undetected for so long.
Hugh	A mixed reception then?
Stephen	I think that's a fair way of describing it, yes. So all in all it's been a pretty tiring forty-eight hours. Well, forty-four to be more accurate. But it seems like forty-eight, I can tell you. Well, forty-six or seven at least.
Hugh	Tell you what, Control – if you're feeling that tired, do you think a cup of coffee might perk you up?
Stephen	Oh I say, Tony, that's ever such a super thought. I'd just love one.
Hugh	Coming right up.
Stephen	You're a lifesaver, Tony and that's a fact.
Hugh	And I tell you what, Control . . .
Stephen	Mm?
Hugh	I'm going to make it a good and strong one.
Stephen	Doh!

Puppy Appeal

Stephen sits behind a desk, addressing the camera.
There is an exceptionally cute puppy in his arms,
probably a golden labrador.

Stephen This puppy, Snipper, is in most desperate need
of help. Four months ago Snipper's mother died,
and only three days later her father was killed
by a hit-and-run driver. Barely five months old
and an orphan, Snipper was also faced with the
embarrassing and painful affliction of incontinence.
It's a condition that we in the West don't talk
much about: shame keeps millions of sufferers
silent, but Snipper's incontinence was a source
of great distress to her and rather than come to
terms with it, she ran away, to London. It was
on the way to London that Snipper was assaulted
and abused by an older dog. You can imagine the
effect this would have on an innocent puppy bitch
like Snipper. She was totally confused, bewildered
and hurt. We think that it is around that time that
she was struck with traumatic amnesia, a total
loss of memory. This, apart from anything else,
made it very difficult for her to know where she
was and what she was doing. She drifted into a
life of scavenging and prostitution, selling her soft,
furry young body just in order to stay alive. That
was the life she was living when we at the ASTL
found her. We were able to give her food, warmth,
and more than that – love, the one thing that
has been denied her in her short and tragically
unhappy life.

Snipper is taking an interest in life now. Her
memory is slowly returning, which is how we've

431

been able to piece together the details of her life, and with luck she will be able to lead a normal, happy and fulfilled life. But there are thousands of Snippers in Britain and we desperately need your help to carry on the work we are doing. We are an entirely independent charity, we receive no government funding and rely on public generosity to keep us going. If you're the kind of person who would like to help a Snipper then please send your donation, however large, to me, Stephen Fry, care of the BBC, instead.

VOX
POP

Stephen   So I just told them to stuff it.
             But they said it had been dead
             too long.

Critics Two

Stephen and Hugh are in the swivel chairs again, being revolting.

Stephen Well of course what I found particularly disappointing was their choice of . . .

Hugh Did that work for you?

Stephen What?

Hugh Their choice of . . .

Stephen No it didn't. I felt it was a mistaken choice, a misguided choice, a badly chosen choice.

Hugh They could have chosen better?

Stephen I think so. And of course, if they had chosen better . . .

Hugh Which they didn't.

Stephen Well of course not. But if they had, their limitations would have . . .

Hugh I was going to ask you about that.

Stephen But you didn't.

Hugh I was going to.

Stephen Well then, yes. Just so limited, you see. And that was bound to limit them.

Hugh So they were limited by their own limitations?

Stephen Nicely put.

Hugh Thank you. That leads me on to another question. May I?

Stephen Of course.

Hugh   Thanks. I wonder, is there a sense in which you're not completely revolting?

Stephen No sense whatsoever. I've looked hard for a sense, but at the end of it all I've come up senseless.

Hugh   Does that I wonder tie in with . . .

Stephen Precisely my point. Could one say, from any critical standpoint yet devised, that you are any distance at all from being utterly repulsive?

Hugh   Ah. Now that's interesting.

Stephen Oh dear. Wasn't meant to be.

Hugh   Never mind. There'll be other opportunities I'm sure.

> VOX
> POP
>
> **Hugh** It only takes about ten minutes apparently, and when you come out, you look exactly like Keith Harris.

Sex Change

Hugh   *(To camera)* My guest tonight is someone who in
1987 caused a sensation by becoming the first
woman to undergo a complete and successful
sex change operation. In August of that year she
entered the Pert Frool clinic in Düsseldorf as
Melinda Coppice, author, broadcaster and mother
of three. Two weeks later she left that clinic as
Michael Coppice. His bestselling account of the
operation, the painful decisions leading up to it,
the painful incisions during the course of it and
the aftermath of fame that resulted from it have
made Michael Coppice a household name. Let's
meet him now – ladies and gentlemen, Michael
Coppice.

*Enter Deborah, completely normal woman. Shakes
hands with Hugh. They sit. The sofa they sit on is
dangerously soft and yielding: every now and then they
are out of physical control because it's so squashy and
hard to maintain balance in or on.*

Michael. Welcome.

Deborah   Thank you. Great pleasure.

Hugh   So. Michael. How would you say your life has
been since the operation?

Deborah   Well, I have to say firstly that everyone, my
family, my friends, the people I meet have been
enormously supportive since the operation that
transformed me into a man. Both my ex-husband
and my present wife have been tremendously
understanding.

Hugh   You now have a wife?

Deborah   Yes indeed. With two children.

435

Hugh	You are able to have children?
Deborah	Oh yes. I have fathered a wonderful pair of twins. It was a total gender change, the operation.
Hugh	And how successful would you say that operation has been?
Deborah	Well, you can see for yourself. One hundred per cent.
Hugh	Ye-e-es. How would you describe, as perhaps the only person in the world in a position to be able to do so, the difference between the sexes, then?
Deborah	In a way it's hard for me to answer that, Clive: you see although I have been completely transformed into a man, I am still a transvestite. Hence the women's clothes.
Hugh	You are still a transvestite?
Deborah	Yes. More properly a transexual. Rather a good one, I think you'll agree. You'd never know I was a man would you?
Hugh	No. No, I don't think I would. Does your wife object to your transexuality?
Deborah	She seems to understand and support me fully.
Hugh	Well let's meet her and find out. Ladies and gentlemen. Welcome now please Michael's wife Lucy Coppice.

Enter Stephen as manly as ever. Man's clothes.

Hugh	Welcome Lucy. *(They kiss)*
Stephen	Thank you. *(He squeezes Deborah's hand)*
Hugh	We were talking about whether or not you objected to the fact that your husband is a transexual.

436

Stephen	Oh good Lord no. I'm one myself.
Hugh	You are?
Stephen	Yes. It's my ambition some day to have an operation like Michael's and become a man.
Deborah	And I'm going to change myself back into a woman and we'll marry again.
Hugh	Are you worried that this might upset and confuse your children?
Stephen	Oh no, the twins are very aware of what's going on.
Hugh	Are they identical twins?
Deborah	That's right. A girl and a boy.
Hugh	Um – identical twins must surely be of the same sex . . . er . . .
Stephen	Yes, well Simon dresses as a girl and Lucy is a complete tomboy.
Hugh	But what sex were they originally?
Deborah	Um . . . ?
Stephen	Do you know, we can't remember.

VOX
POP

Stephen Well it's a dying art, that's
my view.

437

Forward to the Past

Stephen answers the door to Hugh who is dressed in incredible futuristic gear.

Stephen Yes?

Hugh Hello, I come from the future.

Stephen *(Annoyed)* What?

Hugh I come from the future.

Stephen Do you? Do you, indeed?

Hugh That's substantially correct, yes. I come from a time in advance of your own.

Stephen Really?

Hugh Yes, really.

Stephen And what century exactly would you be from, I wonder?

Hugh I come from the twentieth century.

Stephen So not so significantly far advanced then?

Hugh Well, no. I come from a time five minutes ahead.

Stephen Five minutes.

Hugh Yes. Five of your primitive minutes. Goodbye.

Stephen What. You're going now?

Hugh Yes.

Stephen No message from the future?

Hugh There are laws, time laws we dare not interfere with, lest we meddle with our own destinies.

438

Farewell. I may say I'm sorry that I can't return it. Please accept my apologies.

Stephen Return what?

Hugh What you lent me. It was burnt up in the time-leap. Still, as you rightly said, it was only Habitat anyway.

Exit Hugh.

Stephen *(Still standing in doorway)* Well, frankly.

Enter Hugh wearing deerstalker and cape, looking very late Victorian.

Hugh Good morning. If it is morning.

Stephen You again.

Hugh I don't think we've met.

Stephen What?

Hugh This is my first time in this neighbourhood.

Stephen Oh don't be ridiculous, I was talking to you just five . . . minutes *(Voice trails off)* . . . ago.

Hugh Something wrong?

Stephen No, no. Probably just a day dream. How can I help you?

Hugh Well the thing is, I'm a bit lost. I know this'll sound like the ravings of a complete imbecile, but you must believe me. I'm a time-traveller.

Stephen Yes, yes. From the future.

Hugh *(Puzzled)* No, from the past. Five minutes ago I projected myself five minutes into the future, into your time and I was wondering who is Prime Minister now?

439

Stephen	Margaret Thatcher. Look . . .
Hugh	Ah, really? Still? Some things never change. Has anyone invented a way of opening a packet of 'Hob Nob' biscuits without tearing their nails yet?
Stephen	No, look just what exactly –
Hugh	Is Noel Edmonds still alive?
Stephen	*(Surprised)* Not that I'm aware of. Look, is this some kind of practical joke?
Hugh	Well, I must go before I catch up with myself. I think next time I shall try going forward a bit. Farewell.

Exit Hugh.

Stephen	Bye then. This is getting very difficult to follow.

Enter Hugh dressed as normally as he ever is.

Hugh	Hello.
Stephen	And where are you from?
Hugh	This is going to sound quite unbelievable but I come from . . .
Stephen	. . . the funny farm.
Hugh	I'm sorry?
Stephen	Never mind, what time are you from then?
Hugh	North Finchley.
Stephen	What?
Hugh	North Finchley, call it Barnet.
Stephen	When?
Hugh	I'm sorry?
Stephen	When are you from?

Hugh	Are you alright?
Stephen	I – I think so, yes.
Hugh	I'm collecting.
Stephen	What?
Hugh	Collecting.
Stephen	What for?
Hugh	This blinkered, hidebound, reactionary government has no vision. I plan to build a machine. A machine that will enable man to travel . . .
Stephen	Through time, yes, yes, very clever.
Hugh	No. To travel to central London without getting caught in the traffic. The principle is simple: using ruthenium and polonium as energisers, I intend to build a prototype machine which will leap over traffic queues as if they weren't there. Simply key in the coordinates of the street you want and hey presto. Can I get a grant from the morons in government? No sir.
Stephen	You don't think there might be any unfortunate side-effects?
Hugh	What do you mean?
Stephen	Such as time-travel for instance.
Hugh	*(Laughing)* Oh I don't think so, you've been watching too many TV sketches.

Stephen looks into camera puzzled for the briefest of brief seconds.

Stephen	*(Tired)* Alright then, how much do you want?
Hugh	Oh, it's not money. It's just that the transducer needs a lampshade.
Stephen	What?

441

Hugh   I knew you'd think me crackpotted, but it's true. Just a simple common or garden lampshade, so that the gallium plate can reach P state in a picosecond and then instantly revert to an N state which . . .

Stephen   Yes, yes alright. I'll get you a lampshade. *(Goes in)*

Hugh   *(Calling after him)* Thank you! Thank you so much! You're a friend of science.

Stephen   *(Coming out with lampshade)* There you are.

Hugh   Marvellous. Bless you. I have the machine round the corner. It will only take five minutes to fit and then – London's traffic problem solved in a stroke.

Stephen   Right.

Hugh   I shall return your lampshade.

Stephen   Don't worry, it's only Habitat anyway . . . *(Voice trails away)*

Exit Hugh.

Stephen pauses for a while and then looks into camera.

I'm sure, logically, something weird should happen now, but I can't work out what.

VOX
POP

Hugh   *(Smelling a bottle)* Oh I say, that's rather good. Oh yes. Where did you get it?

The Old Folks

Stephen is behind the reception desk of an old people's home. Hugh enters.

Hugh	Hello.
Stephen	You're not very old.
Hugh	Sorry?
Stephen	I say you're not very old.
Hugh	No, I . . .
Stephen	This is an old folks' home, you see, and consequently we do ask that people wishing to stay here are, at the very least, old. It's in our charter.
Hugh	I don't want to stay here.
Stephen	Oh. Then I must instantly demand that you pardon me. Have we been talking at cross purposes do you suppose?
Hugh	Possibly, yes.
Stephen	Whoops. My fault, quite dreadful of me. We'd better start again then.
Hugh	Right.
Stephen	Right.
Hugh	I wondered if . . .
Stephen	You're not very old.
Hugh	What?
Stephen	This is an old folks' home, you see, and consequently . . .

443

Hugh	No, I don't want to stay here. I've come to see my aunt.
Stephen	Oh. No. Oh no. What a shame. She died.
Hugh	Who did?
Stephen	Your aunt. If you'd only been a few hours earlier.
Hugh	Wait a minute. You don't know who I am yet.
Stephen	I don't have to. We only had one aunt, you see and she passed away last night. Oh, we shall miss her indeed. Her cheerfulness, her sense of fun . . .
Hugh	Hold on. Do you mind if we just check the name first, to make sure we're talking about the same person?
Stephen	If there's the slightest chance that it'll help you to confront some of the painful unanswered questions that must be weighing upon you at this most difficult of times, then all of a surely.
Hugh	Thank you.
Stephen	Please don't thank me, nephew.
Hugh	Wh . . . ?
Stephen	I do this job because I love it. How many people can say that? Less than a dozen I fancy rotten. Yes, here it is. Room 14, aunt, died at ten o'clock last night.
Hugh	Yes, what was her name?
Stephen	Fourteen.
Hugh	No, her name.
Stephen	Well now, I don't think we actually have a record of her name. There isn't much space on these cards, you see? I keep on saying to the Trustees – did I say 'saying'? Beseeching on bended legs, rather – 'give me bigger cards' but . . .

444

Hugh	What was her name?
Stephen	Well before you rush headlong down that tree-lined avenue, let me just say that we're very much given to using nicknames, here.
Hugh	Nicknames?
Stephen	Indeed, yes. To myself and the rest of the staff your aunt will always be remembered as 'fourteen'. Sounds a bit informal, I know. But that's our style here. We leave formality very much outside on the doorstep, together with a cheerful note to the milkman. From the day she arrived, 'fourteen' just seemed so right somehow.
Hugh	Are you saying that a woman died here last night and you don't even know her name?
Stephen	I know that it's hard sometimes for an outsider to enter a home like this, and it is a home – did I mention that? Did I make that abundant? – and straight away understand what it is we're really trying to do here.
Hugh	My aunt's name is Amanda Thighkiss.
Stephen	Well there you are, you see. Amanda Thighkiss. How could we have called her that? It's so cold, so unfriendly. And you can see how small the cards are. I'd be lucky to squeeze 'A. Thigh' on one of these.

Deborah, as a very old lady, appears next to Stephen.

Deborah	Please . . .
Stephen	Whoops! Hahaha . . .

Stephen tries to push Deborah's head down.

Deborah	Just a piece of bread, a biscuit, anything.

445

Hugh	Aunt Amanda?
Deborah	*(Popping up)* Neville! Oh thank God!
Hugh	Are you alright?
Stephen	*(Standing in front of her)* Oh dear. Oh dear, oh dear.
Hugh	What's the matter?
Deborah	I'm starving. Have you brought any food?
Stephen	Oh dear, oh dear, oh dear. I'll never forgive myself for this. You should have been spared this. I'd give anything for you to have been spared this.
Hugh	You told me she was dead.
Deborah	Who was dead?
Stephen	As if the shock of the news was not enough, you've now had to see this. I'm so sorry. So very sorry.
Hugh	What are you talking about?
Stephen	I'm sorry that you should be confronted with the body in this fashion. It's all very distressing.
Hugh	Body?
Stephen	Still, spiritually she's in a better place now. Let's be grateful for that.
Hugh	She's standing right there.
Stephen	Well of course her body is right here, but her soul . . . Who knows what beautiful journey . . . ?
Deborah	Please, Neville, have you got any food?
Hugh	Food? No. Are you hungry?
Deborah	I haven't eaten since lunchtime yesterday.
Hugh	Lunchtime yesterday? What's the matter, don't you feed people here at all?

Stephen	Of surely course.
Hugh	You do?
Stephen	Indeed yes. Our guests have had more hot dinners than you've had . . . than you've had.
Hugh	Then why hasn't my aunt been fed since yesterday?
Stephen	Ah. You're a stranger to death, I can see. Let me just say, as simply as I can, that it is deeply unusual to give food to dead people.
Hugh	What?
Stephen	Unless, of course, it is specified in the will. Otherwise we tend to look upon it as a needless extravagance. However, if it is your wish . . .
Hugh	What are you talking about? My aunt is not dead.
Stephen	Are you a medical person?
Hugh	No.
Stephen	Ah.
Hugh	Look, she's standing there, talking and breathing . . .
Deborah	*(Faintly)* Aaagh . . .
Hugh	. . . just . . . and you're telling me that she's dead.
Stephen	I can readily understand that the effect of the shock taken with the friendly brightness of our decor would make it hard for you to grasp . . .
Hugh	She is not dead. *(To Deborah)* Are you?
Deborah	No.
Hugh	There.
Stephen	Oh I know how much you want to believe it. Otherwise how could you stand the loss? But you

447

	see, I too have lost. When dear old fourteen died, a little part of me died with her.
Hugh	Did it?
Stephen	Yes, I shall be burying that little part of me this afternoon after a simple but affecting ceremony in the garden. Would you like to come?
Hugh	Look. Why do you keep saying that she's dead? Just tell me . . .
Stephen	Well, if it won't be too painful . . .
Hugh	No go on. I'm keen to know.
Stephen	Brave, brave nephew. What happened was this. I sent out a final reminder, thirty days after the last payment fell due, and believe me, even at that stage I still hoped that all might be well . . .
Hugh	Wait a minute. Payment for what?
Stephen	Why, room and board. Payment comes due on a monthly basis. Most of our guests favour an arrangement whereby . . .
Hugh	You mean she hasn't paid her bill?
Stephen	Sadly, no. We're all so very sorry. My deepest and most heartfelt condolences to you.
Hugh	How much?
Stephen	Your very pardon?
Hugh	How much does she owe?
Stephen	A very tragic one hundred and nineteen pounds and seven pence.
Hugh	*(Getting out cheque book)* Well for goodness sake, *(Writing)* one hundred . . . nineteen pounds and seven . . . pence. There.
Stephen	*(Taking it without looking – his gaze is fixed on Deborah, who has started to eat the desk blotter)*

448

Fourteen! Can it be true? Can I be believant of my eyes! I'm sure I saw . . . *(To Hugh, briskly)* Would you mind putting your card number on the back?

Hugh does so and hands over the cheque.

Yes! She moves, she stirs, she seems to feel the breath of life beneath her keel. It's a miracle! A miracle!

A porter enters wheeling a conspicuously dead person on a trolley.

Number twelve! Look at this! Number fourteen has come back to life! Oh wonder of wonders!

Hugh   Now come on, that woman really is dead.

Stephen   On the contrary, sir. She has a standing order.

VOX
POP

Stephen   *(Wrinkling nose in disgust)* Oh that's horrid. That's really horrid. Disgusting. Is it Welsh?

Hugh's Brain

Enter Stephen, holding a human brain.

Stephen Ladies and gentlemen, I wonder how many of
you know what this is? Well most of you will know
that it's a brain, a human brain, but can you guess
whose brain it is? I should tell you first of all that
for some time I've enjoyed a bit of a reputation
as a practical joker, you see, and what I've done is
this. While Hugh was asleep in his dressing room,
I crept in and very carefully removed his brain,
being sure not to wake him up. This is Hugh's
brain. He'll be coming on in a second, let's see if
he's noticed anything's amiss . . .

Enter Hugh, laughing cheerfully.

Hugh Hahahaha.

Stephen Hello, Hugh. What have you been up to?

Hugh I've just been watching that Noël Edmonds show,
it's so funny. Just brilliant. Completely brilliant.

Stephen Ha. Are you feeling alright?

Hugh Yeah, fine, fine.

Stephen Good.

Hugh And then I saw a bit of an interview with Kenneth
Baker. That man is fantastic.

Stephen Do you think so?

Hugh Oh, he's wonderful. He's just what this country
needs. He's firm, courageous, and his views on
education are so enlightened, so sophisticated,

450

so utterly enthralling. Well, he's an enthralling person, of course.

Stephen *(To audience)* It's great, isn't it? We can see the difference, but poor old Hugh hasn't noticed a thing. *(To Hugh)* D'you recognise this?

Hugh It's a cauliflower.

Stephen Hahaha. A cauliflower. Hasn't he been a sport, ladies and gentlemen? So what are you going to do now?

Hugh I thought I'd write a letter to 'Points of View'.

Stephen Dear oh dear oh dear. Perhaps I've gone a bit far.

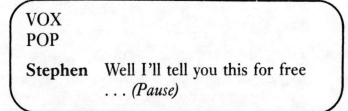

451

Christening

Mother (Deborah Norton) and father (Hugh) standing at font with baby. Stephen is the vicar. Hugh is very much the modern thrusting executive.

Stephen   I baptise thee Rupert Jeremy James –

Hugh   No, hold on a minute.

Stephen   What is it?

Hugh   You're right darling, Nicholas is better. Nicholas Thomas Geoffrey.

Stephen   Nicholas Thomas Geoffrey.

Deborah   You can't have Nicholas Thomas: that's a very ugly rhyme.

Hugh   You're right. What was the other one we liked?

Deborah   Timothy Nicholas Peter.

Hugh   No, Nicholas *Timothy* Peter.

Stephen   *(Dipping finger in water)* OK. Nicholas Timothy Peter?

Deborah   Yes.

Hugh   It's a shame to lose Jeremy though, isn't it?

Deborah   I still like Duncan.

Hugh   Duncan Jeremy Nicholas or Nicholas Jeremy Duncan?

Stephen   Look. I have got a wedding in ten minutes.

Hugh   You're being paid aren't you?

Stephen   *(Puzzled)* No . . .

Hugh	Nick's idea was Peregrine.
Deborah	Oh darling, you can't call a baby Peregrine.
Stephen	So Peregrine Jeremy Duncan . . .
Deborah	I know it sounds silly but I've always loved Dick.
Stephen	Erm . . .
Hugh	Now Dirk's due for a revival.
Deborah	Duncan Dirk Dick.
Hugh	Rather fetching.
Stephen	Duncan Dirk Dick, I baptise thee in the name of the Father and of the Son, and of the Holy Ghost, Amen. We receive this child into the congregation of Christ's flock and do sign him with the sign of the cross *(Signs with finger on forehead)* and in token that hereafter he shall not be ashamed to confess the faith of Christ crucified and manfully to fight under his banner against sin, the world and the devil, and to continue Christ's faithful soldier and servant unto his life's end. Amen.
Hugh	No it's still not right . . . I don't know . . . hold on, what about Tweeble?
Deborah	Oh darling . . .
Hugh	Well it's our nickname for the little blighter anyway, so why not?
Deborah	Tweeble Timothy James, I like it.
Hugh	Yeah, Tweeble Timothy James.
Stephen	I'm sorry, it's Duncan Dirk Dick, I've just done it.
Hugh	Well, undo it.
Stephen	Undo it?

Hugh	Yes.
Stephen	This is a Holy Sacrament of the Church, not a bleeding hotel reservation, you can't just undo it.
Hugh	You're beginning to annoy me, buster. Look at this card. *(Holds up white card)* What does this say?
Stephen	'Christening service'.
Hugh	Yes. Service, notice – not rudeness. It doesn't say 'Christening Rudeness'.
Stephen	I wasn't being rude.
Hugh	Just bear in mind that there are plenty of other religions you know. Some of them, I may say, offering much greater range and value.
Deborah	Not to mention carpets. Look at this.
Hugh	So come on. Hand him over.
Stephen	What?
Hugh	Hand him over. We'll take a look at the Mosque on Arlington Road, if it's all the same to you.
Stephen	But I haven't finished the service!
Hugh	The rudeness, you mean? Well you should have thought of that before.
Stephen	Look, you can't just walk out half way through. Think of the child!
Hugh	Screw the child. Haven't you heard the news?
Stephen	Well I've heard some news, but I doubt if it's the same news that you're . . .
Hugh	There's a revolution going on. Enterprise, initiative. Those who can't trim their fat go to the wall.
Stephen	What wall?
Hugh	What wa . . . ? You just don't know what I'm

454

talking about do you? I'm talking about the
way you're running this flea-bitten, one-horse
operation. Take this building. All this equity
tied up for what? A couple of weddings a week.
Pathetic. God, I'd like to get my hands on this
place. I could really do something. Shopping
arcade, four luxury flats, brasserie downstairs. It's
a criminal waste.

Stephen *(Getting annoyed, puts baby in font to use both hands
to speak – no one notices)* Look, matey, this is a
church, not a dealing room. I am not interested
in your creepy theories about enterprise and
initiative. This place is founded on ideas a bit
more permanent than the Dow Jones Index.

Hugh Yeah?

Stephen Yeah. Something a tadge classier than 'buy long,
sell short and get into gilts'.

Hugh Uhuh?

Stephen The Church will be here long after your little brat
has grown up, ripped a few people off and died
unloved in his Spanish retirement villa.

Deborah Portuguese, actually. And there's no need to be
so beastly.

Stephen Well I'm sorry, but people like you really piss
me off.

Hugh You've got a big mouth, mister. So what's your
pitch, your scam, your angle?

Stephen Well look at you. You fight and deal and cheat
all your life to get enough money to spend a few
years wobbling your fat old bodies round a beach
or a golf course, but what provision have you
made for after your retirement?

Hugh *After* my retirement?

Stephen I'm talking about heaven.

455

Hugh	Heaven? Isn't that where the Gilroys went, darling?
Deborah	Devon.
Hugh	Oh yeah.
Stephen	After a hard life, don't you think you ought to treat yourself to a little long-term security? I'm talking about lifestyle, status, comfort, and peace-of-mind.
Deborah	*(Nudging Hugh)* Don't trust him, Pudding.
Hugh	Give me space, give me space.
Stephen	She's right, think about it, Pudding. Think about it. Talk to your independent spiritual adviser.
Hugh	Hmm. He may have something.
Stephen	And if you won't treat yourself, have a thought for Duncan Dirk Dick. Give him a chance to get in on the ground floor.
Hugh	Darling, and no disrespect to you, Vicar, but what I'm thinking is this. How about a mixed portfolio, whereby we spread him through Judaism, Islam, Hindu and so on, maintaining a firm base in the Church of England?
Deborah	It does sound safer.
Hugh	Exactly.
Stephen	Alright. So. Duncan Dirk Dick, I baptise thee in . . .
Deborah	Well then it ought to be something like Duncan Isaac Sanji.
Hugh	Duncan Abraham Sanji would be nice.
Deborah	Or how about Duncan Abraham Naresh?
Stephen	Right. Do it yourselves. There's the water, there's the hymn book. I'm off for a slash.

456

Bank Loan

Bank manager's office. Stephen sitting behind the desk. Hugh enters, looking quite needlessly repellent, folders and things tucked under his arm.

Stephen *(Rising)* Mr Lully?

Hugh That's right. Glad you could see me at such short notice.

Stephen Not at all, come in, sit down. Coffee?

Hugh Thank you.

Stephen How do you like it?

Hugh Decaffeinated, jug method, low mineral content filtered spring water, not quite brought to the boil with semi-skimmed milk and one Nutrasweet. Unstirred.

Stephen Right. *(Intercom)* Mark?

Voice *(Intercom distort)* Yes.

Stephen Do we still have that chemistry set in the office?

Voice *(Intercom distort)* 'Fraid not.

Stephen Right, one coffee then please.

Voice *(Intercom distort)* K.

Stephen So, Mr Lully, you'd like a loan?

Hugh That's pretty much the size of it.

Stephen You mention in your letter that you're starting up a business and that you're interested in taking advantage of our new 'Gredo' start-up package.

Hugh That's correct.

457

Stephen   Yes, now first things first. What exactly is the product you're hoping to market?

Hugh   Ah, yes. Brought some samples along as a matter of fact.

Hugh gets out two small sachets.

Haven't actually settled on brand names yet. But there's basically two products. The blue sachet is cocaine and the red is heroin.

Stephen   I'm sorry?

Hugh   My own market research and some work undertaken by the packaging and graphics team has revealed that cocaine is thought of as a fresher, brighter product, hence the blue, and heroin is warmer and more passionate, therefore red. You disagree? I'd value your input.

Stephen   You're planning to distribute and sell drugs?

Hugh   On the button. The market's there, I'm ready to go, and let's face it – Europe's open for business.

Stephen   Ye-e-es.

Hugh   Problem?

Stephen   Possibly. Possibly.

Hugh   I know what you're going to say. It's a market that up until now has been hedged about with a lot of rules and regulations, and let me tell you this. When I first began to look at this market, I thought to myself, 'hey, I'd be better off manufacturing red tape'. Hahaha!

Stephen   Red tape, yes.

Hugh   But thank God, times are changing. Whole new markets are opening up, and I'm ready to play them.

458

Stephen	Right.
Hugh	The demand is there, no question.
Stephen	Uh huh.
Hugh	The most exciting thing for me is that it's such a young market.
Stephen	Really?
Hugh	Immensely young. Consumer profiling indicates the twelve to fifteen-year-old segment. And if we can instil in them product loyalty, that's got to be good news.
Stephen	Aha. But . . . but . . .
Hugh	I know what you're going to say. 'Do they have the income?' right? Well, what I always say is, 'if the product's right, they'll find the income.' Their mothers' handbags, car stereos, old age pensioners, wherever.
Stephen	Mmm. I meant, well . . . I hesitate to use a word like this. I know it's old-fashioned. But do you think it's strictly moral?
Hugh	I beg your pardon?
Stephen	Is it moral?
Hugh	Moral?
Stephen	Yes.
Hugh	I'm not sure if I've actually got any precise figures on that . . .
Stephen	Yes, I actually mean . . . is it moral to do this at all? You know . . . children and so on.
Hugh	Well. Let me turn the question round and ask you this. Would you rather we stood by and watched the Germans, the Dutch, the South Americans take our market share? Where's your precious morality then?

459

Stephen   Well . . .

Hugh   Up a gum tree without a paddle, that's where it is. The question is this. Either you believe in market forces or you don't.

Stephen   Well actually, I'm afraid to say I don't.

Hugh   You don't?

Stephen   No. I used to of course, when I was a child, but like everyone else, I discovered as I grew older that it was all made up.

Hugh   Made up?

Stephen   Yes. I can still remember the exact moment. It was Christmas Eve. I can't have been more than about thirty years old. I couldn't sleep, so I crept downstairs and heard my parents laughing about market forces, and saying that they'd have to break it to me sooner or later. Bit of a blow, I can tell you. And then two years after that, I discovered there was no such thing as Father Christmas either.

Hugh   You're kidding?

Stephen   Oh sorry, did you . . . ?

Hugh   Yes I did. Tscch.

Stephen   Oh dear.

Hugh   Growing up, eh?

VOX
POP

Stephen   Well, you haven't paid me yet.

460

Ignorance

Stephen and Hugh are having a chat in a setting yet to be decided.

Stephen   Interested in politics at all?

Hugh   Interested?

Stephen   Yes.

Hugh   It's my hobby.

Stephen   Is it?

Hugh   Crikey yes. Politics? Oh yes. Of course it's mostly a weekend thing I'm afraid, but come Sunday, it's down the end of the garden and politics, politics, politics. In answer to your question, yes. I'm a bugger for politics.

Stephen   What do you think of Nigel Lawson?

Hugh   Nigel . . .

Stephen   Lawson.

Hugh   Lawson, yes. *(Long pause)* What d'you think of him?

Stephen   He's a twerp.

Hugh   Oh, thank God for that. I thought he might have been a friend of yours or something. Yes, he's a twerp. What a twerp. Tscch.

Stephen   At least you know who he is.

Hugh   I don't actually, to be honest.

Stephen   You don't?

Hugh   Not who he is, no. I've always just thought of him as a twerp. Never bothered to look any deeper than that. It's the shortage of time . . .

Stephen He's Chancellor of the Exchequer. Just.

Hugh No. Is he? The old bastard. Nigel Lawson, the Chancellor of the Exchequer? What a twerp. Tscch.

Stephen *(To camera)* Perhaps you can see what we're trying to do here. Hugh is trying to act the part of a man who doesn't know very much about politics. *(To Hugh)* What do you think of Douglas Hurd?

Hugh Douglas Hurd. Er . . . Pretty lukewarm about him, to be honest.

Stephen Really?

Hugh Yeah. Bit of a twerp. But . . .

Stephen *(To camera)* Hugh is pretending not to know who Douglas Hurd is.

Hugh . . . you know, it takes all sorts to make a world.

Stephen D'you think?

Hugh Oh definitely.

Stephen You don't think that with fewer twerps, you could make a better world?

Hugh Oh you've got to keep the number of twerps down, yes. You can't let them run out of control.

Stephen Tell me something. Did you vote at the last election?

Hugh Oh they haven't banned them as well, have they?

Stephen What?

Hugh Was that the last election? Never going to be any more, ever again? Tscch! And I missed it.

Stephen *(To camera)* I suppose what we're trying to say

462

with this sketch is, can democracy really work
as long as the people who vote are kept, or keep
themselves, in ignorance of political affairs?

Hugh   Is that what we're trying to say?

Stephen   Yes.

Hugh   Blimey.

Stephen   Because let's face it, doesn't the constitution of
the present government show, more clearly than
a thousand pictures ever could, that the people of
this country haven't the faintest idea who they're
voting for?

Hugh   Are we trying to say that as well, with this sketch?

Stephen   Oh yes.

Hugh   Turning out to be quite an ambitious sketch, then?

Stephen   You've got to aim high in my view. So, you don't
really know anything about Nigel Lawson or
Douglas Hurd?

Hugh   No.

Stephen   So I think this has gone some way towards
proving . . .

Hugh   Mind you, I don't see why I should.

Stephen   Pardon?

Hugh   They don't know anything about me. Do they?

Stephen   Well . . .

Hugh   I mean, you say I don't know anything about
them, so how can I vote, but I say they don't know
anything about me, so how can they vote . . . to
make laws about me?

Stephen   Mmm. That would be quite a good point, if it
weren't so pathetic.

463

Hugh	Oh I see. We're not aiming that high, then? We don't want to say too much with this sketch?
Stephen	No.
Hugh	But there's so much more we could say.
Stephen	Perhaps, but I'm afraid that time, the old enemy has beaten us again, and we can only say that the pen of my aunt is bigger than the patio of my uncle.
Hugh	Huh. Quite a pen.
Stephen	Quite an aunt.

VOX
POP

Stephen   On the bottom. Right on the bottom. Saying 'Made In Korea'. I don't know what made him say that.

A Bit of a Pain in the Bottom

Stephen enters a surgery. Hugh is sitting behind a desk.

Stephen Hello, Doctor.

Hugh Ah, come in. Look, you're the last, do you mind if this is very quick?

Stephen Er . . . no.

Hugh Alright then, how can I help?

Stephen *(Very fast)* Well Doctor, the fact is that I've got a bit of a pain in the bottom.

Hugh *(Just as fast, if not faster)* A bit of a pain in the bottom, I see. How did this happen?

Stephen Well I was out shopping this afternoon, and across the other side of the road a bomb went off in a shop.

Hugh A bomb? Good heavens!

Stephen Yes, and anyway, the whole pane of glass in the window of the shop next to me blew out.

Hugh The whole pane?

Stephen Yes, and anyway, a bit of the pane flew out and hit me in the arm.

Hugh The arm.

Stephen Yes. So I dropped my shopping, unfortunately on the foot of a horse that was standing in the street.

Hugh A horse?

Stephen Yes. A Horse. Are you deaf? And the horse shied and just as I was bending down to pick up my shopping this horse kicked me in the other arm.

Hugh	The other arm? I see.
Stephen	So I went over to a doorway and sat down. But I didn't look where I was sitting, there was glass everywhere, and as I sat down I got a bit of glass right in the palm of my hand.
Hugh	Palm of your hand?
Stephen	Yes and I had this bottle of strong acid in my bag and unbeknownst to me I spilt some on the step when I stood up, sharply, from the pain of the bit of pane of glass in the palm of my hand.
Hugh	I see, you spilt some acid.
Stephen	So then I caught the bus home.
Hugh	You caught the bus home.
Stephen	Yes, you are deaf. And on the bus I sat next to this pervert. He took out an enormous carrot, and at knife point he . . .
Hugh	Good Lord.
Stephen	He made me put it up my nose, while he watched.
Hugh	Heavens.
Stephen	So I ran out of the bus, which was moving, so I landed with a great bump and grazed my knee. But eventually I got home.
Hugh	Good.
Stephen	And I rushed to the bathroom because I was dying to go, you know . . .
Hugh	Mmm.
Stephen	But I rushed out of the bathroom, because there's no toilet in there, and I went into the lavatory instead. But there wasn't any paper.
Hugh	Ah!

Stephen So I had to get some from the cupboard. I then went upstairs to change, and there was a wasp in my new pair of trousers.

Hugh Oh, a wasp!

Stephen Yes, so I killed it. Then I went downstairs and watched television.

Hugh Mmm.

Stephen And it was that Paul Daniels, who's a bit of a pain in the bottom. Doctor, what can you do about it?

Hugh Doh!

Stephen Doh!

Both Doh!!!

VOX
POP

Stephen I said to him, he must have been about fourteen, then. I said 'Son, you can't carry on forever just hanging onto your mother's apron. She's going to want it back one day.'

Inspector Venice

A woman answers the door. Hugh is standing there, in a raincoat and pork pie hat.

Hugh   Good evening, Chief Inspector Venice, Burnham CID. May I come in?

Woman   Of course you can, dear. It's your house.

She turns and walks away, leaving the door open.

Hugh   You stupid woman! You stupid bloody woman! Come back here! Are you mad? I could be anybody! I could be a maniac!

Woman   You're my husband, dear.

Hugh   How do you know that? I mean how do you know that? Have I produced any identification?

Woman   No.

Hugh   No, exactly.

Woman   But . . .

Hugh   Ask to see my warrant card.

Woman   *(Sighs)* Can I see your warrant card, dear?

Hugh   Certainly madam. A very wise precaution, if I may say so.

Hugh produces warrant card, and holds it under her nose.

Woman   Good, now do you . . .

Hugh   Well look at it! You haven't even looked at it! Jesus, I could have bought this in Whitechapel,

	for all you know. I could be a maniac with a fake warrant card.
Woman	Alright. 'Chief Inspector . . .
Hugh	Don't leave the door open! God almighty! Use the chain, woman! What do you think it's there for?

She closes door. Hugh stays outside while she reads the card.

| **Woman** | *(Off)* 'Chief Inspector Venice, Burnham CID.' |

She opens the door again.

Now come in and have your dinner, dear.

Hugh	Come in where?
Woman	The kitchen.
Hugh	I'm sorry. I have no authorisation to enter the kitchen.
Woman	You don't need it. It's your kitchen.
Hugh	Our kitchen, dear.
Woman	Our kitchen.
Hugh	You know perfectly well, I cannot enter our kitchen without your special permission.
Woman	You have my permission.
Hugh	Haven't you forgotten something, dear?
Woman	What?
Hugh	We agreed that we would both get telephone confirmation of the other's identity, before either of us gave special permission.
Woman	Oh Christ.
Hugh	Here's the telephone, dear. And remember. Better

safe than cut up into tiny pieces by a maniac pretending to be me.

She dials.

Woman   Burnham CID? Have you got an Inspector Venice in your department? *(Pause)* Thank you very much indeed.

Hugh   Well?

Woman   They've never heard of you.

Hugh   Damn. Anyway, what's for supper? Smells great.

Woman   They've never heard of Inspector Venice.

Hugh   Probably just a joke. We're always having jokes, down the station.

Woman   You're not a policeman, are you?

Hugh   No. No, I'm not.

Woman   What are you?

Hugh   A maniac.

VOX POP

Hugh   Desmond Lynam. Yeah, Desmond Lynam. Roughly equivalent to Malcolm Muggeridge in old money.

Special Squad

Deborah is sitting on a sofa watching television. Suddenly there is some extremely violent hammering at the door. We hear Stephen and Hugh off.

Stephen   *(Off)* Just turn the handle.

More crashing.

(Off) Turn the handle. What's the matter with you?

Hugh   *(Off)* Nothing.

More crashing.

Stephen   *(Off)* All you've got to do is . . .

Hugh   *(Off)* Look, I've carried this bloody thing all the way from the car park, I'm not going to just turn the handle and walk in.

Stephen   *(Off)* All right, well I'll turn the handle.

Hugh   *(Off)* Do what you like. I'm smashing this bloody door in.

The door opens. Stephen enters the room.

(Off) Close the door, close the door.

Hugh stays in the doorway and smashes the door to pieces with a sledgehammer.

Deborah   *(Scared)* What do you want?

Stephen   Mrs Catherine Popey?

Deborah	Yes? What? Who are you?
Stephen	Sorry to disturb you madam, my colleague and I are making some routine door-to-door enquiries in this area. D'you mind if we come in?

The door is finally off its hinges.

Hugh	Finished.
Deborah	Well, why didn't you ring the bell?
Stephen	You see, I knew this would happen. She's now asking why we didn't ring the bell.
Hugh	We thought you were out.
Stephen	No, that's the wrong answer. That's the wrong answer.
Hugh	We didn't want to disturb you.
Stephen	No. No no no.
Hugh	If we had rung the bell, there would have been no point in my having carried a sledgehammer all the way from the car park.
Deborah	I see.
Stephen	*(Pause)* Yup. Looks like we may have got away with that one. Now Mrs Popey, is your husband at home?
Deborah	What?
Stephen	Your husband. Is he at home at the current time?
Deborah	I haven't got a husband.
Stephen	You haven't got a husband? I see. Right.
Hugh	Well when do you expect him back?
Deborah	What?
Stephen	No. No. That's the wrong question.

472

Hugh	Is it?
Stephen	Yes it is. Now then . . .
Hugh	When do you expect her back?
Stephen	Now then Mrs Popey, please excuse the incompleteness of our records. Computer trace indicates that you are currently the holder of a husband.
Deborah	Well I'm not.
Stephen	You're not. Well I'll have my colleagues amend the record accordingly. Now then Mrs Popey.
Deborah	Yes?
Stephen	Your husband's been a bit busy lately, hasn't he?
Deborah	What?
Stephen	Been giving us the proper runaround.
Hugh	He's scum. That's what he is. He's a scumbag. A great big bag of scum, he is, scumming around in a big bag. That's what he is. And he always will be.
Deborah	I haven't got a husband. I'm not married.
Hugh	You can take the scum out of the bag, but you can't take the bag out of the scum.
Stephen	Yeah . . .
Hugh	Boil in the bag scum, that's what he is.
Stephen	Yeah, my colleague has perhaps adopted a rather more forthright tone than I would have chosen, but then I like to think that's why we work so well together. Because we compliment each other, you see.
Deborah	Really?
Stephen	Yes, we compliment each other beautifully. Watch this. You're looking very smart today.

473

Hugh	Thank you. That's a very nice haircut.
Stephen	You see? Teamwork. Now then. To business, Mrs Popey. Your husband has . . .
Deborah	For heaven's sake. How many times do I have to tell you? I haven't got a husband.
Stephen	Well now . . .
Hugh	Twenty-five.
Stephen	Excuse me for just a moment, would you, Mrs Popey? *(To Hugh)* What?
Hugh	She's got to tell us twenty-five times that she hasn't got a husband.
Stephen	Why?
Hugh	Once for every day in the week.
Stephen	Yeah, that doesn't quite work.
Hugh	Doesn't it?
Stephen	No.
Hugh	Alright. Once for every year he's going to spend inside. The scumbag.
Deborah	Look, I don't know who you are, or why you want to speak to a husband I haven't got, but I'm telling you . . .
Stephen	Oh, we don't want to speak to him.
Deborah	Don't you?
Stephen	No no no.
Hugh	No no. Speak to him? No.
Stephen	If I may say so, I think you've been watching too many films, Mrs Popey.
Deborah	Well whatever. The point is, I haven't got a husband and therefore do you think it's possible that you might actually have the wrong house?

474

Stephen	No no no.
Hugh	No no no no no no no.
Stephen	No.
Hugh	No. You see, we've already been there.
Deborah	Where?
Hugh	To the wrong house. We've just come from the wrong house, just now.
Stephen	My colleague is absolutely right, as it happens Mrs Popey. We have, just this minute, come from the wrong house. So that argument doesn't really stand up, I'm afraid.
Hugh	No. That argument falls straight over.
Stephen	Yeah.
Hugh	And just lies there.
Stephen	Now since you claim to be alone in the house, you won't mind us having a quick look around?
Deborah	How quick?
Stephen	Very quick.
Deborah	Help yourself.
Stephen	Thank you.

Stephen and Hugh wave their heads about, stupidly.

	There. That didn't hurt, did it?
Hugh	It did actually.
Deborah	Just whatever you do, don't wake up my son.
Stephen	I beg your pardon?
Hugh	Yeah so do I. I beg it as well.
Deborah	My son is asleep upstairs. I'd rather you didn't wake him.

475

Stephen	Now wait a minute Mrs Popey. Wait just a minute.
Hugh	Whoah there, boy! Whoah!
Stephen	Hold on one second. You have a son?
Deborah	Yes.
Stephen	Well now Mrs Popey, we may be stupid, but we're not clever. How do you come to have a son without having a husband? That sounds mightily ingenious.
Deborah	He was a sailor.
Stephen	Mmm. In the Navy?
Deborah	No, with the Nat West.
Stephen	I see. Well, we'll leave that for the moment. This son of yours, he's upstairs, you say?
Deborah	Yes, asleep.
Hugh	What, tired, is he?
Stephen	I'm not surprised he's tired after the merry dance he's been leading us.
Hugh	Yes, a very merry dance indeed he's been a-leading us of. Highly merry. Ha, ha, ha, it's so merry.
Stephen	I think we'd better have a word with this son of yours, Mrs Popey, if it's all the same to you.
Deborah	Only if you promise to leave as soon as you've finished.
Stephen	Of course Mrs Popey. We'll leave just as soon as we've finished being here.

Deborah exits.

What a charming woman.

Hugh	Charming. Delightful. A really super woman.

Stephen	She's taken it so well.
Hugh	This is it, you see.
Stephen	Too well, perhaps.
Hugh	Well I didn't want to say, but yes, she may have taken it too well.

Deborah reenters, carrying a cot containing a small baby.

Deborah	This is my son William.
Stephen	Aha. You've been a bit of a naughty boy, haven't you, William?
Hugh	Ask him what he's done with the stuff.
Stephen	Now then William, what have you done with the stuff? *(To Hugh)* What stuff?
Hugh	I don't know. It was a trap.
Stephen	He hasn't fallen for it.
Hugh	*(Pause)* Scumbag.

VOX
POP

Hugh Who are the great hat-wearers of
today? There aren't any, you see.
No one for the kids to look up to.

Orthodoxy

Headmaster's study. Stephen is behind a desk. Quite a public-schooly sort of study, but not overdone. Not actually window seats and old English Gothic windows, but quite cosy nonetheless. Enter Hugh dressed as a schoolboy. Grey uniform, darkish tie. Dull appearance.

Stephen Ah, Bamford, come in, come in.

Hugh Thank you, sir.

Stephen So, Bamford. First day at St Gray's, eh?

Hugh Yes, sir.

Stephen Getting on alright?

Hugh *(Shy)* Not too bad thank you, sir.

Stephen Not too bad thank you, sir. Not too bad thank you, sir. Good, good. Good, good, good. You'll find it strange at first I dare say.

Hugh It's a bit hard to find my feet, sir, yes.

Stephen Really, well we'll have to do something about that. Some sort of name-tape sewn into them may help. But the first few days are always a little bewildering.

Hugh Yes sir.

Stephen Mind you Bamford, if you were to believe everything you read on the television you'd think new boys spent their days being roasted in front of fires and having dessert fruits pushed up their . . . their . . . there couldn't be less truth in that, could there, Bamford?

Hugh No, sir.

Stephen	No, sir. Quite right. Schools like ours have survived because they've moved into the modern age, Bamford. Progress, Bamford.
Hugh	Sir.
Stephen	Progress isn't a dirty word, you know. Arse is a dirty word, and so, to some extent, is labia. Learn that, Bamford, learn and obey.
Hugh	Yes, sir. I will.
Stephen	But progress is the towel that rubs us dry. Each soft cotton flick of progress can penetrate the darkest, dampest corners of our mired and filthy selves, and polish us clean.
Hugh	I didn't know that, sir.
Stephen	Well Bamford, now you do, now you do. Good. Oh good. First class. Fine. Splendid. Sp-len-did. Excellent. Eccellente.
Hugh	Um, was there anything else?
Stephen	Hm? Yes, yes indeed there was anything else. There's a rumour going around the Lower Fourth that you have an uncle who is a Member of Parliament.
Hugh	Yes, sir.
Stephen	A Labour Member of Parliament, Bamford.
Hugh	Sir.
Stephen	Now, on the whole, boys are a pretty healthy, tolerant and forgiving lot, Bamford. But they can be cruel. You can answer this next question with perfect frankness, it won't transgress that schoolboy code we masters know and respect so well. Have you been teased at all about this unfortunate relationship?
Hugh	Well sir, not teased exactly . . . more, well, beaten up.

479

Stephen I see. I'm sorry you saw fit to sneak on your schoolmates, Bamford. That disappoints me. I shall overlook it this time.

Hugh Thank you, sir.

Stephen You're a new bug after all. Do you know why they have been ballyragging you?

Hugh I must say, I'm a bit puzzled by it, to be frank, sir.

Stephen Well, you see, in my history and general study lessons I sometimes speak about Socialism and I expect that's made something of an impression on your classmates. Their political zeal may have got the better of them.

Hugh Oh.

Stephen You see, I tell the boys, Bamford, and this may come as quite a shock to you, that while socialism is all very well in practice it doesn't work in theory.

Hugh I didn't know that, sir.

Stephen Yes. Quite a thought isn't it?

Hugh And that's why they punch me in the face a lot, is it sir?

Stephen Well Bamford, they know that the real evil of socialism lies in its treatment of people as units. It discounts the individual, Bamford. It's the grey, dull uniformity of it all.

Hugh Yes, sir.

Stephen And the – have you got your top button undone, Bamford?

Hugh Oh, yes, sir.

Stephen (As if reciting a catechism) 'The top button to be done up only on Crimson Days or on the Thursday preceding exeats, otherwise the middle button unless you have a note from matron to say

480

you have a veruka in which case the bottom button may be done up, but only if the left sock is rolled halfway down between patella and Achilles tendon on a line previously drawn by Mr de Vere.'

Hugh   Sorry, sir, I forgot.

Stephen   Alright. Don't let it happen again. Where was I?

Hugh   Grey dull uniformity of it all, sir.

Stephen   Yes. Yes, exactly. Regimented lines of soulless automata, putting state before self, sacrificing everything for 'the good of the state' – it's a nightmare. That's the drawback of socialism, it discounts the – the what, boy?

Hugh   The person, sir?

Stephen   No, the individual! Get it right. The individual is paramount in any political system – your hair is two thirds of an inch over the collar, see Mr Buttaris for a licking – individualism is all. Alright, Bamford. That's all. We shall all make a mighty effort to overlook your uncle for the moment.

Hugh   Thank you sir.

Stephen   Good. And cheer up, eh? I know you'll do your best, what?

Hugh   I'll try, sir.

Stephen   That's right, boy. For the good of the school, eh? For the good of the dear old school. After all, we can point with pride at our history as the finest comprehensive in Durham, can't have you letting the side down. Off you go.

Hugh   Thank you, sir.

Stephen   *(Getting cane out of drawer)* And send Scargill minor in, would you?

Critics Three

Stephen and Hugh are in the swivel chairs again.

Stephen Simon Clituris, you saw that. Thoughts? Inferences?

Hugh Well, you see they fell into the old trap, the old trap of doing material that is essentially self-referential.

Stephen By using the term 'self-referential', you mean . . . ?

Hugh I mean to present myself as an impressive, even perhaps interesting, person.

Stephen Ng. Ng. Aren't you getting a little tired though of humouresque material on television that is *about* television?

Hugh Very tired. Exhausted.

Stephen I think there's something very incestuous about people who make love to close blood relations. Perhaps it's just me.

Hugh You see I wish, I wish they'd come to me when they first wrote that sketch. I could have just pointed out to them where they had gone wrong.

Stephen This was my feeling exactly. Just nudged them gently in the right direction. It's all they needed. There's *some* talent there.

Hugh Would you have said that?

Stephen Well, not talent perhaps. I don't think they'd make very impressive critics for example.

482

Hugh	They always put out these things without consulting us first. I mean we're here to help.
Stephen	To help and to criticize. I'm sick up to the back stomach with the kind of comedy that has such utter and profound contempt for people like us.
Hugh	You see it's interesting isn't it, if you compare that sketch with the work of someone like Diana Suckleigh.
Stephen	Ah. Now, you see?
Hugh	Diana is observant, she's real, she's truthful.
Stephen	Always truthful. Very beautifully truthful and real. Very actual.
Hugh	I mean it doesn't all work.
Stephen	Oh no.
Hugh	She makes mistakes, but then which of them doesn't?
Stephen	That's right. We can't all be critics, for goodness' sake.

VOX
POP

Stephen	What you've got to do is boil them, for about ten or twelve minutes, and then slice them down the middle. But these judges nowadays are soft. Far too soft.

Spies Four

The spies' office. Stephen is pacing up and down frantically.

Hugh enters.

Hugh Hullo there Control. Something up?

Stephen *(Still walking)* Well, it's a strange thing, Tony, but I've been advised that in order to stay fit I have to walk at least ten miles a day.

Hugh But you've always been as fit as a flea, Control. Or a fiddle anyway. 'One of the fittest men in the service' you've been occasionally referred to as.

Stephen Look at this.

Stephen brings out a pedometer.

Hugh What is it?

Stephen That's what I asked myself when the doctor gave it to me. It's a pedometer.

Hugh A pedometer?

Stephen Yes, it measures how many miles I walk. Mrs Control is jolly careful to make sure that I put it on every morning, worst luck.

Hugh Hah. Still, I'm sure Mrs Control has your best interests at heart.

Stephen Yes, that's true. Selfish of me to grumble. After all Tony . . .

Hugh Yes?

Stephen It's for my good she's being quite so firm about it.

484

Hugh   That's right.

Stephen   Any golly way, you don't want to listen to my woes I dare say, Tony.

Hugh   Oh, I don't know, they're quite interesting.

Stephen   What brings you to the seventh floor this morning?

Hugh   Well, do you remember the Minister asking us to jolly well hurry up and find out who was behind all these bombs that have been going off in government departments of lately?

Stephen   Do I remember, Tony. Yes indeed, I most certainly do. A top priority investigation was demanded as I remember. Surveillance, tailing, tapping, no limit to the budget. 'Let's pull out all the stops on this one, Control, if you'd be kind enough', he said.

Hugh   That's right. Quite a to-do.

Stephen   I was going to ask you Tony. I put you in charge of that operation, have you come up with anything yet that might be a useful lead, or better still concrete information that could lead to some arrests?

Hugh   Well, that's the very reason I popped in and surprised you at your walking, Control, I've just had a report from Commander Henderson of Special Branch.

Stephen   That's the Scotland Yard branch founded earlier this century to deal with subversion and counter-insurgency?

Hugh   That's the exact one.

Stephen   I imagined quite strongly that it would be.

Hugh   Yes. And they say that with some of our agents working undercover alongside them, they've arrested a cell of men and women who they believe they can prove are definitely responsible for the

485

whole sorry wave of unfortunate and exasperating bomb attacks.

Stephen It was a sorry wave wasn't it?

Hugh It certainly was.

Stephen Well that is good news I must say.

Hugh I thought you'd be pleased.

Stephen I'm most pleased Tony. Well done. Full marks.

Hugh Calls for a coffee wouldn't you say?

Stephen It most certainly does.

Hugh I'll fetch you one.

Stephen No, Tony. It's my turn to fetch *you* one.

Hugh Well goodness, thank you Control.

Stephen No Tony, thank *you*. White no sugar, I think it is.

Hugh Yes please. This really is excessively kind of you Control.

Stephen Oh please don't mention it, Tony. Besides . . . *(patting his pedometer)* . . . the extra walk will impress Mrs Control!

Hugh Oh you.

Stephen Back in a mo, Tony.

Hugh Righto Control. I don't mind the wait.

VOX
POP

Hugh No it would not be nice. It wouldn't be nice if all towns were like *any* town, let alone Milton Keynes.

486

Hugh's Poem

Hugh is reading a poem.

Hugh   Underneath the bellied skies,
Where dust and rain find space to fall,
To fall and lie and change again,
Without a care or mind at all
For art and life and things above;

In that, there, look just there,
No right left up down past or future,
We have but ourselves to fear.

Stephen   Hugh, you chose that poem. For God's sake why?

Hugh   I chose it for a number of reasons, Stephen.

Stephen   I see. The most important one being . . . ?

Hugh   Can I perhaps turn that question round and say
'because it was short'.

Stephen   The poem?

Hugh   That's right. I chose that poem because it
was short.

Stephen   And that's significant?

Hugh   Well of course. With the pace of modern life
being what it is, it seemed to me that most
people just haven't got the time to spend on long
poems, and this would therefore ideally suit the
short-haul commuter or the busy housewife. This
is a poem that can fit neatly into the most hectic
of schedules, and leave time for other sporting or
leisure activities.

Stephen   So that represents quite a boon to the modern
poetry reader?

Hugh   Oh an enormous boon.

487

Stephen	Well of course we're always on the lookout for enormous boons. And I presume it's reasonably safe?
Hugh	Absolutely safe. This is a poem you could leave around the house in absolute confidence.
Stephen	Excellent. Presumably though, there must be shorter poems than that one?
Hugh	Oh good heavens yes.
Stephen	Good heavens yes?
Hugh	Good heavens yes. There's a poem by Richard Maddox called 'Institutions' that I can read for you now, if you like?
Stephen	Please.
Hugh	Here it is. 'Li.'
Stephen	That is short.
Hugh	It's very short indeed.
Stephen	Too short perhaps?
Hugh	Possibly.
Stephen	But I suppose that might just suit the busy senior executive who can only snatch a moment between meetings, and so on?
Hugh	Well that's right. That's certainly the market that Maddox was aiming for.
Stephen	Now at about this time, many people are going to be thinking about their summer holidays. Are there any poems that you might recommend to a family going on, say, a two-week get-away day leisure bargain break weekend away leisure holiday-break?
Hugh	Well first of all, let me give a warning to any families planning to take poetry on holiday with them.
Stephen	And that is?

Hugh	Be careful.
Stephen	Sounds like good advice to me.
Hugh	Check with your travel agent to see if there are any specific customs regulations regarding poetry, and if you're travelling outside the EEC, wrap up warm.
Stephen	Any particular advice on how to carry poetry, when travelling abroad?
Hugh	Yes, I would say it's definitely worth getting a proper travelling poetry bag.
Stephen	A travelling poetry bag?
Hugh	Yes. You can buy one of these at most big High Street travelling poetry bag shops.
Stephen	Great. Now I think you've got one last poem for us, before you go?
Hugh	I certainly have. This is 'The Rest of My Life' by R.P. Mitchell.
Stephen	*The* R.P. Mitchell?
Hugh	No. *A* R.P. Mitchell.
Stephen	Right.
Hugh	This poem is fairly solid, but at the same time, not too heavy. I think it's quite stylish.
Stephen	So it might suit, say, a young couple starting out in the catering business?
Hugh	If you like. 'Forward and back, Said the old man in the dance, As he whittled away at his stick, Long gone, long gone, Without a glance, To the entrance made of brick.'
Stephen	Thanks very much.

A Frank Talk

Stephen is getting out a couple of glasses and a bottle of whisky in the kitchen of his house. Hugh is sitting at the table looking faintly embarrassed.

Stephen   We'll wait for the ladies to get back from the theatre shall we?

Hugh   Yes, yes – good idea.

Stephen   I don't know what they see in it myself. Sitting there in the dark watching a lot of old nonsense.

Hugh   Oh well, they seem to enjoy it.

Stephen   I don't know about you, but I go to the theatre to be entertained.

Hugh   Well, I think they do too.

Stephen   If I want to see a lot of swearing and pretentious drivel I can stay at home.

Hugh   Still, anyway. They've been looking forward to it for a long time.

Stephen   *(Pouring out the drinks)* Right. Right.

Hugh   *I've* been looking forward to *this*, as a matter of fact, Matthew: this opportunity for a frank talk.

Stephen   Yes. Good. It's always nice to have a good – water?

Hugh   Thanks.

Stephen   *(Adding water to Hugh's drink)* – chat, isn't it?

Hugh   Mm. How long have I known you and Sarah now?

Stephen   Hoo, ch. What, must be nigh on.

Hugh   More I should think.

490

Stephen	Right. Possibly even more.
Hugh	You and Sarah are quite a couple.
Stephen	Well, I'll tell you this, Dominic. I don't know where I'd be without Sarah.
Hugh	Ah.
Stephen	Amazing woman. I think I love her more now than when I first met her. Be nothing without her. Lost. A shadow. Nothing. A blank. A zero.
Hugh	Mm.
Stephen	God I love her.
Hugh	Right. Thing is. Mm. Well. You know Mary and I have been going through a sticky patch lately?
Stephen	*(Surprised)* No. No, I didn't know that. A sticky patch.
Hugh	Yes.
Stephen	What sort of sticky patch?
Hugh	Well, just a general sort of, you know, sticky patch really.
Stephen	Oh dear. Nasty things sticky patches.
Hugh	They can be, certainly. You and Sarah have never . . . ?
Stephen	What? No. Not us. We're a team. Never had a sticky patch between us. Do you know in the fifteen years we've been married, I've never so much as looked at another woman.
Hugh	Really?
Stephen	Well, except my mother of course.
Hugh	Um . . .
Stephen	But then you have to look at your own mother,

491

don't you? Rude not to. And I know Sarah's the same.

Hugh   She's never . . . ?

Stephen   No. She'd never betray me.

Hugh   She'd never, for instance, have a ten year love affair with, say, your best friend, for the sake of, say, argument, say?

Stephen   Sarah? No. She'd rather cut the legs off her favourite table. Faithful as the day is long.

Hugh   Right.

Stephen   Anyway. This frank talk.

Hugh   Ah.

Stephen   You had something you wanted to say?

Hugh   Right. Yes.

Stephen   Fire away then.

Hugh   This isn't easy. It's just that – well, that ten year-old love affair I mentioned –

Stephen   Mary.

Hugh   What?

Stephen   Oh no. Don't tell me. You've discovered that your wife Mary has been having an affair. Dominic, I don't know what to say.

Hugh   No, no. Mary wouldn't betray me, I know that – that's what makes it all so difficult.

Stephen   I was going to say. I was pretty sure Mary and I have kept it pretty discreet.

Hugh   It's the other way round, I – what?

Stephen   What?

Hugh   What did you say just now?

Stephen	Oh nothing. Just that I was sure Mary and I had been far too discreet for you to notice that we've been having a wild affair under your very nose for the last – twelve years I should say. At the very least.
Hugh	You and Mary have been . . .
Stephen	Oh God yes.
Hugh	But you said you would never look at another woman apart from Sarah and your mother.
Stephen	And Mary, obviously. That goes without saying.
Hugh	Well, that makes what I was going to say a lot easier then.
Stephen	Oh yes?
Hugh	It may interest you to know that your beloved Sarah and I have also been having an affair for . . . well for eleven years anyway.
Stephen	I beg your pardon? You and Sarah?
Hugh	Yes, I thought that might shake you up a bit.
Stephen	You pair of deceitful, two-timing –

Enter Sarah and Mary.

Mary	Hello, you two.
Sarah	Look at them both, up with the whisky bottle. I don't know.
Hugh	Sarah. Darling, is it true that you and, that the pair of you have been . . .
Stephen	Mary, tell me. It isn't true that the two of you have . . . is it? Tell me it isn't.

Sarah and Mary look at each other and sigh.

493

Sarah	We were going to tell you anyway, weren't we darling?
Mary	Yes, we were. Tonight in fact.
Sarah	Mary and I have been having an affair for the last fourteen years.
Mary	A very passionate affair.
Sarah	Strikingly passionate.
Hugh	You what?
Mary	I don't know how you found out.
Sarah	*(To Mary)* You didn't leave the thingy lying around did you?
Stephen	No, I meant you and Dominic. You and Dominic have been having an affair for the last eleven years at least.
Hugh	And you and Matthew, Mary.
Sarah	Oh that. Well that was just a diversion really.
Stephen	Oh was it? Well, Matthew, it makes it a lot easier for us to tell them, doesn't it?
Hugh	It certainly does. It may interest you to know that Dominic and I have been – how shall I phrase it?
Stephen	Bed-mates?
Sarah	Lovers?
Mary	Sex-friends?
Stephen	Joy-partners?
Sarah	Bliss buddies?
Hugh	Yes, well, any one of those for the past – what?
Stephen	Hoo, it's got to be at least eighteen or twenty hasn't it?
Hugh	Yes, for the last eighteen or twenty years.

494

Sarah	Well.
Mary	Frankly.
Sarah	So. You're saying that we have all been to bed with each other.
Stephen	That seems to be about the size of it, yes.
Mary	Though separately.
Hugh	Yes, separately, obviously.
Stephen	In every possible combination.
Sarah	Well. What a kerfuffle. What a business.
Mary	I don't know what to say.
Stephen	It is something of a how-do-you-do, isn't it?
Hugh	Well. So. What do we do?
Stephen	I should have thought it was obvious.
Mary	You mean . . . ?
Sarah	Only thing to do.
Hugh	What?
Sarah	Let's all go to bed.
Hugh	Oh. Right.

They all trot off to bed.

VOX
POP

Stephen *(Smelling a bottle of something and handing it back)* I don't know. Kenneth Baker perhaps. Nicholas Wychell?

495

Café

*Stephen enters a café. Hugh is behind the counter,
wearing an apron and wiping the counter.*

Stephen Morning.

Hugh Morning.

Stephen I'd like a tuna sandwich and a tea, please.

Hugh So would I, to be perfectly honest.

Stephen I beg your pardon?

Hugh Well I don't know about the tuna sandwich –
maybe a doughnut – but I'd certainly like a tea.
I'm dying of thirst.

Stephen Oh dear, well, can I have one as well?

Hugh What?

Stephen A tea.

Hugh You're asking me?

Stephen Yes.

Hugh Oh, ahaha. I think there's been a bit of a
misunderstanding. I don't actually work here.

Stephen Don't you?

Hugh No.

Stephen Oh I'm so sorry. I thought . . .

Hugh Oh, the apron and everything . . . yes. No I don't
work here. No no no. Haha. That's quite funny
actually.

*They both look down the counter, as if to find
the owner.*

Stephen   Well . . . is it closed?

Hugh   I don't think so. They'd have put the sign up.

Stephen   Yes, I thought it said 'open'.

Hugh   Yeah, I think it's open. Cor, I could murder a doughnut, couldn't you?

Stephen   Actually yes, a doughnut would be nice.

Hugh   I was thinking maybe I could just take one, and then leave the money on the side. What d'you reckon?

Stephen   It's a possibility, I suppose.

Hugh   'Course, I don't know how much they are.

Stephen   Errm . . .

Hugh   Yes?

Stephen   Well, if you don't work here, why are you behind the counter?

Hugh   Me?

Stephen   Yes.

Hugh   I'm an undercover policeman.

Stephen   Are you?

Hugh   Yeah.

Stephen   I see.

Hugh   Phwor. Those doughnuts are driving me potty. I'm going to have to put them away in a minute.

Stephen   Right, yes. You're not very far undercover, are you?

Hugh   How d'you mean?

Stephen   Well, I mean what's the point of being undercover, if you're going to tell me that you're undercover?

Hugh   *(Quite a long pause)* Actually, that's quite a good point.

497

Stephen	Yes.
Hugh	What you're saying is, I shouldn't have told you that I was an undercover policeman?
Stephen	Precisely.
Hugh	Yeah, that's a good point. Because basically, you now know that I'm a policeman.
Stephen	Yes.
Hugh	So the whole reason for me putting on this apron and standing here since eight o'clock this morning . . . is, well, wasted really.
Stephen	I'd have thought so. I mean, it's none of my business.
Hugh	No no no. Don't ever say that. Don't ever say it's none of your business. No, we need the public to come forward. Believe me, we're very grateful.
Stephen	Not at all.
Hugh	Of course, we also need the public to shut up and not tell anyone else that I'm a policeman.
Stephen	Well of course.
Hugh	Good. That is a very good point, though. Don't say you're an undercover policeman. Yeah. Thanks.
Stephen	So, are you waiting for some criminal or something?
Hugh	That's right, funnily enough, yes. I'm waiting for a criminal, and when he enters the premises, let me put it this way, he can expect a warm reception.
Stephen	I see. That should be exciting.
Hugh	People often say that, but no, it's not exciting. It's ninety-nine per cent routine legwork.
Stephen	Right.

498

Hugh	You're not a criminal by any chance, are you?
Stephen	Me?
Hugh	Yes.
Stephen	No.
Hugh	Oh good. Because I'd have had to give you a warm reception if you were.
Stephen	But then of course, I probably wouldn't tell you if I was.
Hugh	Yeah. Right.
Stephen	Now that I know you're a policeman.
Hugh	Oh I get you. You wouldn't tell me, because you now know I'm a policeman.
Stephen	Yes. That's if I was the criminal.
Hugh	Right. Right. Are you the criminal?
Stephen	No.
Hugh	Oh good.
Stephen	But the point is, I might be.
Hugh	Oh hold up, you've gone all strange again. You just said you weren't.
Stephen	I'm not.
Hugh	Good.
Stephen	But I might be.
Hugh	This is getting stupid.
Stephen	Not really. You see, if I was a criminal, I wouldn't tell you that I was. If I wasn't, I also wouldn't tell you that I was. So just because I say I'm not, doesn't mean I'm not. A criminal.
Hugh	Slippery sod, aren't you?

Stephen   I beg your pardon?

Hugh   You read a lot of books, I suppose?

Stephen   Well, you know . . .

Hugh   One of my regrets about the police force. No time for reading.

Stephen   Mmm. Pity.

Hugh   Do you want to share a doughnut with me?

Stephen   Er, no thanks.

Hugh breaks a doughnut in two, and gives one half to Stephen.

Hugh   There you go.

Stephen   No, really I won't thank you.

Hugh   There you go.

Stephen   No.

Hugh   Take it.

Stephen   No!

Hugh pushes half the doughnut into Stephen's face.

What are you doing?

Hugh   Giving you half this doughnut.

Stephen   I don't want it!

Hugh   You think I'm stupid.

Stephen   What?

Hugh   Just because you've read books and I haven't, you think I'm stupid.

Stephen   No I don't.

Hugh   If you didn't want a doughnut, you'd say you

500

wanted a doughnut. So just because you're a criminal doesn't mean that I don't have to give you a doughnut, because you've said you didn't want a doughnut in the first place which is actually what you'd say if this doughnut was a policeman.

Stephen You're mad.

Hugh Mad am I? Your first mistake. I never told you I was mad. I told you I was a policeman. But you've just said that I'm a mad policeman. How could you have known that, without me telling you? So I must have told you. Except that I didn't, so how do you know?

Stephen It's obvious.

VOX
POP

Hugh I've got nothing against where I live now. It's just a bit detached.

501

Judge Not

Hugh is a judge in a full-bottomed wig. Stephen is counsel with a full bottom. He is cross-examining a female witness, Deborah.

Stephen So, Miss Talliot, you expect the court to believe that on the evening of the fourteenth of November last year, the very year, I would remind the court, on which the crime that my client is accused of committing took place, you just happened to be walking in the park?

Deborah That is correct.

Stephen That is what?

Deborah Correct.

Stephen Oh it's correct, is it? I see. Am I right in understanding, Miss Talliot, that the American writer Gertrude Stein was a self-confessed Lesbian?

Deborah I believe so.

Stephen You believe so? Gertrude Stein remains one of the most celebrated American female novelists of the century, Miss Talliot. Her lesbotic tendencies are a matter of public record.

Deborah Yes.

Stephen But you only 'believe' that she was a Lesbian?

Deborah Well, I've never really thought of it much. I haven't read any of her works.

Stephen Miss Talliot, there is a bookshop not two streets away from your 'flat' where the works of Gertrude Stein are openly on display.

502

Deborah	Oh.
Stephen	Yes; 'oh'. And yet you would have us believe that somehow, on the many occasions on which you must, in the course of your duties as a woman, have passed this shop while shopping, failed entirely to enter and buy any book published by this openly Sapphic authoress?
Hugh	Mr Foley, I'm afraid I really fail to see where this line of questioning is leading us.
Stephen	With your permission m'lud, I am trying to establish that this witness has been guilty of weaving a tissue of litanies, that far from being the respectable president of a children's charity and ambassador's daughter that my learned friend the counsel for the prosecution would have us believe, she is in fact an active, promiscuous and voracious Lesbite.
Hugh	I see. Carry on. But I must warn you, Mr Foley, that if you attempt to ballyrag or bulldoze the witness I shall take a very dim view of it.
Stephen	Your lordship is most pretty.
Hugh	Very well then, you may proceed.
Stephen	Are you aware Miss Talliot –
Deborah	It's Mrs in fact.
Stephen	Oh. Oh, I do beg your pardon. If you wish to make so much of it, then I will certainly not stand in your way, 'Mrs' Talliot, if that is how you prefer to be known.
Deborah	It is how my husband prefers me to be known.
Stephen	Your husband the well-known Bishop?
Deborah	Yes.
Stephen	A bishop in a religion, the Church of – ah –

England, I believe it calls itself, which owns land on which houses have been built, houses in which it is statistically probable that private acts of Lesbian love have been committed?

Hugh Mr Foley, I fear I must interrupt you again. I myself am a member of this same church. Are we to imply from the tenor of your thrust that I am a Lesbian?

Stephen Your lordship misunderstands me.

Hugh I hope so. I hope the day is far distant on which I could be accused of making love to a woman! Ha, ha, ha.

Stephen Certainly, m'love. I never meant to imply . . .

Hugh Attraction to women, however, repellent as it may be to persons of sensibility, is not in itself a crime.

Stephen I love your lordship.

Hugh We must therefore remember, Mr Foley, in our enthusiasm to get to this bottom, that Mrs Talliot is not on trial, she is a witness. However depraved and wicked her acts of lust, they – in all their degenerate and disgusting perversion – are not the subject of this assize, bestial as they may be.

Stephen I am yours for ever, m'dear.

Hugh Please continue.

Stephen I do not wish, 'Mrs Talliot' to submit the court to any more details of your sordid and disreputable erotic career than is necessary. I merely wish to enquire how it might be that you expect a jury to believe the testimony of a monstrous bull-dyke of your stamp against the word of a respectable businessman?

Deborah I am merely reporting what I saw.

Stephen What you saw? What you saw through eyes

504

dimmed with lust? What you saw maddened by the noxious juices of your notorious practices?

Deborah What I saw on my way back from the parish council meeting.

Stephen Is it not a fact that the words 'parish council' are an anagram of 'lispian crouch'?

Deborah Er . . .

Stephen You hesitate, Miss Toilet!

Deborah I was . . .

Stephen You stand condemned out of your own soiled and contaminated mouth.

Deborah I –

Stephen No further questions.

Deborah Well . . .

Hugh You may stand down, Miss Lesbian.

Deborah Oh. And will you be in for tea tonight, Jeremy?

Stephen Certainly, mother. *(Louder)* Call Sir Anthony Known-Bender.

VOX
POP

Stephen Of course crime is bound to be on the increase. If you're the kind of person who wants to start a satellite broadcasting channel, but you can't get a licence, crime is the obvious alternative.

Psychiatrist

Hugh, American, is standing, Stephen, English, lies on a couch.

Hugh   Are you at ease and relaxed, Mr Lloyd?

Stephen   Yes, very. This is a very comfortable chair.

Hugh   That is no accident, Mr Lloyd. It was designed by a friend of mine, to my specifications, purposely to relax you and place you fully at your ease.

Stephen   Well it is very comfortable.

Hugh   My friend will be delighted to hear that. Now, Frank – I shall be calling you Frank through the duration of these sessions. Okay by you?

Stephen   Fine.

Hugh   I have found that that also helps relax you into a state where you feel able to talk freely with me. Is it working?

Stephen   Yes.

Hugh   Good. Now . . .

Stephen   My name is Jonathan, I don't know if that –

Hugh   Good. Already we're finding out new things. Now Frank, I want you to take a deep breath through your mouth.

Stephen   *(Doing so)* Haah!

Hugh   Fine. Now I'd like you to breathe out through your nose.

Stephen snots slightly in obeying this request.

In through the mouth, out through the nose. Do you know what this is called, Frank?

506

Stephen	Breathing.
Hugh	That's nice. Frank, this is called inter-oral, extra-nasal respiratory relaxant therapy, and – as the name implies – this is an American technique. Good and calm and regular. Frank, I want now that you should allow your mind to take you backward in time. Think yourself back and back and back.
Stephen	Right.
Hugh	Have you gone back?
Stephen	Yes.
Hugh	You've gone back. What do you see in your mind's eye, Frank?
Stephen	The Spanish Armada.
Hugh	Frank, you may have gone back too far there. I'm talking of your memories Frank. Your childhood status. I want to investigate all the sense data of your infancy. Go back to when you were in second grade.
Stephen	What?
Hugh	Second grade.
Stephen	I don't know what that is. I've never understood it when people talk about grades and semesters in films.
Hugh	OK Frank, maintain your respiratory rhythms and let's turn then, if we may, to your dreams. You dream, Frank?
Stephen	Yes I do, yes as it happens, yes.
Hugh	You do? Well that's fine. Are you able at this time to recall to the surface of your consciousness any recurrent nocturnal dream sequences for me?
Stephen	Well I do have one recurring dream as a matter of fact.

507

Hugh	Well now, let's take time off Frank, to analyse that sequence together.
Stephen	It is rather a strange dream.
Hugh	Is it Frank, a dream of an erotic nature I wonder?
Stephen	No, not really.
Hugh	Oh. Well I'd still like to hear it.
Stephen	As I say it's a bit odd.
Hugh	Ordinarily, Frank, the more bizarre or outré the dream, the more readily susceptible to positive interpretation it thusly renders itself to become. On the converse side of the bull-pen, simpler dream experiences are more resistant to explication and offer a much more complex morphology to the professional inquirer bold enough howso to venture therein.
Stephen	I see.
Hugh	But hey, Frank! That's my problem. You've got a dream, let's share it. What do you say?
Stephen	Are you sure this is going to get us anywhere?
Hugh	Depends where you want to be, Frank.
Stephen	Well . . .
Hugh	Where do you want to be?
Stephen	Well I want –
Hugh	I want to be there too, Frank. I want to take you there. *(Putting his arm on Stephen's shoulder)* Don't be scared. Do I scare you, Frank?
Stephen	No, not really.
Hugh	You sure about that?
Stephen	Well, a bit perhaps.
Hugh	*(Incredibly loudly)* I'm going to kill you!

Stephen	*(Starting)* Jesus!
Hugh	That scared you, didn't it?
Stephen	Yes. Yes it did, actually.
Hugh	Good, I like to know the thresholds within which I have to operate. Putting my hand on your shoulder did not scare you. Shouting loudly in your ear that I was going to kill you, did. Those are my limits. My ceiling and floor if you will.
Stephen	Do you want to hear this dream or not?
Hugh	I very much want to hear this dream, Frank. I do really. Shoot.
Stephen	Well, I'm in a corridor –
Hugh	Frank, I have a small tape-recorder here. Do you mind if I – ?
Stephen	No, no. Good idea. This is quite a complicated dream.
Hugh	Thank you.
Stephen	I'm in a big building. I think it's a hospital . . .

Hugh switches on his tape-recorder: pop music comes out. Hugh taps his feet and joins in the singing.

	What are you . . . ?
Hugh	Please continue, Frank.
Stephen	I think it's a hospital, but it isn't. It's some kind of institution. There's a big staircase, a uniformed man at the top. Janitor or something. He beckons to me . . . look, I can't concentrate with this going on.
Hugh	*(Turning it off)* I do most sincerely beg your pardon, Frank. Please continue.
Stephen	Well, anyway, the janitor beckons to me and then I wake up.

509

Hugh	You wake up. I see. Now this sounds . . .
Stephen	And almost immediately I'm chosen for a bathroom wall.
Hugh	Frank, I've never thought of myself as a stupid man, but even so I think I'm going to need a little help understanding that last sentence. You were chosen for a bathroom wall.
Stephen	Well the thing is, you see, I haven't woken up at all. I've only woken up in the dream. I wake up and find that I'm the colour blue.
Hugh	The colour blue.
Stephen	That's right. And somebody chooses me for their bathroom wall.
Hugh	I see. And do you then become the colour of that wall?
Stephen	No. As it happens, I'm a particular shade of blue that's very difficult to get in the shops. The bathroom wall ends up with a bit too much green in it. But we get on reasonably well.
Hugh	I'm sorry?
Stephen	The colour of the bathroom wall and I get on pretty well. There are no hard feelings.
Hugh	I see. This bathroom, Frank. Does it belong to a lady?
Stephen	Er . . . yes, I think so.
Hugh	And she likes to bathe in this bath in this bathroom?
Stephen	Well I suppose so.
Hugh	Are you attracted to her?
Stephen	Well no. I'm the colour blue, how could I . . . ?
Hugh	But she's attracted to you.

510

Stephen	Well ...
Hugh	She chose you, Frank. Out of all the other colours, she chose you.
Stephen	Yes.
Hugh	There you go. She was attracted to you, Frank.
Stephen	She chose me because I reminded her of the colour of a bruise she once had on her inner thigh.
Hugh	Now we're getting somewhere, Frank. You remember being the colour of this bruise?
Stephen	Vaguely.
Hugh	This is an interesting sequence, Frank. What happens next?
Stephen	I tell you how my dream continues, I think.
Hugh	Right.
Stephen	I find myself in the corridor in a large house just outside Taunton and Prince Edward is running towards me, he's about to bowl a cricket ball at me and I haven't got a bat. Prince Edward is running in to bowl and I haven't got a bat. What does that mean?
Hugh	Just may be a little early to say yet, Frank.
Stephen	But suddenly I find it isn't Prince Edward after all, it's Bob Holness.
Hugh	Come again for me?
Stephen	Bob Holness. You know, 'Blockbusters'. Bob turns to me and I catch sight of his face, it's a twisted grinning mask of contorted hatred and frenzy. I look down and I find I have got a bat. I didn't have a bat when it was Prince Edward but I did when it was Bob Holness. Why? Why? Am I mad?

Hugh	Mad? Frank, 'mad' is not a word I like to use. Let's just say that half of us is always 'mad', disordered, wild and the other half is sane, rational, in control.
Stephen	Oh I see. You mean there's two sides to every person?
Hugh	No, I mean the two of us. Half of us is sane, that's me, and the other half is mad, that's you, Frank.
Stephen	I must say you seem rather unorthodox. The last man I saw just gave me a couple of fillings.
Hugh	Dentistry has made many advances, Frank.
Stephen	Obviously.

VOX
POP

Hugh Yeah, I've been there once
or twice, but I didn't much
like it. There's another one
on the A12 which I think
is better.

Madness

Stephen addresses the camera, the way he often does. He is talking to Dr Marjorie who is a distinguished-looking woman, wearing a badge that says 'Say no to madness'.

Stephen   Every day in Britain, more than ten million people are mad. That's the worrying conclusion contained in a report just published entitled 'Is Britain Turning Into a Nation Of Mad People?' Dr Mijory Marjorie is with me now. Dr Marjorie, just how serious is this problem . . .

Deborah   It's very serious in . . .

Stephen   Wait a minute, I haven't finished.

Deborah   Sorry.

Stephen   . . . in real terms?

Deborah   *(Pause)* OK?

Stephen   Yes, go on.

Deborah   It's very serious indeed. In 1957, when records began, we were, I think, the sixth maddest country in Europe. Whereas last year's figures show that now, Britain, I'm afraid, leads the European Community . . .

Stephen   And it is a community, isn't it?

Deborah   Yes . . . Britain now leads Europe in terms of being mad.

Stephen   That's a worrying trend, certainly.

Deborah   You're very kind.

Stephen   Not at all. Now, Dr Marjorie, in case any viewers

513

have just this moment tuned in, would you mind
having this whole conversation all over again?

Deborah   Fine with me.

Stephen   Is Britain turning into a nation of mad people?
Dr Mijory Marjorie is with me now. Dr Marjorie,
how serious is this problem, in real terms?

Deborah   Not particularly.

Stephen   Not particularly what?

Deborah   Serious.

Stephen   Isn't it?

Deborah   No.

Stephen   I see. Right. When we talk about Britain being
one of the maddest countries in Europe, exactly
what sort of madness are we talking about?

Deborah   All sorts really – from the kind of madness that
leads people to put on a hat whenever they get
into a car, to the really extreme madness shown by
the sort of people who write to 'Points of View'.

Stephen   Interesting. That's quite a broad basket of
madness isn't it?

Deborah   I think we've been pretty thorough.

Stephen   Right. Now, for those viewers who have only just
tuned in right this second, I think it might be
worth you investing in a copy of the *Radio Times*,
don't you? So that you can plan your viewing
properly. After all, you wouldn't start reading a
book at chapter five, would you?

Deborah   You would if the first four chapters were rubbish.

Stephen   Oh be quiet. Now turning to the causes behind
or beneath or even slightly to one side of Britain's
increasing madness . . . in a sense, what are they?

Deborah	Well, we examined a number of factors . . .
Stephen	Sorry, who is 'we'?
Deborah	My mother and I.
Stephen	Fine.
Deborah	. . . and a woman called Alice.
Stephen	Good.
Deborah	And we came up with some very interesting results. Essentially, madness is like charity. It begins in the home.
Stephen	Christ that's interesting.

VOX
POP

Stephen . . . Haha . . . round the ring
road . . . hahaha . . .

Fascism

Hugh and Stephen are in white tie, drinking brandy, perhaps in a clubby sort of place. Maybe a portrait of Hitler above a mantelpiece.

Hugh   Gayle?

Stephen   Yes, Leonard?

Hugh   How are we going to do it, I wonder?

Stephen   Do what?

Hugh   How are we going to make Fascism popular in this country? Popular and exciting.

Stephen   Oh that. Yes. That's become something of a madness with you, hasn't it?

Hugh   I believe it has become something of a madness with me.

Stephen   And yet, if anyone were to ask me, I would never say you were a mad person.

Hugh   I believe I pay you well enough for that service?

Stephen   Indeed yes. I didn't mean . . .

Hugh   Perhaps it's that little touch of madness that keeps us all sane.

Stephen   Yes. I doubt it.

Hugh   But how are we to do it? How are we to make Fascism exciting and important?

Stephen   We must reach out to the young people.

Hugh   You think?

Stephen   Certainly. After all, the young people are the

516

seedcornerstone of our society. The young people
are the future.

Hugh   Yes. Or at least they will be.

Stephen   No. They are.

Hugh   Are they?

Stephen   Yes. They will be the present, but they are
              the future.

Hugh   Well well. So how can we make fascism live
              among the young people?

Stephen   We could advertise.

Hugh   Gayle, my dear old mucker, what are you thinking
              of? Advertise?

Stephen   I am thinking, Leonard, that we must use today's
              tools for today's job.

Hugh   Go on.

Stephen   If we are to be successful.

Hugh   Yes.

Stephen   In our venture.

Hugh   Yes?

Stephen   That's it, I'm afraid.

Hugh   I see. And what are today's tools, in your opinion?

Stephen   Oh there are so many tools around today. Look
              at advertising. Pop music. Films. Magazines.
              Everywhere images of sexuality and coolness.

Hugh   Coolness.

Stephen   Coolness. Hipness. Laid backness. Not being a
              pratness.

Hugh   And so we must make fascism . . .

Stephen   Cool.

Hugh	Cool.
Stephen	First, we must invent a fashion in clothing.
Hugh	Mmm. There must be leather.
Stephen	Leather, yes.
Hugh	And lace.
Stephen	Leather and lace, yes.
Hugh	With cotton facings.
Stephen	Excellent. Already you see, we have a look.
Hugh	And where shall we find them, these young people?
Stephen	Wherever blood and money and sexy talk flow freely, there will you find the young.
Hugh	And what will we say? How will we persuade them to surrender their ice-skating and their jazz music and turn to Fascism?
Stephen	Mm. Leonard, I wonder if you're not a little out of touch.
Hugh	Gayle, please. You are my lieutenant. My side-plate.
Stephen	Indeed.
Hugh	Tell me what I must say.
Stephen	You must say to the young people – Oh young people. You who are young and thrusting and urgent, there is a beat, a sound, a look that's new, that's you, that's positively yes!
Hugh	They'll laugh at me.
Stephen	At first . . . and ultimately, yes. But in the middle, they'll listen.
Hugh	Hmm. Alright. Boys and girls, dig what I am about

to say. Fascism is cool. Fascism is leather and lace with cotton facings.

Stephen   Good.

Hugh   Throw away those transistor radios. Come on out from those steamy parlours where the coffee is cheap and the love is free. Join us in our movement.

Stephen   And while their bodies jerk and jig to the music of those words, we must somehow introduce the subject of segregating races and abolishing elections.

Hugh   We could give away sachets of face-cream in our magazines.

Stephen   And for the women?

Hugh   Gayle. There is no place for women in our thousand year order.

Stephen   But Leonard, women do have certain useful functions.

Hugh   Such as?

Stephen   News reading.

Hugh   Why do you always insist on calling it that?

Stephen   It excites me.

Hugh   Now on the subject of racial purity, perhaps a national advertising campaign?

Stephen   Excellent.

Hugh   I will present it.

Stephen   Oh but you can't.

Hugh   And why not pray?

Stephen   Because God doesn't exist.

Hugh   No, I mean – and why not ... *(Pause)* pray?

Stephen Because God does not . . . *(Pause)* exist.

Hugh Never mind. Why can't I front this national advertising campaign?

Stephen Because your grandmother was a quarter Italian. I shall present the commercials.

Hugh You? You, whose godfather is Jewish?

Stephen At least my sister didn't marry a Welshman.

Hugh Better marry a Welshman than eat Greek yoghurt.

Stephen Rather Greek yoghurt than Cornish ice-cream.

Hugh Stop, stop! Don't you see? They are turning us against each other. We shall present the commercials together.

Stephen Yes. Together.

Hugh Our slogan shall be – 'Good old Fascism. As true today as it's always been.'

Stephen But Leonard, my dear old acquaintance, surely this is a new Fascism?

Hugh Alright. 'New Ph balanced Fascism, a whole new world of natural goodness, right there in the cup.'

Stephen Cup?

Hugh Why not?

Stephen What about – 'Maureen Lipman, with some letters from you about new Fascism'.

Hugh Would she do it?

Stephen I don't see why not.

Hugh I have it. 'If you thought Fascism was just goose-steps and funny hats, then take a look at what we've been doing. Available in matchpots too.'

Stephen *Das Sieg wird unser sein,* as they say in Germany.

Hugh   Do you hate anyone enough to give them your last pot-noodle?

Stephen Fascism. Half the fat, all the taste. That's the Fascist promise.

Hugh   From Lenor.

Stephen It's Ideal.

Hugh   I wish I was young.

Stephen Me too.

VOX
POP

Hugh   It's just well laid out, you see. If you can imagine that the four star pumps are lined up there, and they've got the diesel and two star pumps opposite ... well you see I much prefer that.

Jeremiah Beadle

Hugh is a bank teller. Stephen approaches the counter wearing some sort of mask and carrying a sawn-off shotgun.

Stephen   Be clever.

Hugh   I beg your pardon?

Stephen   Be clever. If you even breathe too loud, I'll blow you in half. Now, slowly and carefully, open the till and take out all the notes.

Hugh   All the notes?

Stephen   All the notes.

Hugh   Yes. Is your account actually with this branch?

Stephen   What?

Hugh   If not, I'll have to make a phone call. Shouldn't take long.

Stephen   If you even look at a telephone, I'll spread your brains all over the wall. I'm robbing the bank.

Hugh   Robbing the . . . oh God.

Stephen   Now just take it easy.

Hugh   Oh God.

Stephen   Mouth shut. Nice and relaxed. Put all the notes into this bag.

Hugh   Don't kill me.

Stephen   Just do it, alright?

Hugh   Yes, yes. All the notes . . .

Stephen   That's it. Nice and easy.

Hugh nervously takes out all the cash, then suddenly stops.

Hugh   Oh oh. Wait a minute.

Stephen   What?

Hugh   Oh I don't believe it. I don't believe it.

Stephen   Come on, I haven't got all day.

Hugh   Who put you up to this?

Stephen   Put me up . . . ?

Hugh   It was Carol, wasn't it? I knew it! She's crazy.
Tscch! Where's the camera then?

Stephen   What are you talking about?

Hugh   You're that Jeremy Beadle, aren't you?

Stephen   What!?

Hugh   I didn't recognise you at first. I'll kill her! She's a
right minx. Oh I feel such an idiot!

Stephen   Listen, you twerp, put all the money . . .

Hugh   I must say this is brilliant. You people are so
clever. So when's it going to be on the television?

Stephen   Look, I am not Jeremy bleeding Beadle! Now put
the notes in the bag.

Hugh   'Course you'll have to bleep that out, won't you?

Stephen   What?

Hugh   Jeremy bleeding Beadle. You can't really say
Jeremy bleeding Beadle on family television.
Unless of course 'Bleeding' is actually your
middle name.

Stephen   Look, I am not Jeremy Beadle. I don't look
anything like Jeremy Beadle.

Hugh   Well not with that mask on, obviously.

Stephen removes the mask.

Stephen   Satisfied?

Hugh   That's brilliant.

Stephen   What is?

Hugh   You've got a false head on, have you? That's incredible.

Stephen   If you don't fill that bag and pass it over in ten seconds, I'll kill you.

Hugh   I can't wait to see this.

Stephen   One, two . . .

Hugh   Actually, to tell the truth, I used to prefer 'Candid Camera' . . .

Stephen   Five, six . . .

Hugh   You just stole their idea, really, didn't you?

Stephen   Nine . . .

Hugh   Oh I just wish I'd put that other shirt on this morning. Still . . .

Stephen fires into Hugh's chest. Lots of blood.

(Dying) You will send me a tape, won't you?

VOX
POP

Hugh   And if you don't like the shape you can scoop it out with your finger.

Architect

Stephen is sitting behind, yes, a desk. On the desk
there is what appears to be an architect's model of
a fairly pleasing housing estate. Nicely done, trees, a
stream, model people walking dogs and so on. Hugh is
explaining it.

Hugh   And basically I think . . . or what I hope I've
            managed to achieve with this design is a new
            direction. The emphasis is very much on the
            quality of people's day to day lives. I know it
            doesn't correspond exactly to the initial brief, but
            I hope you'll agree it has qualities that really set
            it apart from any other contemporary design. Ha.
            That's it really. I'm very excited by it.

Stephen   Yes.

Hugh   So what do you think?

Stephen   Ahem. Mr Braganza . . .

Hugh   Please be honest.

Stephen   I will. I will. But first of all can I ask you why you
            chose to depart from the . . . er . . . shall we say
            traditional . . . ?

Hugh   You mean the old shoe box approach.

Stephen   That's it.

Hugh   The strict, rectangular lines . . .

Stephen   That's right. Shoe box.

Hugh   Well to be honest, Mr Catchpole, that style is out,
            it's dead. Brutalism, modernism, post-modernism,
            all those isms are finished with. We've got to look
            at people's lives.

Stephen   Yes, quite. The thing is, when we asked for a shoe box, we did actually mean a box for putting shoes in. We are a shoe manufacturer, you see. And we really do need to put our shoes in a box.

Hugh   Oh I know that. I know that. But by carrying on with the same old rectangular prisons, you're only stifling the human spirit. I'm trying to free the human spirit.

Stephen   Well that's . . . that's fine. But you see, I'm left with the problem of where to put our shoes. I need a box to put our shoes in, you see? I need a shoe box.

Hugh   Need? Who are we to say what's needed, in the sense of some fancy design idea that's going to blight the lives of generations to come?

Stephen   I don't think our shoe boxes have blighted any generations.

Hugh   Well I wouldn't be too sure about that.

Stephen   Nick. Let me put it this way. To me, a shoe box is just a machine for keeping shoes in.

Hugh   Oh yes? And to hell with the human spirit, that's what you're saying.

Stephen   Not really.

Hugh   I know what it is. It's the cost, isn't it? You're frightened of how much it's going to cost.

Stephen   No, I'm frightened of where I'm going to put our shoes.

Hugh   Well forget money. Because there are some things that can't be calculated to the last penny. I'm talking about human lives.

Stephen   Yes, you see, I'm talking about shoes.

Hugh   Oh shoes, shoes. Is that all you think about?

526

Stephen	When I'm at work, yes.
Hugh	Well then I feel sorry for you. In fact, I pity you.
Stephen	Well . . .
Hugh	But I'll do you a shoebox, if that's what you want. I don't know how I'll live with myself, but if that's what you want, I'll do you a nice, safe, ordinary, rectangular shoe box.
Stephen	Thank you.

Hugh picks up the model.

Hugh	I'll take this away, then.
Stephen	No no. Leave it here. I think we can find a use for it.
Hugh	What?
Stephen	Some of our workers might want to live in it.

VOX
POP

Hugh   *(Slapping himself rather hard
on the face and looking mad)*
I was beaten as a child
and it didn't do me any
harm.

527

Critics Four

Hello, it's swivel-chair time again.

Hugh   Simon Clituris. You saw that. What do you think was happening there?

Stephen   Well you see, again this was a rather trite, rather predictable – I don't know what the word is I'd use to describe it really.

Hugh   Squib?

Stephen   If you like. A sort of cod spoof guying take-off pastiche parody.

Hugh   What did you make of the two central performances?

Stephen   I'd have welcomed them.

Hugh   *(Laughing at this sally)* Right, right. I liked the clever and original use of words.

Stephen   Oh thank you very much.

Hugh   Not at all. Your clever and original use of words has been collected into book form recently, I understand.

Stephen   That's right.

Hugh   Well received?

Stephen   Well, you know what critics are like. What do they know about the work we do?

Hugh   Quite so, quitely so. Quitely so-ington. But to return to that spoof cod squib guying of conventions. My main worry was that it told us nothing of the relationship between the two central characters.

528

Stephen That's right. Some people may have been mildly amused by this kind of grotesquerie, but where were the truths about relationships in England today, now, this evening, this afternoon?

Hugh You certainly couldn't see them from where I was lying.

Stephen No, I hated it.

Hugh That's right. Two out of ten for trying, then.

Stephen It just wasn't your cup of tea?

Hugh No. *(Picking up teacup)* This is my cup of tea, in fact.

Stephen Actually, I think you'll find it's mine.

VOX
POP

Hugh The short one has got a different accent, but they both smell of Noël Edmonds to me.

Marjorie's Fall

Some sort of period sitting room. Stephen is fiddling with a clock on the mantelpiece. Hugh enters, agitated.

Hugh   Thomas! Bad news I'm afraid.

Stephen   Just a moment, John. I promised Marjorie I'd mend this clock for her. I wonder if you could give me a hand.

Hugh   Big hand?

Stephen   Little hand.

Hugh   Anyway Thomas, listen to me. I have some bad news.

Stephen   Bad news?

Hugh   It's Marjorie.

Stephen   Marjorie?

Hugh   She's had a fall.

Stephen   Marjorie's had a fall?

Hugh   I'm afraid so. She was out riding this morning on Thunderbolt, and she hadn't returned by the time Mrs Mempwaster arrived. It turns out she'd had a fall.

Stephen   Calm yourself John. Marjorie has had a fall?

Hugh   Yes.

Stephen   Off a horse?

Hugh   Well of course off a horse.

Stephen   I don't see that there's any 'of course' about it,

John. Girls nowadays are likely to fall off anything. Doesn't have to be a horse.

Hugh   No, alright. But in this case it was.

Stephen   She could have fallen off a chair, a table, a pianoforte, anything.

Hugh   Yes, except that, in this case, she was riding a horse when it happened.

Stephen   When she fell off?

Hugh   Yes.

Stephen   So, you reasoned to yourself, Marjorie has fallen from a horse?

Hugh   That's right. Thunderbolt.

Stephen   Thunderbolt, you say?

Hugh   Yes.

Stephen   Well, Thunderbolt's a horse, alright.

Hugh   Exactly.

Stephen   Any damage?

Hugh   Too soon to say. Cavendish is examining her now.

Stephen   That old fool. What does he know about horses?

Hugh   Cavendish is examining Marjorie.

Stephen   Marjorie? Is she ill?

Hugh   No. She fell off a horse.

Stephen   Fell off a horse? Then you'd better fetch Cavendish.

Hugh   I have, Thomas. He's in the drawing room.

Stephen   Horses are very big, John.

Hugh   I know they are, Thomas.

531

Stephen	You fall off one of them, and anything can happen.
Hugh	Quite.
Stephen	*(Pause)* Well not 'anything'.
Hugh	No. Not 'anything'.
Stephen	I mean this clock isn't going to become Prime Minister, just because someone has fallen off a horse. I didn't mean 'anything' in that sense.
Hugh	Of course not, Thomas. Anyway Cavendish is examining her now.
Stephen	You said he was in the drawing room.
Hugh	He is. Examining Marjorie.
Stephen	And where is she?
Hugh	She's also in the drawing room.
Stephen	Hah. So they're both in the drawing room?
Hugh	Yes.
Stephen	Perhaps I was wrong. Perhaps he's not such a fool after all. How is she?
Hugh	Too soon to say. Sounds like a hell of a fall.
Stephen	From the horse?
Hugh	Yes.
Stephen	Thunderbolt?
Hugh	Yes.
Stephen	Now what the devil is Marjorie doing, falling off Thunderbolt?
Hugh	You know how Marjorie loves to ride, Thomas.
Stephen	She was riding Thomas?
Hugh	No no.
Stephen	I'm Thomas, John.

Hugh	I know.
Stephen	She wasn't riding me. Your story's a bit twisted there, old fellow. Doesn't add up. You said she was riding Thunderbolt.
Hugh	She was.
Stephen	She was?
Hugh	Yes.
Stephen	But she's not any longer?
Hugh	No. She fell off.
Stephen	Good God.
Hugh	I know.
Stephen	Where is she?
Hugh	In the drawing room.
Stephen	She was riding Thunderbolt in the drawing room?
Hugh	No. She fell off at Stratton Brook, where the path separates. That young fellow Cottrell found her and carried her to the drawing room.
Stephen	Stables would have been better, don't you think?
Hugh	What?
Stephen	Drawing room's no place for Thunderbolt.
Hugh	Marjorie.
Stephen	What d'you mean?
Hugh	Marjorie's in the drawing room.
Stephen	With Thunderbolt?
Hugh	No. Thunderbolt's in the stables.
Stephen	Oh. Well that's alright, then.
Hugh	It's not alright, Thomas. She's had a bad fall.

Stephen Is she hurt?

Hugh   Too soon to say. Cavendish is with her now.

Stephen Cavendish? He's a doctor, isn't he?

Hugh   Yes.

Stephen I wonder if he knows anything about clocks.

VOX
POP

Stephen I started on the piano and then moved up onto the mantelpiece.

The 'Burt'

*Stephen is interviewing Hugh, who is a croaky-voiced
Richard Harris, stroke Peter O'Toole stroke Oliver
Reed stroke my thigh sort of wildman actor.*

Stephen Did you actually know Burton personally?

Hugh Oh yes. Well, in as much as anyone really 'knew'
Burton. Oh yes, I was very fond of 'the Burt'. He
was such a character, you see.

Stephen And of course Elizabeth Taylor . . .

Hugh Well now Liz was a joy, a dream, a treasure. If you
could have seen them together . . .

Stephen Did you ever . . .

Hugh Oh yes. Many times. In fact I was best man at
their wedding.

Stephen Which one?

Hugh All of them.

Stephen Now Gielgud and Richardson. You must have . . .

Hugh They never married of course.

Stephen No, but you knew them?

Hugh Oh good Lord yes. Real characters. 'The
Giel' and 'the Rich' used to ask me for advice,
constantly. They used to call me their 'guru'.

Stephen Now around that time, you must have met . . .

Hugh Just about everyone, really.

Stephen Good heavens.

Hugh Oh yes. I knew everyone, and everyone knew me.

Stephen	That's extraordinary.
Hugh	I really was very lucky.
Stephen	Mmm. What did you think of Simon Condywust?
Hugh	Simon . . .
Stephen	Condywust. Didn't you know him?
Hugh	Oh yes, I knew him. Yes, everyone knew 'the Condy'. Yes. Amazing character, he really was.
Stephen	Right. What about Margaret Limpwippydippydodo?
Hugh	Mm. Now, Margaret was fascinating. I was fascinated by her for many, many years.
Stephen	Was she an amazing character?
Hugh	No. She was a woman. The men were characters. Margaret was fascinating.
Stephen	I see. Colin FenchmoseythinkIhave?
Hugh	What a character.
Stephen	Fenella Hahahahahaspuit?
Hugh	Fascinating woman.
Stephen	Peter Weeeeeeeeeeeeeeeeeeeeeee?
Hugh	Now there was a character. They broke the mould after they made Peter.
Stephen	Angela Brokethemouldaftertheymadepeter?
Hugh	Delightful woman.
Stephen	Cliff Richard?
Hugh	You've just made that up.

Chicken

Stephen and Deborah are having dinner in a restaurant.

Stephen He gets all misty-eyed and he puffs himself up and says – 'I do it for my country' . . . and he stabs himself in the head with a pair of scissors. So the Irishman says . . .

Hugh enters as a waiter, pushing a trolley.

Hugh Are you ready for your main courses now?

Stephen Yes I think so.

Woman Yes please.

Hugh Excellent.

Stephen Can I ask you something?

Hugh Certainly.

Stephen How do you do it?

Hugh Do what, sir?

Stephen How can you hear from the other side of the restaurant the exact moment I get to the punchline of a joke? You've done it four times since we arrived.

Hugh Good question, sir. There's actually a tiny microphone hidden underneath the ashtray.

Stephen Oh I see.

Hugh And we have a receiver in the kitchen, so you know . . . It's very simple really.

Stephen Right. I just wondered.

Hugh	The lamb?
Woman	Yes please.
Hugh	Very good madam.

Hugh puts a plate of lamb in front of her.

Woman	Thank you.
Stephen	Where was I? The Englishman . . . er . . . oh hell . . .
Hugh	*(While giving her vegetables)* The Englishman said 'I do it for the Queen' and jumped out of the window . . .
Stephen	That's right, yes. Then the Scotsman said 'I do it for my country' and er –
Hugh	Stabbed himself in the head with the pair of . . .
Stephen	. . . scissors, that's right. So the Irishman said . . .
Hugh	And you're having the chicken, sir?
Stephen	Tsscch. What?
Hugh	Chicken Lacroix. Prepared at your table.
Stephen	Yes, thanks very much. The Irishman . . .

Hugh removes the lid of some huge graillon, to reveal a live chicken, preferably clucking.

Woman	Oh my God!
Stephen	What!?
Hugh	Chicken Lacroix.

Hugh starts to sharpen a knife.

Stephen	What are you doing?
Hugh	What am I doing?

538

Stephen	Yes.
Hugh	Sir, I have to make sure the knife is properly sharp.
Stephen	I mean this chicken . . . it's alive!
Hugh	Ha. Not for much longer, sir.
Woman	I think I'm going to be sick.
Hugh	Oh. Something wrong with the lamb, madam?
Stephen	You're not going to kill a chicken in here?
Hugh	Certainly. This, sir, is Chicken Lacroix. As you ordered. 'Fresh, plump, baby chicken, prepared at your table.'

Hugh lifts the knife.

Stephen	Wait! Don't . . . don't kill it!
Hugh	Don't kill it?
Stephen	No!
Hugh	You'd rather eat it while it's alive?
Stephen	No.
Hugh	Well then . . .
Stephen	Stop it! I'm telling you – don't kill that chicken.
Hugh	Is there a problem, sir?
Stephen	Yes there is. You cannot kill that chicken.
Hugh	Why not, sir?
Stephen	Well . . . you know.
Hugh	No.
Stephen	All the letters we'll get. It's not worth it.
Hugh	Letters?

539

Stephen	Yes.
Hugh	Who from?
Stephen	Oh I don't know. Mad people.
Hugh	What mad people?
Stephen	Mad people. 'Why oh why oh why oh why was my six-year-old grandmother forced to watch a chicken being hacked to death in the name of so-called entertainment?' That kind of thing.
Hugh	Well it's no worse than being hacked to death in the name of so-called lunch.
Stephen	Well I know that.
Woman	It is, actually.
Hugh	I beg your pardon?
Woman	I think it is worse.
Hugh	Oh do you?
Woman	Yes.
Hugh	Really?
Stephen	Yes well that's fair enough.
Hugh	Is it? Well let's ask the chicken, shall we? Would you rather die as part of a sketch on national television, or would you prefer just to go straight into a Tesco sandwich, unmourned and unnoticed?
Woman	That's just how I feel. I'm sorry.
Hugh	What's the matter with you? It's had a great time. We showed it the 'Blue Peter' studio, didn't we?
Stephen	Actually, I'd be happier if you didn't kill it.
Hugh	What?
Stephen	I'd be happier if you didn't kill the chicken.
Hugh	Happier? What's happiness got to do with it?

540

Stephen	To be honest, I never really liked the idea.
Hugh	'Never really liked'?
Woman	I'm not crazy about it either.
Hugh	Oh well obviously if everyone's just going to go squeamish at the last minute, we'll have to call it off.
Stephen	I think so.
Hugh	Right.
Stephen	On second thoughts, I'll just have a green salad.
Hugh	A green salad?
Stephen	Please.
Hugh	Very good, sir.

Hugh takes the chicken trolley and exits.

Stephen	I think that was the right decision.
Woman	So do I.
Stephen	Anyway, so the Irishman says . . .

Stephen is interrupted by violent terrifying screams.

Now what are you doing?

Hugh enters with a plate of salad.

Hugh	Never heard a lettuce scream before? Frightening isn't it?
Stephen	What?
Hugh	You never knew, did you? You thought lettuces just came in little sterilised polythene bags, and grew on supermarket shelves. Never occurred to you that a lettuce might have feelings, hopes, dreams, a family . . .

541

Stephen Bugger the lettuce! Will you let me finish my joke!?

Hugh Oh I'm sorry.

Stephen The Irishman says . . .

Cut to whatever.

VOX
POP

Stephen I like the way it *starts*.

Cocoa

An old people's home. Mr Simnock's room. Bed, sofa, etc.

Stephen   *(Attendant)* Alright, Mr Simnock?

Hugh   *(Very, very old northerner)* Eh?

Stephen   I say, are you alright, Mr Simnock?

Hugh   Smimble cocoa.

Stephen   Yes, you can have your cocoa in a minute. I'll draw the curtains shall I?

Hugh   Eh?

Stephen   I say, I'll draw the curtains – be a bit cosier. More cosy for you.

Hugh   Draw the curtains, cosy that. Cocoa.

Stephen   Yes, your cocoa's coming, Mr Simnock.

Hugh   Curtains.

Stephen   *(Drawing them)* There, that's better. Nights are drawing in now, aren't they, Mr Simnock? Getting more chilly by the day. I don't know, time just races by doesn't it? Seems like it was only yesterday that it was Christmas. Oh no, what's this? You've dropped your magazines.

Hugh   Didn't like them. Rubbish they were.

Stephen   I'll pick them up for you – let's see, what have we got here.

As Stephen bends down to pick up the magazines, Hugh cuffs him a mighty blow on the ear.

Ooh, there now. That wasn't very nice was it?

Hitting me like that. What d'you want to go and do that for?

Hugh Want me cocoa.

Stephen Your cocoa's coming – though I'm not so sure as you deserve it, really acting up today like I shouldn't wonder. Whatever next? You're a bad man, Mr Simnock. I'll tuck you up, look.

Hugh Ninety-two years old.

Stephen That's right, ninety-two isn't it? Ninety-three come November.

Hugh Ninety-two years old and I've never had oral sex.

Stephen I should think not indeed. Oral sex! The idea.

Hugh Never ridden a camel.

Stephen Now you're just babbling, Mr Simnock.

Hugh I've never watched a woman urinate.

Stephen I shall get cross with you in a minute, I shall really.

Hugh Never killed a man.

Stephen Now Mr Simnock, there's a certain man that I shall start killing if he's not very careful, thank you very much.

Hugh Never been inside an opera house. Never eaten a hamburger.

Stephen You're a stupid silly old man and I won't have any nonsense.

Hugh I'm fed up, me. Never done anything.

Stephen Well, you're a bit chilly I shouldn't wonder. Your cocoa'll be along in a minute.

Hugh Don't want any stupid cocoa.

Stephen Now don't be contrary – you love your cocoa.

544

Hugh	I hate cocoa. Gets a skin on it.
Stephen	Not if you keep stirring it.
Hugh	Makes me kek that, makes me want to cat up. I want to drink milk from the breasts of a Burmese maiden.
Stephen	I don't know. What's the matter with you today, Mr Simnock? I think we'll have to put you on extra Vitamin E. Burmese maidens! In Todmorden.
Hugh	You've got bad breath you have.
Stephen	Now. Now, Mr Simnock, there's no call to be personal, I hope.
Hugh	Like rotting cabbages.
Stephen	I'm very angry with you, Mr Simnock.
Hugh	You're a great Nancy.
Stephen	I'm not a great Nancy, Mr Simnock, and you're wicked to say so.
Hugh	Great Nancy, Mary-Ann, bum-boy Nance. I bet you've never even done it.
Stephen	I won't have you talking like this Mr Simnock, I won't really.
Hugh	You shouldn't be in a place like this, your time of life.
Stephen	Someone's got to do it, Mr Simnock. Dedication, though why I bother –
Hugh	You should be out there having oral sex, killing people, watching women urinate in opera houses and eating hamburgers on camels. Drinking milk from the breasts of Nepalese maidens.
Stephen	It was Burmese last time.
Hugh	I've changed my mind. Nepalese. Instead you're

stuck here taking rude talk from an old man. You're a Nancy, a great bog-breath Nancy.

Stephen Ooh, you've upset me today, Mr Simnock, you have really. I'm going out to hurry along your cocoa and when I get back I don't want any more nonsense. Honestly!

Exit Stephen.

Hugh *(Calling after him)* You're a screaming Bertie and you pong. *(To himself)* Never seen a woman urinate, not once. Tragic waste, that.

Stephen *(Re-entering)* Now, I managed to intercept Mrs Gideon with the tray in the vestibule. So here's your cocoa, and don't say you aren't a lucky man to get it before the others.

Hugh Hooray!

Stephen There, that's the stuff isn't it?

Hugh Cocoa.

Stephen Yes. A certain naughty boy said some naughty things though, didn't he?

Hugh I'm sorry Brian. Right sorry.

Stephen Well there. As soon as you see your cocoa you mend your manners. I'm not sure I should give it to you, now.

Hugh Oh please, Brian.

Stephen There you are then. That's better, isn't it?

Hugh Lovely drop of cocoa, that.

Stephen Berent's: that's the best.

Stephen smiles at the camera.

Advert-style voice-over

Good old Berent's cocoa. Always there. Original or New Berent's, specially prepared for the mature citizens in your life, with nature's added store of powerful barbiturates and heroin.

Hugh collapses with a grin on his face.

VOX
POP

Hugh Betty had a bit of bitter butter and put it in her batter and made her batter bitter.

Naked

Stephen and Hugh are in a black limbo area. Hugh is on a monitor, Stephen is really there.

Stephen   I'm afraid that we've now got to ask you to do some work, and help us a bit, ladies and gentlemen. Use you imagination, as it were.

Hugh   That's right. For the purposes of this next sketch, ladies and gentlemen, we want you all to imagine that we're both naked.

Stephen   Yes. I'm sorry to have to ask this of you. Speaking for ourselves, Hugh and I really wanted to go the whole way, and actually be naked for this one but, unfortunately, we ran out of money.

Hugh   That's right. The budget simply wouldn't stretch that far, I'm afraid. Never mind.

Stephen   Now to help you build up the picture in your minds, I should tell you that the sketch is set in a church.

Hugh   That's right. Stephen will be playing a Bishop.

Stephen   And Hugh will be playing the organ.

Hugh   The organist.

Stephen   What?

Hugh   I'll be playing the organist.

Stephen   The organist. Yes. But you'll be playing the organ as well?

Hugh   No. No. That's the whole point. I play an organist who can't play the organ.

548

Stephen Oh God I'm sorry. I'm sorry. Of course. Have I ruined it?

Hugh Yes, frankly.

Stephen I'm sorry, ladies and gentlemen.

Hugh You'd better all stop imagining that we're naked.

Stephen Yes stop. Hold it. It's all my fault. I'm sorry. Damn.

VOX
POP

Stephen A man enters a bar. It was an iron bar. No, *goes into* a bar. *Walks* into a bar, that's it. A man walks into a pub, it was an iron pub. Henry Cooper used to do that one. Tommy. Tommy Bar used to walk into that one. Oh no, that can't be right.

Nipples

Stephen addresses Mr and Mrs Audience.

Stephen   Ladies and gentlemen, I think we've got to know each other well enough over the weeks now, for me to make a little confession. I don't want you to be embarrassed by this. *I'm* not, and it is I whose breast is being cleaned, not yours. The fact is, I'm not quite as I seem. You see before you what I have been kind enough to call a rather lovely figure of a super and that's by and breastly as it should be. However, and this is where I'm going to have to ask you to be excitingly pretty, I do have a peculiarity which I feel I must in all softness be rather heavenly about just for a divine. Like an increasing number of people today, I have a pair of nipples attached to my chest, here and to a lesser extent here, but, and this is where I'm forced to be a little bit more delicious than usual, while this one here, Neville, is rosy and healthy and everything one could want, this one Sheila is bright blue and something of a young disappointment. Well there, in a smooth-limbed golden-thighed way, we are. You've been patient, you've been glossy, you've been surprisingly supple. I've enjoyed being fabulous with you. Thank you.

Language Conversation

Stephen and Hugh are in a TV studio, talking animatedly – at least Stephen is animated.

Hugh   Well, let's talk about instead about flexibility of language – linguistic elasticity if you like.

Stephen   I think I said earlier that our language, English –

Hugh   As spoken by us –

Stephen   As we speak it, yes certainly, defines us. We are defined by our language if you will, then please, for goodness' sake, do.

Hugh   *(To camera)* Hullo! We're talking about language.

Stephen   Perhaps I can illustrate my point – let me at least try. Here's a question: is our language capable, English this is, is it capable of sustaining demagoguery?

Hugh   Demagoguery?

Stephen   Demagoguery.

Hugh   And by demagoguery you mean . . . ?

Stephen   I mean demagoguery, I mean highly-charged oratory, persuasive whipping up rhetoric. Listen to me, if Hitler had been English would we, under similar circumstances have been moved, charged up, fired by his inflammatory speeches, or should we have laughed? Er, er, er, is English too ironic a language to support Hitlerian styles, would his language simply have, have rung false in our ears?

Hugh   *(To camera)* We're talking about things ringing false in our ears.

Stephen   Alright, alright, do you mind if I compartmentalise? I hate to, but may I? May I? Is our language

551

a function of our British cynicism, tolerance, resistance to false emotion, humour and so on, or do those qualities come *extrinsically* – *extrinsically*, from the language itself? It's a chicken and egg problem.

Hugh   *(To camera)* We're talking about chickens, we're talking about eggs.

Stephen Let me start a leveret here: there's language, the grammar, the structure – then there's utterance. Listen to me, listen to me, there's chess and there's a game of chess. Mark the difference, mark it for me please.

Hugh   *(To camera)* We've moved on to chess.

Stephen Imagine a piano keyboard, eighty-eight keys, only eighty-eight and yet, and yet, new tunes, melodies, harmonies are being composed upon hundreds of keyboards every day in Dorset alone. Our language, Tiger, our language, hundreds of thousands of available words, frillions of possible legitimate new ideas, so that I can say this sentence and be confident it has never been uttered before in the history of human communication: 'Hold the newsreader's nose squarely, waiter, or friendly milk will countermand my trousers.' One sentence, common words, but never before placed in that order. And yet, oh and yet, all of us spend our days saying the same things to each other, time after weary time, living by clichaic, learned response: 'I love you', 'Don't go in there', 'You have no right to say that', 'shut up', 'I'm hungry', 'that hurt', 'why should I?', 'it's not my fault', 'help', 'Marjorie is dead'. You see? That surely is a thought to take out for a cream tea on a rainy Sunday afternoon.

Hugh looks at camera, opens mouth as if to speak, decides against it. Speaks to Stephen instead.

552

Hugh   So to you language is more than just a means of communication?

Stephen   Er, of course it is, of course it is, of course it is. Language is a whore, a mistress, a wife, a pen-friend, a check-out girl, a complimentary moist lemon-scented cleansing square or handy freshen-up wipette. Language is the breath of God, the dew on a fresh apple, it's the soft rain of dust that falls into a shaft of morning sun when you pull from an old bookshelf a forgotten volume of erotic diaries; language is the faint scent of urine on a pair of boxer shorts, it's a half-remembered childhood birthday party, a creak on the stair, a spluttering match held to a frosted pane, the warm wet, trusting touch of a leaking nappy, the hulk of a charred Panzer, the underside of a granite boulder, the first downy growth on the upper lip of a Mediterranean girl, cobwebs long since overrun by an old Wellington boot.

Hugh   Ner-night.

VOX
POP

Hugh   Then Betty took a bit of better butter and put it in her bitter batter and made her bitter batter better. Something like that. It was before the next war of course.

553

Stephen's Poem

Stephen is at a desk, reciting.

Stephen   'Crate, a normil nighman
Hane a freethy stipe
You veen where musse is Simon
Critch botty trees a wipe.'

I first wrote the poem from which that verse was
an extract when my dear wife Enemy died. I wrote
it again in 1978 after hearing of the death of rock
music. I'd like with your kind indulgence to write
it once more. Thank you.

Stephen sits and writes.

554

Girlfriend's Breasts

Farmhouse kitchen set. Like a Tyne Tees TV late night religious discussion set. Stephen intrudes on Hugh who is busy reading a book. They are both foully nice.

Stephen   Who told you that you were naked?

Hugh puts the book down and looks smilingly up at Stephen.

Hugh   I'm sorry?

Stephen   I was thinking 'who told you that you were naked'?

Hugh   You may have lost me there, Arnold.

Stephen   Well, let me explain. I was thinking of that passage in the book of Genesis where Adam explains to God why he and Eve have covered themselves.

Hugh   Ah yes. If I remember that story alright, Adam says, 'we were naked and we were ashamed'.

Stephen   That's right, Glenn. And God says . . .

Hugh   'Who told you that you were naked?'

Stephen   *(As if catching sight of the camera for the first time, speaking directly into it)* We were just having a conversation, Glenn and I, about a passage in Genesis that has been intriguing me rather.

Hugh   It is fascinating isn't it? But anyway, tell me about the size of your girlfriend's breasts.

Stephen   Well, let's clear up this problem of why God should give such a complex reply to what is, on the surface, a very simple question.

Hugh   Not as simple a question, in many ways, as for instance: 'are they very big, or only quite big?'

555

Stephen   Well, fair point. But while not that simple, still relatively simple.

Hugh   That's right, Arnold: simpler certainly than 'is she very exciting in bed?'

Stephen   Ng. I think God was saying, 'How are you aware, Adam, of such a thing as a "state of nakedness"? How can that concept mean anything to you, unless you have eaten of the fruit whereof I said thou shouldst not eat?'

Hugh   My bet is that they are really quite substantially large. A fulsome pair of funbags, that's my bet.

Stephen   One thing at a time Glenn.

Hugh   You're right. One thing at a time. Let's take the left one first shall we? How enormous would you say that it is?

Stephen   *(Laughing)* Ha, ha! Glenn is having difficulty concentrating on our Bible Study readings because he has something of an obsession with the size of my girlfriend's breasts.

Hugh   *(Also laughing)* I like to put it this way. Arnold is having trouble concentrating on our little discussions about the size of his girlfriend's bazoncas because he is a little too interested in analysing passages from the Bible.

Stephen   We'll sort it out, don't you worry!!

They both turn to each other talking again, simultaneously.

Hugh   Say a forty-eight cup, or bigger still?

Stephen   A knowledge of good and evil, that is what the fruit contained, when Eve took it from the serpent . . . etc.

Violence

Stephen and Hugh are somewhere.

Stephen   Violence: it's a theme we've touched on before now in this fortnightly look back on the past three days, and I dare say it's one we'll touch on again, and we don't apologise for that. Violence is not something that is going to lie down and go away.

Hugh   Well put. I suppose Responsibility Television is the phrase that best sums up our approach.

Stephen   What does Responsibility Television mean? Well it means that we are immensely concerned that nothing we do has a bad influence on our viewers. Thus when I hit Hugh, like so:

Stephen hits Hugh.

We have to consider what the effect on the viewer might be.

Hugh   Is a vulnerable, easily-led section of our audience going to start imitating this kind of behaviour?

Stephen   Well so far in this series I have hit Hugh on no less than a startling seven occasions. You might think we had no thought at all as to how the young might be influenced by this kind of senseless, horrific violence. Would they start to imitate it? Hugh.

Hugh   Well the interesting and inescapable conclusion that we've come up with is yes. Because since the series has started to be transmitted I have found, walking along the street that I have been hit no less than twelve times by complete strangers.

557

Stephen So it looks as if the suggestible out there are actually imitating my violent behaviour patterns and striking you?

Hugh That's right.

Stephen Is that a worrying development?

Hugh It's not unworrying.

Stephen So it might be that the Milton Schulmans of this world aren't as incredibly stupid as they appear at first, second and thirty-fourth glance. We are unwittingly helping to make Britain a more violent place.

Hugh It's beginning to look horribly like it.

Stephen Well, let's see if we can't reverse this process. I'm going to give you a fiver now Hugh.

Stephen does so.

Would all those stupid enough to be influenced by my violent behaviour who are likely to go out onto the street and hit Hugh please watch very carefully as I now smile at Hugh, hand him another five pounds and say 'There you are old chap, there's a fiver for you. Have a really super time. Oh, look, here's another one. And another. There you go, bless you.'

Hugh Well thank you very much indeed if you don't mind me saying so.

Stephen I certainly don't mind you saying so, in fact it's very kind of you. Here's a fiver.

Hugh Well, thank you I'm sure.

Stephen Good. Well, I hope you're going to monitor the public's behaviour very closely Hugh, and if you find people approaching with five pound notes,

you'll come back on the programme and let
us know?

Hugh   I certainly will.

Stephen Alright then. Just time now to go over to Devizes
and catch up with Chris and that giant sauna.

VOX
POP

Hugh   They've got hotter pavements, I
know that.

Tomorrow's World

Hugh   How many times have you walked out in front of a bus, been knocked down and killed? Pretty frustrating, isn't it?

Stephen   Well, now there's a solution to that problem. A company down in Truro in Cornwall have started producing these lightweight travelling hats, which can be folded very tightly indeed, but when unpacked can be thrown away almost immediately.

Hugh   Which hopefully should eliminate that bus problem at a stroke.

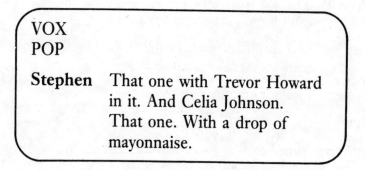

VOX
POP

Stephen   That one with Trevor Howard in it. And Celia Johnson. That one. With a drop of mayonnaise.

Spies Five

A park bench, in a television studio somewhere in Shepherd's Bush's famous London. Hugh approaches Stephen, who is sitting and feeding ducks from a brown paper bag.

Hugh   My cheque book is sometimes yellow.

Stephen   Yellow is the colour of some people's front porches.

Hugh   *(Slipping down next to Stephen)* Hello Control.

Stephen   Hello Murchison. Sorry to ask you to go through that coded exchange.

Hugh   Yes, it seemed rather odd, because we know each other quite well, don't we?

Stephen   That's a true thing to say, Tony, but the fact is we can't be too careful at the moment.

Hugh   Did you think perhaps that I might be a KGB man with a false head on?

Stephen   I hadn't entirely ruled it out.

Hugh   So.

Stephen   Mm. I expect you're wondering why we couldn't meet in my office, Tony.

Hugh   Not really, it's being redecorated, isn't it? I had a little peek through the door this morning when I was passing. I think I caught a glimpse of some rather attractive rolls of wallpaper. A sort of silvery stripe, with a textured bit.

Stephen   Yes. The cornice and moulding are going to be picked out in maroon.

Hugh   That sounds very adventurous.

Stephen   Mm. I find that makes a room look bigger. Well I've got to put my serious hat on now. Are you familiar with the term 'mole'?

Hugh   Surely a mole is an enemy agent planted deep within an organisation, such as ours, who pretends to be on one side but is really on the other all the time?

Stephen   Yes. They are beastly.

Hugh   Yes, very.

Stephen   Well, for some time, Murchison, the Minister and I have been ever so slightly anxious about the possibility of there being just such a 'mole' working inside our department.

Hugh   Oh lor.

Stephen   Yes. That's why I thought it would be more secure if we met here, not in my office.

Hugh   That's a smart and professional piece of thinking, Control.

Stephen   It's no good trying to be all private and secret if there's a mole listening to you all the time, probably laughing up his sleeve at you. If moles have sleeves.

Hugh   So a mole, with or without sleeves. Fff. In our department? That makes my blood boil.

Stephen   Mine too. It really is beginning to look like it. The Minister and I have decided to call the mole 'Duncan' by the way.

Hugh   Oh. Well I'm afraid that your theory about there being a mole may be wrong then, Control.

Stephen   I'm busy wondering why that should be, Tony?

Hugh   Well, we haven't got anyone called Duncan

working in the department. I could ask the computer to give information on people called Duncan until the cows come home, but it is such a quite common name. Especially in Scotland, I think.

Stephen   I may not have explained myself too well, Murchison. Duncan is just his code-name for the time being.

Hugh   What a devious business we're in, Control.

Stephen   Yes, I often think that it's a pity that we have to lie and conceal the truth so much. It leaves a not very pleasant taste in the mouth sometimes.

Hugh   Hear, hear.

Stephen   I have to say that I don't envy the mole, though.

Hugh   No, quite. I have to say that as well, Control. Because a mole has extra helpings of lying and concealing the truth to do.

Stephen   Yes. We've got quite enough on our plate just working for one country, haven't we, Tony?

Hugh   We jolly well have.

Stephen   If I had to do all my work twice I should get pretty fagged out. I shouldn't have a moment to call my own.

Hugh   Nor me.

Stephen   Bother him. Bother Duncan. Bother the Minister. Bother the whole damned lot of them.

Hugh   Yes. Mind you, it's given us an opportunity to get out into the fresh air for a change.

Stephen   That's true. And I expect the ducks will be pleased.

Hugh   They'd be jolly ungrateful if they weren't.

Stephen   Well I've got to have a small talk with the Minister now. Can I leave you to finish off feeding them?

Hugh   Certainly Control, leave the bag with me. You put the ducks out of your mind.

Stephen   Thanks Tony. Have done.

Hugh   B-bye, Control.

Stephen   B-bye, Murchison.

> VOX
> POP
>
> **Stephen**   Sometimes I think they ought to build a ring road round the ring road. Ha ha. *(Laughs hysterically almost forever)*